Your Father, Your Self

How Sons and Daughters Can Understand and Heal Their Relationships With Their Fathers

Barry H. Gordon, Ph.D.

A Birch Lane Press Book

Published by Carol Publishing Group

A Birch Lane Press Book
Published by Carol Publishing Group
Birch Lane Press is a registered trademark of Carol Communications, Inc.
Editorial, sales and distribution, rights and permissions inquiries should be addressed to Carol
Publishing Group, 120 Enterprise Avenue, Secaucus, N.J. 07094
In Canada: Canadian Manda Group, One Atlantic Avenue, Suite 105, Toronto, Ontario M6K 3E7

Carol Publishing Group books are available at special discounts for bulk purchases, sales
promotion, fund-raising, or educational purposes. Special editions can be created to specifications.
For details, contact: Special Sales Department, Carol Publishing Group, 120 Enterprise Avenue,
Secaucus, N.J. 07094

Manufactured in the United States of America
10 9 8 7 6 5 4 3 2 1

Library of Congress Cataloging-in-Publication Data

Gordon, Barry, H.
　　Your father, your self : how sons and daughters can understand and
　heal relationships with their fathers / Barry H. Gordon.
　　　　p.　cm.
　　"A Birch Lane Press book."
　　Includes bibliographical references.
　　ISBN 1-55972-378-5 (hc)
　　　1. Father and child.　2. Fatherhood—Psychological aspects.
　I. Title.
　HQ756.G587　1996
　306.874'2—dc20　　　　　　　　　　　　　　　　96-24926
　　　　　　　　　　　　　　　　　　　　　　　　　CIP

Excerpt from "Even If You Weren't My Father" by Camillo Sbarbaro, translated by Shirley
Hazzard, reprinted by permission; © 1990 Shirley Hazzard. Originally in the *New Yorker*,
August 6, 1990.

Excerpt from "My Father's Back" from *The Night Parade* by Edward Hirsch, copyright © 1989
Edward Hirsch. Reprinted by permission of Alfred A. Knopf, Inc.

Excerpt from "My Father's House" by Bruce Springsteen, copyright © 1982 Bruce Springsteen
Publishing. Reprinted by permission.

To my father, for the love
he gave in his own way

To my wife, Eileen, and my
daughters, Jessie and Nora,
for their unending support and love

Contents

Father, even were you not my father,

were you some utter stranger,

for your innocence, your artless tender heart

I would above all other men

so love you.

Camillo Sbarbaro, Italian poet (1888–1967)
Translated by Shirley Hazzard
Excerpted from "Even If You Weren't My Father"

Author to Reader

About a dozen years ago, when I was in my mid-thirties, I was talking with my close friend about our reactions to the aging of our parents. He knew I had a difficult and complicated relationship with my father. Out of curiosity and probably intending to make me think, he asked me how I would react if my father died. I responded, almost reflexively, that I did not think I would be sad. I believed at the time that my dad had caused me and my brothers so much pain and had been so difficult to relate to that I would be relieved to have him dead. My friend was silent for a moment. Then he said, "I think you're wrong."

I thought a great deal about my friend's question and my answer. I understood my friend was right. I realized I did not want to let things stand as they were.

This conversation with my friend was the catalyst for a ten-year journey that spanned the remaining years of my father's life. Through a combination of self-reflection, work at understanding my father, and conscious attempts at altering the patterns of the past I was able to arrive at the point where his death at the age of ninety was deeply sad for me. Yet I was also truly at peace with him and with myself over our relationship.

Throughout my years of therapy practice, helping other people come to terms with their hurt about their fathers had always been a central theme. I knew it was often the primary avenue to inner healing. My personal mission with my father, however, served as a profound awakening to the power of denial about our paternal relationships over the years. I have seen so many men and women who were unaware of their longing for more connection to their fathers. These individuals did not know, without someone to help them examine their feelings, that having their dads play a truncated role in their lives had harmed them. Others were living with buried pain or crippled emotions and did not know that the source flowed back to the father-child relationship. This book was written in part to open the eyes of the unknowing, so they can understand themselves better and decide whether they want to change their relationship with their fathers.

An increasing number of men and women today are becoming conscious of the mistakes made by their fathers. Men with families of their own may be motivated by their wish to be more active as fathers and husbands. They want to change the present and future, but may not know what to do with the past. Both women and men are trying to deal with their pain and sense of loss. They are trying to figure out how or if they can do anything to repair the torn relationship with their fathers. Many don't know how to move forward with these concerns. This book was written in part to show them some pathways.

Your Father, Your Self is intended as a loving statement and a forceful message that fathers are important. Fathers, mothers, and children have too often conspired in denial of the fact that it has been normative for dads to underplay or, at times, overplay their basic functions without facing the consequences. I will describe in this book what it is that we look for from our fathers and what we need from them for our own healthy psychological development. I will point out many of the ways we may be affected when we don't receive what we need and instead try to adapt to what we get. I want to erase the myth that a father's disconnection from his children is psychologically neutral.

Fathers are disconnected from their children when their behavior leaves them emotionally unavailable and unable to adequately meet the emotional and developmental needs of their children. This disconnection can come about in many different ways—through physical absence, intimidation, being consumed by their own problems, or emotional withdrawal. I will describe in *Your Father, Your Self* the different ways fathers commonly disconnect from their children. Each way affects a child somewhat differently. I will explore these paternal differences and address how efforts to work on the relationship must take them into account.

I use an original framework in looking at how disconnection with fathers occurs. I describe nine different types of fathers according to their uses of power, their weaknesses, and the ways in which they may have been absent. Any father may exhibit one or more of these characteristic patterns; however, fathers are not stereotypes who will neatly fit into categories. My intention is to humanize fathers, not to constrict our views of them and certainly not to paint them as villains or all bad. All of you will find parts of your own paternal experience here, and none of you will find your exact experience reproduced.

This is not a book that romanticizes fathers or tries to capture the ways in which fathers have endeared themselves and devoted themselves to their children, though most fathers have loved their offspring in their own ways. Many dads were loving, supportive, and closely connected to their children. Many were unsung heroes. But we have paid too little attention to the ways in which many fathers have missed their opportunity and responsibility to carry out the fullest potential of their role. There are indeed many fathers who themselves sense they have not done their best by their children and carry a grievous pain about this.

A growing number of men of all ages are realizing they want to be closer to their children. Many, especially the older ones, may not know how. This book is for them as well. I hope it will motivate them to try, to see paths they might take, and to be receptive to their children when they make efforts to relate.

Part I of *Your Father, Your Self* clarifies the nature of many father relationships and explains why a journey to bring about healing is needed. These chapters also offer guidance about how to overcome the emotional wounds that result from the failure to connect with your father.

The second half of the book offers a blueprint for how to conduct the journey. There is important preparation needed for any challenging venture. In this case we are talking about emptying our backpacks as much as about what we need to bring along. The emotional preparation and outlook needed to make this journey effectively are described. Many common myths and mistakes about approaching our fathers are pointed out. The difference between reconciliation with the father himself, which is not always possible, and inner resolution about the relationship, which is possible for everyone, is highlighted.

Your Father, Your Self provides a practical and emotional guide for healing your relationship with your father. It presents specific ways to approach fathers as well as what to avoid. The difficulties and pitfalls in trying to engage our dads in improving the relationship are included.

The personal experiences of many clients and individuals whom I have observed or helped through the process illustrate what the path looks like in practice. Just as the different ways fathers behave have their particular impact, our psychological needs in the healing process vary according to the nature of the father. I will offer ways to satisfy these needs through matching reconciliation efforts with the type of dysfunction in the relationship. Finally, I will describe the emotional growth and interpersonal rewards that are gained through accepting the challenge of this journey toward healing.

Your Father, Your Self is not an academic exercise or an aloof clinical manual. I am certain that writers write at least partially from our own unconscious needs. As I have indicated, I made my own personal journey of coming to terms with my relationship to my father. The writing of this book was a further leg of the journey, one that took me deeper into myself. A good guide will have made the trip on his own and directly discovered the danger spots and the points of wonder. He will freely share his own experience without using it to define what his fellow traveler must do. Pieces of my personal journey are included with this perspective in mind.

From both my personal and professional work I have learned to appreciate the enormous emotional struggle the journey represents for others. I also see how universal the need for the journey is, whether one intends to run for the presidency of the United States or to learn to change a baby's diapers. I know I am in good company.

In writing *Your Father, Your Self* I wanted to represent accurately what happens between fathers and their children. In focusing closely on a given subject, we inevitably add refinements and detailed accuracy to our central vision, but the peripheral matters—what we are not zeroing into—may blur. Many of the things said about fathers' behavior and its impact could as well have been said about mothers. Statements made about how mothers' actions shaped fathers' functioning in the family have a context from the mothers' perspective that may have been shortchanged. This is not a book about mothers, though, and in shining a light on fathers we dim it in relation to mothers. Ultimately, the hope is to illuminate the whole family system thoroughly.

In looking to make meaningful distinctions that are universal about fathers, major areas of difference among fathers were not examined. The principal distinctions are cultural, racial, and socioeconomic. Certainly, fathers whose backgrounds and economic resources are markedly different will tend to approach their role with different expectations. The population from which I drew my knowledge base and examples was predominantly white and middle class. The ethnic backgrounds were diverse and there was a broad representation economically, from working- and lower-middle-class through upper-class fathers. The numbers for any one category, however, did not allow for generalizations along these lines.

I am convinced that the distinctions made about the power, weakness, and absence of fathers are valid for fathers from any background. We know that abusiveness, alcoholism, emotional problems, divorce, and death are not isolated within a single class. All children need and benefit from the role a father can play in family life. That is a far more important acknowledgment than the fact that shades of difference exist across cultural, racial, and economic groups.

I did attempt to focus on the distinctions between daughters and sons. At one point during my writing a male client told me about a work-related dinner he had had with two men and a woman. The conversation centered on the experience the men had with their fathers. They bemoaned how difficult it had been to get affection and support from their fathers and how unavailable their fathers were. At the point when one of the men became concerned they were leaving out their woman colleague, she told the group that she was identifying with everything they were saying.

The more I wrote about experiences with fathers, however, the more invalid it seemed to make broad generalizations about how daughters were affected compared to sons. There are certainly major differences in how daughters and sons commonly interact with fathers. There is a romanticism that frequently pervades father-daughter relationships when fathers view a daughter as "Daddy's little girl" and daughters seek to retain this favored status. Sons have a different favored position that has its own double-edged sword—the need to follow in a father's footsteps. This need to identify psychologically with the father is, in my mind, the one variable that most affects the intensity and depth of impact of fathers on their sons versus their daughters. The self is usually more centrally and fully defined for sons through their fathers than it is for daughters.

There are, however, an infinite variety of family system dynamics that can eradicate the validity of any generalizations about sons and daughters: whether one is an only child; where in the order of siblings the child comes and the talents and character of the other siblings; whether the family consists only of sons or daughters; how assertive, confident, or functional the mother is compared to the father. There are multigenerational issues that operate as well, namely, the sibling and family dynamics of the father's and mother's families of origin.

Throughout the book I noted differences that I have observed and believe to be valid, but anyone can come up with a specific family situation that will contradict these generalizations. There are certainly many daughters who identify psychologically with their dads and even seek to follow in their footsteps.

My focus in writing *Your Father, Your Self* has been on adults who grew up with traditional fathers. In my mind and in the pool of people who represent the case examples of this book are people who range from their later twenties to their seventies. Often, however, when I started talking about my own generation of adults I ended up finding that what I was saying applied equally to children growing up today. Postmodern fathers, though generally much more involved with their kids, have by no means escaped all or even most of the mistakes of the past. We are destined to repeat the errors of past generations if we don't learn the lessons reflected in our present pain. That is the best reason of all for me to have undertaken this project.

Throughout the book I refer to sons and daughters as "children," even though I am commonly referring to them as adults rather than young children. To parents we remain their children through their entire lives. My father unabashedly referred to me as "his baby" all his life. I accept that parents are entitled to this outlook. It is not an endorsement of this perspective, however, but a poverty of language that led to this non-age-specific use of the word 'children.'

As you begin your own journey through this book I want to pass on to you a direct quote from a college commencement speech delivered by science fiction writer Ray Bradbury:

> Sometimes we need to fuse our lives again with those people who seem at times to be antagonists—you young men especially, because it is hard for us men to profess our love. It is quite often very difficult for your fathers and for you. So for you young men, when the ceremony is over, I want you to run over to the old man. Grab him, hug him and kiss him and say, "Dad, I love you and I thank you for all the years." That's part of the ceremony. . . . It will save you a lot of trouble getting to know your fathers ten years from now.

He needed to invite the daughters to do the same. Perhaps it takes a science fiction writer to both be aware of the future struggle we can expect from our relationship with our fathers and to think that it could so easily be averted with a hug. It's not a bad place to start, though.

Acknowledgments

There is an African folk saying that has become popular: "It takes a whole village to raise a child." So it is with the development and writing of a book. *Your Father, Your Self* was initially conceived in a long car ride with my close friend Rob Pasick. On that day Rob drew me out in my thinking and encouraged me to pursue my dream of writing a book about healing relationships with fathers. Since that initial inspiration, Rob, his wife, Pat, and a whole host of friends, family, and colleagues has offered support, interest, optimism, advice, and even consolation when it was needed. My love and appreciation go to all of you.

Two colleagues and friends merit special mention: Kathy Cole-Kelly and Joseph Zinker. Both of these caring, creative, and supportive friends read through the first draft of the book, making insightful suggestions and bolstering my resolve to complete the project.

My special friend, Jeff Ackerman, voluntarily read the second to last version of the manuscript, offering loving support and sage advice that was not only helpful, but almost overwhelmingly touching. Paul Shane, a writer and editor, kindly read portions of the book and shared his skillful observations extensively with me.

There are many clients whose personal stories were used to illustrate the ideas in *Your Father, Your Self.* I am deeply honored for the trust they placed in me by sharing their emotions, reflections, and insights during therapy. I am grateful to those from whom I needed releases for the added trust of allowing me to make use of their experiences in the book. There were also a handful of loyal individuals among my clients who asked to read the manuscript in an earlier version. I was moved by and am most appreciative of their confidence in me and the enthusiastic reception they gave the book. Their interest played a critical part in keeping me on track.

My editor, Hillel Black, provided the greatest gift, believing in the promise of the book enough to publish it. He also provided me with a clear blueprint and some fatherly guidance for finalizing the text. I also want to thank Renata Somogyi, Production Editor at Carol Publishing Group, and Susan Higginbotham, my copy editor, for their excellent editorial help.

My agent, Jim Levine, was faced with far more than he bargained for in bringing *Your Father, Your Self* over all the hurdles required to eventually find itself in print. I am extremely grateful to Jim for his determination, loyalty, integrity, guidance, and wisdom. His staff—Melissa Rowland, Arielle Eckstut, and Daniel Greenberg—were timely with their follow-through on details and cheerfully supportive. It was a pleasure to work with and be able to count on them.

The typing of a manuscript requires far more than meets the eye. Deciphering cryptic notes and meandering arrows and putting up with the tension of the author and pressured deadlines make for difficult, often underappreciated labor. I am thankful for the patient, skillful work of Debbie White and Associates in producing the various clean drafts of the manuscript. In addition to Debbie, I owe her daughter, Tanya Mossbarger, and Linda Lumbert and Lil Bremer a debt of gratitude. I also want to remember the help of my office secretaries, Laurel Bresler and Maureen Graves, for their assistance in the early stages of this effort.

Of course, without the patient, affectionate support of my wife, Eileen, and my daughters, Jessie and Nora, I could never have stayed the course. They had to put up with my moods, my lack of availability, the highs and lows over a prolonged period. Eileen was left with more than her fair share of responsibilities all too often. Throughout I got encouraged, exhorted, advised, and consoled, always with love. I believe I grew as a father and as a husband through this endeavor, not in small part due to the foundation they provided me.

The book and my loving gratitude are dedicated to my family and my father. I wish he were alive to see this book in print. His indomitable spirit to survive and take any task worth doing to its completion helped carry me through this project. I love him for his devotion to me and thank him for all he meant to me in the writing of this book.

Part I

Understanding Our Fathers, Healing Our Wounds

1

Missing Our Fathers

I don't know why we go over the old hurts
Again and again in our minds, the false starts
And true beginnings
         of a world we call the past,
As if it could tell us who we are now,
Or were, or might have been. . . .
        It's drizzling.
A car door slams, just once, and he's gone.
Tiny pools of water glisten on the street.

"My Father's Back,"
Edward Hirsch

A group of fifteen men sit in a circle, uncomfortably awaiting the start of a day-long retreat to explore their identities as men. We begin with a simple directive: to talk about what has shaped their view of themselves as men. Three hours later they are exhausted and bonded from their revelations, often crying unashamedly in empathy with the others and in the purest of recollections of their own pasts. The one topic they have almost all talked about and that has elicited the most passion involved their fathers, the longing to have known them better, to have had more of their nurturing and less of their tempers or their silence or their distance.

3

In the emergence of men's retreats, groups, and workshops that has occurred across the nation in this decade, the release of pent-up grief about fathers is the dominant emotional force. This grief, however, is not the sole province of men, even though it may be the most critical psychological variable with which men must grapple.

A young woman at a mixed-gender workshop on helping men change stood up to relate her tale of a father who used to greet her visits home for college vacations by noting how happy the family dog was to see her. He was unable to voice directly his own pleasure, or at other moments, his great pride and love for his daughter. There was a tangible ache in the room as this woman tearfully told of her experience. The many women in the room were nodding knowingly and drifting back through similar memories, every bit as moved and in pain as the men.

A kind of nostalgia for fathers worked its way through to the national consciousness during the early 1990s. Memoirs and reminiscences of fathers, like Philip Roth's *Patrimony* and Germaine Greer's *Daddy, We Hardly Knew You*, became popular bookfare. Movies such as *Nothing in Common*, *Memories of Me*, *Dad*, and *Field of Dreams* tapped a widespread longing for reconciliation with fathers. It is as though the baby boom generation, having arrived at the stage of parenting that it rebelled against, was now coming to terms with the psychological loss that was the underpinning of that rebellion. And it is as though young parents today, as they encounter the demands of parenting for working mothers and for more involved fathers, have been awakening to the fact that they lack role models. That is a loss for them today as parents, but it also embodies a deeper loss in their own childhood development.

What is it that we long for in our fathers? For some it is the absence of cruelty, the wish that a physically or sexually or verbally violent father had never inflicted his pain and never scarred us with this undying image of a father to be feared and ashamed of. Others of us suffered a tangible loss of our fathers through death, divorce, or extended absences, perhaps due to war service or illness. Often the loss is intangible and the absence is of the soul and not the body. In a hauntingly beautiful recollection of her childhood, "My Father's Love Letters," Tess Gallagher writes:

> My father's sleep was like the rain. It permeated the household. When he was home he seemed always to be sleeping. We saw him come home and we saw him leave. We saw him during the evening

meal . . . he worked hard. It could be said that he never missed a day's work.

It occurs to me that . . . [my] father was among the living dead, and this made my situation all the more urgent. It was as if I had set myself the task of waking him before it was too late. I seemed to need to tell him who he was, and that what was happening to him mattered and was witnessed by at least one other.

These "living dead" fathers are probably the most common. They are the fathers whose souls were consumed by the daily demands of work and worry about adequately providing; they are the fathers who stoically believed this was, their duty to their children and who did not realize their children needed or even wanted something else.

A woman going through a difficult transition as she neared her fiftieth birthday had been in touch with her father and sought his support for the first time in many years. She was surprised to find that he did not criticize her as he always had in the past. A painful memory drifted into her consciousness of how she used to cry, even as a teen, on those relatively rare occasions when he was gentle and supportive. Her experience was so out of kilter with her expectations. In therapy she was only beginning to understand how much of her life's energy had been spent avoiding criticism from others, especially men and, in particular, her father. It still stunned her that this man who had seemed to live on the periphery of their family could have had such an impact on her emotions and behavior. Moreover, she still needed him for support and yet could not seek it without the old trepidation.

Indeed, fathers have far more emotional impact on the lives of their children than their actual involvement in so many cases would lead us to expect. We are influenced because as small children we regard our fathers as knowing how to manage in the larger world much better than we do. Our fathers seem so much stronger and fearless to our naive eyes. And being under the roof, or wishing we were, with someone for all our developmental years accords them hypnotic powers, if not by repetition then by the focus of conscious and unconscious attention.

Like it or not, our fathers represent half of the primary source of fundamental affirmation available to us as we grow. That potential affirmation is like the sun to a plant. Even when it is hidden from us, it still provides the direction for growth.

Most of us, however, think no more about our fathers' role in our lives than we do about the sun. The average person does not go through the self-examination required to understand how deeply he has been affected by his paternal relationship. As a colleague noted, it takes a conscious intent that is usually reserved for the therapist's office to engage in this level of self-exploration.

Many people had loving, supportive fathers with whom they felt well connected and experienced no great conflict or angst. Even with such fathers many of us feel we haven't connected as fully as we wanted or known them as deeply as we wish we had. It is probably more typical, however, for the present generation of adults to feel varying degrees of loss, conflict, and pain in relation to their fathers. Most, lacking the conscious intent to conduct an internal search, are left with an unexamined hurt that may surface only at certain critical junctures or memory-triggering events or evocative interactions. Many of us simply go through our lives knowing we carry an unresolved pain or longing, not believing that it matters any more than yesterday's worst headline.

The Pain—Do We Really Hurt?

I have a story I share with some of my clients—those individuals who tell me, after relating a particularly pathetic tale of a paternal relationship, "It's just bad history and I've put it behind me." The summer before I went off to college was the last time I lived with my father. At that point, it was just he and I, since my two older brothers were already out of the house. One Saturday morning after I had completed several hours of chores I told him I was going to be picked up shortly to go to the art museum. He responded by telling me he first needed me to help him clean the gutters. My sense of fairness was instantly bruised, but I knew the cost of arguing would be greater than the art museum visit could soothe, so I went along, hoping the task could be done in short order.

My father was a carpenter and he had two ladders, one of which he had made himself. He thought the self-made ladder might not reach the gutter, but he wanted to try it. The other ladder was rickety and needed to be secured by another person at the base. The self-made ladder was naturally too short. Not one to give up easily, however, my father tried propping it up on two parallel carpenter horses. When that didn't work, he added a wooden block and then a second block. All the while I had been building a volcanic resentment at this abuse of my time and patience. The second block being put in place aroused a sense of outright fear for him that superseded my anger for the moment and I insisted he take it all down. That left us with the rickety ladder, which was in worse shape than I had thought, but it reached.

The gutters were cleaned, but then my father wanted to hose them out. My frustration rose another notch as I imagined my friend arriving and finding me ensconced in gutter cleaning. Suddenly the hose got away from my father and whipsawed around, thoroughly wetting me down in the process. I leapt on it and shut it off. I looked up at him to let him know of my displeasure and discovered he hadn't even turned around, didn't even know he'd gotten me soaked. He was just waiting to complete his work at my expense. I glared at the seat of his pants, which was insultingly all he seemed to be directing my way. Without any further thought I turned the hose on full blast and sprayed my target. He looked down at me in utter disbelief and demanded to know what had just happened. I unhesitatingly and unflinchingly said, "I didn't know the water was on."

I make use of this story because for many years I told it at certain times to friends or family members in the most laughable way I could. It was a funny story and it illustrated how difficult my father could be at times. It showed me as the victor of sorts in the end. One day I told this bit of family memorabilia to my practice partners at a meeting we were holding to work on barriers to closeness among the four of us. I don't recall why I chose to tell it, but before I finished it I unexpectedly found myself choked with tears.

After several minutes of sobbing and with the support of my partners, I began to understand what my emotions were all about. I realized that the event had marked for me the feeling of being unrecognized by my father. A deep sadness had bubbled forth, expressing the hurt of feeling my father did not seem to be aware of my needs or my personhood as distinct from his own. The tears were evoked by his seemingly not being concerned enough to look at me and see whether the hose had sprayed me and whether that might affect my being ready to leave for something I very much wanted to do. But the tears were accumulated over time and certainly were not about one accidental hosing down.

From this experience of feelings being uncovered that I had no idea were there, let alone existed with such intensity, I learned a new respect for people's ability to bury feelings. I utilize this story to demonstrate vividly to clients that when they tell me they were unaffected by major parental slights or that they adjusted comfortably to such a reality and harbor no negative feelings, they are ignorant of how well we can

deceive ourselves. The pain can be deep and powerful and yet lie as
dormant as a larva in a cocoon. We can hurt without realizing it, just as
our fathers could be absent without knowing that there was any impact.
Usually at some stage of their lives men figure out that they have done
something regrettable by not being with their children more. In time so
do the children.

Our culture has taught men to believe that their principal means of
taking care of their children is through their capacity to earn money.
The harder they work, the better they provide for their children in the
present and future and the more able they are to meet any crises that
might emerge. As one father who worked extremely hard to make ends
meet put it, "Money is my buffer against trouble. When I have some put
away, I know I can take care of my kids. Take that away from me and
I'm a failure."

By defining themselves as taking care of their children through their
labor, fathers are able to view their time away from their children as a
necessary evil; it is something to regret, but can be lived with. It even
becomes easy to act as though the absence is normal and without negative consequences.

Another corollary of males' common view about their provider/
protector role is that men have tended to discount their capacity to be
nurturers. They have ascribed this role to mothers, even when their
wives work too. Most men get great pleasure out of the interaction
they have with their children, and men have become far more involved
as parents. It is still common, however, for men to regard their wives
as the primary source of nurturing. In this way they are able to view
their own involvement as a kind of "icing on the cake," nice but not
necessary.

The fathers of the present generation of young adult and middle-aged
men were largely unaware that their physical absence had any significant affect on their children. If the palpable absence for long hours of
work or travel time was not understood as harmful, it is safe to assume
that the less obvious distance that comes with being emotionally withdrawn, silent, ill-tempered, stressed out, or drugged out—some of the
ways many men cope with the pressures of their assigned role—was
even less recognized.

It is, of course, not just grown men who held this view of men as
providers. When today's adults were children this traditional outlook
framed our own expectations of our fathers as well. As children this

view made it easy for us also to dismiss our fathers' absence as a necessary evil and to absolve them of any behavior that could be hurtful. It is difficult to comprehend within the rubric of emotions that even well-intentioned behaviors can hurt or that we might unconsciously hold our parents accountable for wounds they had no intention of inflicting. It is more comfortable emotionally to attribute motives or define the circumstances to fit a more benign outlook, one that allows us to retain a positive picture of our fathers.

Thus, as adult children it is logical to look back and say to ourselves:

"Dad needed to work that hard to pay the bills. I can't hold that against him."

"Poor Dad, he looked so exhausted all the time I hated to bother him. I'd just talk with Mom."

"He wasn't there, so we just filled in for him. I don't think we really needed to have him around all that much. After all, we grew up just fine the way it was."

"I never thought of him as particularly capable or interested in being involved that way with me. I accepted that he did his part and left the rest to Mom and us kids to handle. It was probably better that way. He might've made things more complicated anyway."

"The little time he did have seemed to go into being with my brother. I found my own ways to feel special, mostly outside the home or with Mom."

"Frankly, he was such a good guy and trying so hard all the time, I just felt I really wasn't all that important to be concerned with or he would have spent time with me."

These rationalizations allow children to be skillful emotional undertakers, putting a positive face on the situation and then burying it. When we were kids the underlying feelings may have come out sideways as adolescent rebelliousness, poor grades in school, or lack of confidence, but typically were not recognized as being related to Dad. In adulthood, then, there may be no basis for connecting emotional pain or troubles to our fathers' behavior unless it was overtly destructive. Moreover, our childhood rationales shield us from believing there is any pain.

Joan was a social worker in her early forties. She was usually prag-
matic, resilient, and strong in the face of adversity. Her husband had left
her a few years earlier for a younger woman. Though she saw in retro-
spect that her husband had seldom supported her except in crises, she
found herself unable to move forward with her life. She was more
depressed about the end of her marriage than made any sense to her.

In the process of trying to understand her reaction we talked about
her father, who was now retired and living on the West Coast. Her initial description of him was idyllic. He was kind and loving, the most
supportive person in her life. Yet, as she detailed her life growing up, it
became apparent that her father was virtually never home. He was a
salesman who worked late a couple evenings a week and routinely had
to work at least one day of the weekend. When he was around, he was
openly affectionate. He liked to wrestle with her, though he was always
careful not to let things get out of control. Her mother was not a warm
person and didn't like to hug or give public displays of affection. Her
father's brief, fun-filled time with her and her siblings was the core of
love she experienced, and she adapted to the fact that it could occur
only in short, occasional interludes.

As Joan looked again at her relationship with her husband it was
obvious that she had married a man similar to her father. Her husband
worked much like her father did, only he would pull out his briefcase
after dinner and work more. They could spend days apart, and it never
seemed to bother her. She was simply used to love being doled out in
tiny portions. It became apparent that her inability to accept her divorce
meant she could not really live without love. She had been repressing a
cavernous yearning to be recognized as a person who deserved a full
measure of affection. This yearning began as a child, but wore the mask
of adaptation and acceptance until her husband's ultimate rejection.

Out of adapting to the emotional shortfall from our fathers we can
readily turn the tables and blame ourselves for the barriers to greater
closeness. Dan was an individual who carried deep guilt over a missed
opportunity to communicate with his father at the time of his death. Dan
remembered sitting by his father's hospital bedside years earlier. He
knew his father would die within a matter of hours or a few days at best.
He had felt a lump of ill-defined anguish rising out of his chest. He had
an irrational urge to grab his father's gown and shake him into consciousness. He wanted to tell him that he loved him, but he couldn't get
the words out.

As he went back in time Dan unknowingly clenched his hands to the point of blood flow being cut off. He reflected on some of the missed opportunities to let his father into his life. Dan talked about his dead father in purely glowing terms—a wonderful man, a great father. He hadn't recalled at his father's bedside that in all his years, except the last few before his death, Dan had heard his father directly tell him he was proud of him only on one occasion—his record-breaking marathon run in high school.

Now Dan was reading a letter to his dead father that I had asked him to write. It was a chance to express some of what he had never said and what he had realized only too late. Dan had never cried at his father's funeral, but he started to cry as he read this letter. He began to understand finally that the lump he had felt years before at his father's side was not only his own guilt about keeping his father at arm's length but his regret his father had not told him earlier what Dan had meant to him.

In the 1982 film *A Voyage Round My Father*, the lead character, played by Alan Bates, has a soliloquy as he stands in his father's bedroom moments after his father has died. His father had been a wholly domineering, rigid, proud man who could not even acknowledge his blindness to his only son. Bates reflects that he had been told he would feel independent and free after his father died, but all he feels is loneliness. When we have been lucky enough to have a close, supportive relationship with our fathers, we expect to miss them. When we have not, we readily deceive ourselves that we have lost little. We may not know our loneliness. When we are lucky we discover it while there is still time to try to do something about it.

The Problem—Are We Really Affected?

Like many people who seek help through psychotherapy, Dan was acutely aware of his symptoms but had no idea of the cause. He knew he had been drinking too much of late, that he was experiencing a high degree of anxiety and a low degree of motivation for much of anything. He assumed that he was having a "midlife crisis" because it fit his age, forty-four, and because he was finding it difficult to take satisfaction in his present position as a branch manager for a major bank. He believed that his job had exhausted him, but he was fearful about leaving the security it represented for him and his family, especially with two children approaching their college years. This combination of circumstances was at the heart of his anxious, depressed state of mind.

What Dan hadn't noticed was that his change in behavior and mood coincided with the retirement of one of the bank's executive officers, a man who had always been there to back him and advise him when bank politics got dicey. Dan had been feeling isolated and alone at work. He said:

"I know that I'm a person who relies a lot on praise and feedback from other people. I used to get that from John before he retired, plus I always felt a little stronger knowing he was there. Until we started talking about my father and how little direction I ever got from him, let alone the fact that he only praised me that one time, I never saw my relationship with John as filling an old need. It just seemed natural to me. Making this connection brings a lot of stuff together."

Though Dan had become aware of his long-standing sadness about his relationship with his father, he still never imagined that those feelings could somehow create significant emotional turmoil in his life. That something he hadn't even been thinking about could upset and nearly uproot his life defied logic. With the emotional bridge to John, his mentor and friend, identified, his symptoms began to make sense. He could see that without clear messages from his father about how well he was doing, he had grown up lacking confidence in himself and always seeking validation from others.

John's leaving had bared this basic insecurity, heightening his anxiety and making him question whether he could continue to succeed at his job. Hence, his thought of making a career change. The increased drinking was in response to his anxiety, but it was also done to stay in favor with some of the other executives who drank together after work. As an adolescent Dan had drunk too much and his father knew it, but never took a stand against it.

The loss of a mentor or father substitute figure is a common and easily discernible life event that triggers problems indicative of unresolved issues with a person's father. Distorted and continuing dysfunctional reactions after an actual father's death are, of course, transparent. One young woman came to see me trying to understand why she had dropped out of school and was sitting at home brooding. Her father had died suddenly on a business trip six months before. When he was due back the two had been going to have a heart-to-heart talk to help her plan her next year's schedule and decide on what her major field of study would be.

Such strong reactions to the loss of a father or father figure reflect the kind of role in which we tend to put fathers. As Lewis Yablonsky notes in the preface to *Fathers and Sons*, everyone would like to have a father who would be a "superman who would soothe his life by helping him solve his problems and give crystal-clear logical directions for attaining a state of emotional nirvana and success." This is consistent with our culture's idyllic "Father Knows Best"–"Little House on the Prairie" representation of the father role.

It is also true that fathers buy into this role themselves and reinforce their children's view. I recall a morning when I was forcing myself to go to work despite being ill. My daughter, who was ten at the time, sweetly and in some awe told me, "Dad, you're such a great father. You're always there to take care of us."

Before I could settle into the gloriously fulfilling reaction I was having, I quickly started to reflect on what a confining, illusory message I was giving my children. Even if I could be there in such a reliable fashion, what was I teaching them about themselves, about how they could manage without me and live their own lives?

When we realize how much we have depended on fathers we can see how devastating their loss is. The loss may be subtle, but it still affects children when they discover their fathers are not available in some of the fundamental ways they need them to be. Both children and adults, however, are especially adept at denying those things that are disturbing or emotionally painful. The psychohistorian Robert Jay Lifton has identified the human capacity for "psychic closing-off" or emotional distancing as a necessary means of survival for many of the traumatic events in life. How else can people emotionally survive a concentration camp or the dropping of an atomic bomb on their city?

The loss of our dads as idyllic, protective figures in our lives, depending on the form that loss takes, can be a psychological apocalypse. Our defenses may then rise in proportion to protect ourselves from the implications. Incest victims are an example of the potency of this self-protective mechanism. It is possible for such victims to have no recollection for years of the perpetration of the sexual abuse. Despite the blockage of memory, incest survivors are subject to a host of physical, behavioral, and emotional disorders. These symptoms are the result of the power of the trauma coupled with the depth of the denial. The pain must be released indirectly somehow.

While incest is shockingly more prevalent than ever believed in the past, it is not normative. A far more common phenomenon is that of emotionally inaccessible fathers. Even at this level of loss people exhibit a broad spectrum of symptoms that can be linked at least significantly to their wounded relationship with their fathers: lack of self-esteem, anxiety, panic attacks, depression; eating disorders; addictive behaviors, including workaholism and promiscuity; sexual identity problems; difficulty in interpersonal and intimate relationships; and psychophysiological problems, such as ulcers, headaches, spastic colon, tics, or muscular tension.

Jeff's physician referred him for psychological help because of continuing chest pains that were clearly not cardiac related. Jeff was a strapping, outgoing man with an optimistic approach to life on the surface. He was uncomfortable seeing a psychologist and believed there was no relationship between "any of the things from the past you psychologists talk about and whatever this tension is that I've been having." Jeff was quite successful at running his own electrical supply company, but he did realize that he seemed much more worried about his business on a day-to-day basis than made sense. He felt as if he was going off "to do battle," as if the world in which he carried on his commerce was a "war zone."

As Jeff became more comfortable talking about himself, he began to unfold a picture of his growing-up years. His father, who had died two years earlier, had been a councilman in the city in which the family had lived all Jeff's life. During the years in which Jeff's father was active in politics, the 1960s and 1970s, the city experienced enormous racial and political turmoil. Jeff's father was heavily involved and as a result was seldom home until late at night during the week and was often away at meetings and caucuses much of the weekend.

Awe was not too strong a word for how Jeff viewed his father. It seemed that everyone in his political circle turned to him for advice. He also was a target of much harassment from his political enemies. Jeff didn't get to discuss politics with his dad as a kid, but he did overhear him talk about the "sons of bitches that want to cut my balls off" or the "back-stabbing bastards that would shoot me in a minute." His father even used to strap on a gun under his sport coat when he went off to some meetings at night.

It never occurred to Jeff that he had actually grown up in fear. He feared his father, who had a short temper, especially when he'd had too much to drink at a political social event. He feared at least as much that one day his father would not come home alive. With all the talk he heard about the "dog eat dog" world in which we live, his own world had actually been defined for him as an unsafe place.

Moreover, because he had so little time with his father and because his father was so uncommunicative about himself, he never learned about what his father really did or how he worked things out. Thus, Jeff had no means of understanding the relative safety of his world. He went through his life doing the things most other kids and young adults did, but he always felt as if he was having to force himself to do so. He was always sitting on a buried terror that something would go wrong and blow up in his face.

When he saw the connection between the world in which he imagined his father functioned and how he had distorted the dangers of his own business world, a light bulb turned on for Jeff. By the third time we met, the chest pains that had been almost constant for several months (beginning within days of the anniversary of his father's death) were virtually gone. That was also about as much therapy as Jeff wanted, and he stopped coming soon after.

People's symptoms do not usually disappear so readily. Life is usually too complicated for symptoms to be neatly packaged all in response to one issue or trauma. It is clear, however, that the hurt resulting from dysfunctional or disappointing aspects of our paternal relationships becomes embedded in and expressed by a broad range of physical and psychological symptoms.

The Impact—Does It Really Matter Anyway?

Jeff was delighted when his chest pains almost entirely vanished. He was stunned to find that by identifying and talking about the emotional impact of past events he could cure the discomfort. It was like magic. He also apparently believed that his life had just as magically been set on a right course. Magicians, however, know that their magical powers lie in misdirection. Jeff's real problems were not in the muscle tension causing his chest pains, but in his concept of himself.

Jeff had developed a picture of his father as an incredibly bold, confident, powerful man. He believed his dad could do anything he set his mind to and he did it without the least sign of fear or self-doubt. When he compared himself to his father, as all children do, Jeff experienced himself as cowardly and weak.

In his father's last few years of life it became apparent that he was not the fearless, all-powerful man he appeared to be. His drinking had masked his reserved personality and considerable inward fretting. He told tales about some of his political misadventures that showed he was not an invincible kingpin.

In spite of the beginnings of some humanizing cracks in the veneer of his father's image, Jeff had never put this together with his own self-view. He continued to regard himself as the one with the false exterior. He believed others would see through his friendly, exuberant public face and know that he was a mistake waiting to happen, an embarrassment in hiding.

As a result, Jeff did a great deal of avoiding in his life: He never went to graduate school, even though he did well in college and wanted to further his education; he kept his friendships to a limited sphere of people, mostly those who had known him when he was young; he managed his employees poorly because he never could confront them. Even as a father he was tentative with his children and found himself encouraging them to "play it safe" in their own activities.

Jeff is representative of the many sons and daughters who bought into an inflated image of their fathers and consequently carried a deflated view of themselves—not understanding that these were two sides of a trick coin. With fathers it may be particularly easy to ignore the extent to which they influenced our life patterns, because they were often not around that much. One man whose parents divorced when he was about five told me, "How could he have been much of a factor in my life when I didn't see him for ten years after the divorce? He wasn't there, so we did without him." Yet this man shared with his father the same hobbies, a similar pattern of moodiness and way of dealing with feelings, and strikingly comparable attitudes about women.

Even with fathers who were not out of the home, it is common to hear that they were around so little or had so little to do with day-to-day life that their influence is discounted. We simply do not appreciate how powerfully we are drawn, albeit unconsciously, to the persona of our fathers. We attribute influence to direct interaction and to presence, but the status fathers have traditionally held has in itself assigned them enormous psychological weight. As a result, the way we approach work and play and relationships with women or men and with our children is drastically affected by what we observed and experienced from our fathers.

For sons, fathers are the template for what a boy is supposed to grow up to be like. It is more than a modeling of a set of behaviors, because there is a psychological fusion that exists. The boy regards himself as homunculus to the man, a miniature who carries the seeds to form the full-grown man. Even when boys see qualities in their fathers they do not like and thus deliberately try to counter in themselves, they fear that as they grow older they may inexorably take on these qualities. Boys, then, identify with the whole as well as the individual parts of the father.

Daughters are generally not aligned psychologically with their fathers' whole way of being. They identify more with specific traits of the father, though of course they are affected by the sum of his parts. Dads can be significant role models, particularly in arenas where mothers have failed to offer positive images. Fathers of middle-aged daughters are often cited as influences for career direction because the mothers were not engaged in work outside the home. Destructive or negative qualities in fathers conjure up external more than internal fears, concern more about dealing with others who share this quality than about actually having the quality oneself.

One simple exercise I often ask clients to do in order to help them focus on what their fathers meant to them is to make a list of things they regret about that relationship. So many people view their fathers in black-and-white terms, remembering them as ogres or as saints, as never around or always there to count on. As Proust said, "Children have always a tendency either to depreciate or to exalt their parents, and to a good son his father is always the best of fathers, quite apart from any objective reason there may be for admiring him." With some gentle probing and a foundation of trust, clients begin to modify these extreme views, which blunt their understanding of their fathers.

When Jim, a forty-year-old university professor, made his list, he felt a need to add those things for which he was grateful. Yes, he knew he had a few regrets, but the other side of the ledger was more important to him. What he recalled positively about his father was that he made sure his family was economically secure and had a nice home, that he always knew his father would be there for him if he needed him, and that he knew he was loved. Reluctantly, Jim did identify a list of regrets: He missed having had intellectually stimulating talks, talks about how to manage his social life, talks about sexuality, physical affection, time to just play. Jim wanted desperately to minimize these regrets. After all, his father did what he most needed him to do.

I pointed out to Jim that what was missing in his relationship with his father were all things that were ideally part of what one would consider by definition a parent's role. More convincing for Jim, though, was the somewhat jolting realization that all these "regret" items were related to issues he came to work on in therapy—his intellectual and social misgivings about himself, his discomfort sexually with women, his difficulty expressing affection, and his struggle to balance his serious, task-oriented side with a free-spiritedness that was too often suppressed. Realizing how interwoven his own perceived limitations were with his relationship with his father motivated Jim to reexamine that relationship and commit to trying to enlist his father in altering it.

Thus, even if we accept the notion that we were affected by our fathers in specific ways and acknowledge that this can result in identifiable physical or behavioral symptoms, we are falling far short of appreciating our fathers' true impact. Fathers represent a blueprint for how to live life in a world that is confusing, often intimidating, and surely offers no owner's manual. Even when that blueprint reflects ways of living that are repugnant or objectionable, we are still being influenced—either to not act the same way or to follow suit, often in spite of ourselves. Most people do some of each.

In the movie *The Great Santini*, there is a scene in which the son, who has resisted and avoided the aggressive, domineering force of his alcoholic, military hero father, succumbs to his father's goading at a school basketball game. He ends up smashing into an opposing player who has been harassing him all through the game. He hits the boy with such force that he leaves him lying in agony with a broken limb. The behavior is totally opposite to what the son believes in, but his behavior and subsequent reaction demonstrate that he is and he is not his father's son. He acted extremely out of character so that he could receive his father's approval while simultaneously rejecting it. This scenario captures the extraordinary lure of fathers to make us one with them even as we seek to differentiate ourselves from them. This power unwittingly shapes us for better and for worse. In the next chapter we will explore in more depth the ways in which fathers can be powerful and how we are affected by the nature of that power.

2

The Power of Fathers

All fathers except mine are invisible in daytime; daytime is ruled by
mothers. But fathers come out at night. Darkness brings home the
fathers, with their real, unspeakable power. There is more to them
than meets the eye.

Cat's Eye, Margaret Atwood

Donald is just over forty years old. He fought in Vietnam, saw his good
buddy blown up beside him, learned rather easily to kill the enemy. He
led a rough life before and after Vietnam. Now he's facing a major cross-
roads: whether he should change jobs and also marry the woman he
loves. It all feels risky and confusing. At night he has a recurring dream.
He can't recall the details, but it awakens him in a cold sweat. He hears
his father's voice call him by name. It is in that same drawn-out, intimidating way his father used when he intended to punish Donald.

His father has been dead for several years, and Donald had not lived
with him for almost twenty, but his father's voice in a dream calling to
him still elicits the familiar dread of childhood. The fear Donald feels
now is the terror of the boy tagging along behind his father in a panic
about taking a wrong step.

The chilling effect of that dream voice after so many years is not an
unusual response to fathers who were overpowering. Such fathers can
cast a long shadow over their children's lives. Indeed, they held a "real,
unspeakable power" way beyond ordinary dimensions. In fact, it's not

really the kind of power we attribute to our father in most of our routine encounters. That's more about authority and control. It is a power fathers often prefer to deny. It is the power of their being and how it shapes our feelings and our outlook on our lives.

When I was about four years old I had done something to make my father extremely angry. He went to give me a swat, and I ran away. He chased after me, and I promptly locked myself in the bathroom. I can still recall my terror at that moment. In desperation I threw open the door, took a blind swipe at that menacing monster (actually felling him with one punch, because at my perfect height for the occasion I had a direct line on his genitalia), and left him stooped in the hallway. That is one of the few memories I have of that age and the only one to which I can actually attach feelings, my terror. I am quite sure my father had no recollection whatsoever of the event.

By the same token, there are times when my own children have "misbehaved" and I catch myself using my most threatening tone. When I let myself, I can hear the power and intensity of that yelling voice and I want to shrivel up. I want to deny to myself that the man using that unnecessary force is really me.

In part fathers can be unaware of the effect they have on their children because their youngsters may be incapable of telling them. For preverbal children this is obvious, but many fathers would be shocked to hear what their offspring would say if they could answer questions about how intimidating or fearful or powerful they are experienced as being by their own youngsters.

Kafka, in his famed *Letter to His Father*, wrote: "You asked me recently why I maintain that I am afraid of you. As usual, I was unable to think of any answer to your questions, partly for the very reason that I am afraid of you . . ." He went on to say, "Even in writing, this fear and its consequences hamper me in relation to you and . . . the subject goes far beyond the scope of my memory and power of reasoning."

Kafka was in his mid-thirties when he wrote these words. The level of fear that a young child might feel is perhaps better captured in the nightmarish undercurrents of Kafka's fiction.

Once we are adults it is hard to appreciate how our size, our articulateness, our knowledge, our tone, our imagined and real power appear to a child. Philip Greven, author of *Spare the Child*, a book about punishment and its roots in the Protestant ethic, recalled the one time in his life that he was spanked: "When a man who weighs over two hundred pounds, stands six feet and has huge hands spanks a small boy hard, it surely must hurt." Greven states the obvious because he actually could not remember being struck, though he recalled the events leading up to his spanking. He understood that he was so afraid at that moment that his memory was blocked.

Fear is the most obvious and identifiable way in which we experience our fathers' power. Of course, most fathers are only fearful to us on occasion. But our reactions are more complex than simply fear. If you have ever had the opportunity to play Santa Claus for a group of young children, you can appreciate the way in which children can respond to what they see as larger-than-life dimensions in an authority figure. You can feel the excitement and awe for them that comes with just being near this magical figure. Children believe that Santa can look in their eyes and see straight through to all their deeds during the year. Dads can be experienced this way by their young children.

Part of the power of fathers is that on an emotional level we do not close the gap over the years. Fathers remain on a throne of sorts long after we have relinquished our magical beliefs. Their increasingly diminishing actual powers remain cloaked with the mantle of paternal authority, with the capacity to be what we need them to be. As Philip Roth so lyrically put it in *Patrimony*, his poignant memoir of his father: "At least in my dreams I would live perennially as his little son, with the conscience of a little son, just as he would remain alive there not only as my father but as the father, sitting in judgment on whatever I do."

I commonly hear clients voice their dismay about regressing into childlike behaviors when they enter their parents' home, in spite of the hard-earned growth and autonomy they have achieved in therapy. A woman who was executive director of a large agency recalled how she was invited to give a luncheon speech in her home town. Despite being the local celebrity for the moment, she said, "Around my father, I immediately felt the old uneasiness. I worried about whether I dressed appropriately and how I sounded. It was as though he was the entire audience."

Robert Bly, in *Iron John*, talks of three kinds of kings: the Sacred King, the Earthly King, and the Inner King. Santa Claus is more like a Sacred King and exists, therefore, in a magical realm that rises above earthly powers.

The Earthly or Political King is more on the plane on which we relate to our fathers, at least at certain critical moments. The fathers around whom we grew up were rulers in the home castle. If they failed to rule effectively they lost something in our imagination, just as political kings would. But as long as they weren't too unkingly in their behavior, within our imaginations they retained royal powers. They could keep us safe, fix what was broken, tell right from wrong, do the complicated tasks in life, and make bad things go away with the right words or touch. They didn't have the supernatural powers of a Santa Claus, but they could be like him at times and they seemed to have lines of communication to the sacred realm. Moreover, we could rely on them whenever our own Inner King, our capacity to manage our own lives, was overwhelmed or unsure.

So fathers can be anointed with vast power whether or not they know it and whether or not they want it. When they knowingly exercise their paternal powers it adds an edge or weightiness to their authority and children may be more intimidated. Regardless of how conscious fathers are of their power, however, their children's lives are inescapably grounded, like gravity, by this force. Not only does the authority of fathers create emotional boundaries, but the greater the power projected onto them, the more children divest themselves of their own capacity. The higher the pedestal for the fathers, the lower the children may end up feeling.

Jerry's dad had been in combat in World War II. Jerry had not heard his father talk much about the war, but for Jerry it was enough that his father had actually fought. His father was courageous and indomitable. Moreover, Jerry looked up to his dad because of how handy he was. It seemed as if he could fix anything. Whenever Jerry tried to be his father's helper he always seemed to screw up and his dad ended up calling him "stupid" and completing the project by himself. Even though Jerry manages to do a lot of the repairs around his own home as an adult, he still gets uneasy and worries that he is doing them the wrong way. His view at thirty-five is no different than it was at fifteen: "My father set the standard and all I knew was that I fell far short."

Whether fathers are good, successful, effective adults does not in itself determine how much their children internalize, take into and upon themselves, the father's identity. Because children so readily ascribe power to their fathers, they can idealize and inflate the abilities of fathers who do not warrant such adulation.

Regardless of whether fathers were, on some imaginable scale of objectivity, good or bad, weak or strong, able to fulfill their children's needs or not, it is still a critical developmental task for children to learn to separate their own identity from their father's. In this way, the father can be seen more realistically for who he is. What is important about seeing the father clearly is not so much to free sons from holding on to their mothers, or daughters their fathers, as inappropriate love objects, in keeping with the Oedipal Complex theory, but rather to be able to see oneself accurately.

When fathers are overwhelming in their strength with their children, they make it significantly more difficult for their youngsters to achieve this differentiation. Such fathers end up defining their children from without, while internally the children's need to formulate their own sense of self is stifled.

Jennifer reflected on one of the last conversations she had with her father, in which he told her about the one time he was truly ashamed of her. She had come home from a date on time, but lingered in the car. Her father assumed she was doing something sexual with her date and locked her out of the house. The message had lasted as long for Jennifer as it had for her father. She accepted her father's judgment that she was bad and continued to guard against being caught doing anything wrong. "I lived in fear of being shamed and rejected like that again. I couldn't let myself be myself. I wore the mask of someone who was good all the time so I could be sure of being accepted." The judgment of others continued to determine Jennifer's vision of herself.

Both sons and daughters are vulnerable to the loss of identity in the face of a strong, judgmental father. In my experience, the loss for daughters often fits the mold of Jennifer—submerging oneself under the facade of goodness or compliance to avoid rejection.

While Jennifer tried to avoid being seen as bad, she didn't believe she was a bad person. Jerry, on the other hand, struggled for years to overcome feeling "stupid" and incompetent. Despite significant successes in his life he continued to lack self-worth because he judged himself by what he believed his father expected of him and not his own values. The children of fathers whose strength dominates them not only feel diminished, then, but may lack the capacity to value and define themselves at all apart from their fathers. As one young man said to me, "I was so focused on who he was that I didn't pay attention to who I was."

Paul was a highly successful attorney who still felt at age fifty that he was the "flop waiting to happen" that his father always told him he would be. Paul never could understand why he continued to buy into this picture of himself. His own depiction of the interaction with his father offered the explanation:

"I had an outgoing personality as a young kid and was a leader among my classmates. My dad never missed a chance, though, to tell me that my 'charm and personality' didn't count for anything. He said he could see what I really was underneath. I felt like an impostor after that—always waiting for others to see who I really was." For children to hear that their father knows who they really are emasculates their capacity to decide their identity for themselves.

As Paul recognized how his father usurped the right to define him, he finally started to feel some of the anger he had suppressed about his dad. Being able to get angry was a freeing step for Paul because it allowed him to experience a separation between himself and his father. Paul could then put his father outside of him and begin to seize the helm of his personhood.

When children lack self-worth vis-à-vis their fathers, they are losers in two ways: Whatever they do get from their fathers is never enough and whatever they don't get they didn't deserve anyway. The sense of emptiness, of being a nonentity, leads to an unquenchable need for validation, protection, guidance, affection. The children may never feel their needs are fulfilled, much the way addicts might worry about their future supply even as they have just obtained a fix.

Any displays of validation or affection tend to be brushed aside as unbelievable because of how inadequate the children feel about themselves. The children are caught, then, in a circular trap: Their internal emptiness leads to the continued need for support from their fathers, which reinforces their inability to see themselves as individuals in their own right, which in turn leaves them feeling empty.

To break the cycle children of overpowering fathers must find their own strength. They must stop looking to the father for validation and work at taking in the message of their own accomplishments. This process requires movement on both sides of the problem: First, the child must see the father realistically and in perspective in order to deflate his magnitude; and second, the child must be willing to act out of his or her own initiative rather than to please or defend against others. When children follow this path, they not only feel stronger but also recognize their sole right to define themselves. Ironically, they are then free to accept validation externally.

The dynamics that emerge from living with overwhelming fathers often carry over to children's relationships with others. One common impact of the loss of identity is to leave these children feeling vulnerable to others imposing their will on them. Jennifer, for example, avoided conflict with others, especially with her husband, because she expected to be shamed and rejected and she did not believe she could successfully resist or counter such a reaction. The feelings of inadequacy and alienation from the self that arise from being defined from without often have been ignored, repressed, or rationalized as to be expected in relation to the father. These insecure feelings may emerge with others, however, as we project our fathers' power onto them.

Another effect of the lack of identity is to leave the children fearful that others will see through them and recognize their inadequacy. Intimate relationships, then, carry the risk that getting close will lead to embarrassing exposure or to losing oneself in the other's identity. To avoid either risk, the children maintain emotional walls to keep others from getting too close.

In order to feel less vulnerable in relations with others and more confident in their self-identity, children must come to the realization that their responses to others are conditioned or learned through their paternal relationship. There are two significant dimensions to this realization: *No one can continue to have power over us the way our fathers did, unless we let him or her; and, as with any learned behavior, we can practice and condition new responses.* Making the connection to our fathers in how we relate socially allows us to see others with objectivity and frees us to take down our emotional walls. We can then practice holding our ground and being ourselves with others. In the process, our fear of rejection and being overpowered diminishes and our self-confidence grows.

Any father may at times use his potential to dominate, including fathers who are normally experienced as weak or ineffectual. There are many fathers, however, whose use of their authority or dominant image represents a consistent, distinct pattern of parenting. I have identified three types of father patterns that represent common excessive and distorted uses of power: ideal, autocratic, and abusive fathers.

These types are not mutually exclusive and, in fact, one could conceivably function in all three ways. It should be noted that fathers don't normally make a conscious choice to follow a particular style of being powerful, let alone decide whether they will dominate their children. Usually they are simply attempting to carry out the role they believe is expected of them. Most men, despite the fact that we still live in a patriarchal society, are not very aware of the power they wield and may not feel powerful at all. That is one of the primary reasons for their distorted uses of power.

Of the three types, perhaps the most subtle and therefore the most confusing in its impact is that of the ideal father. On the surface, what could be a problem with having a dad who seems thoroughly competent and all-knowing? The difficulty lies, as we shall see, in what messages are communicated to the children of such fathers as they live out their elevated status.

The Ideal Father

Near the end of the movie *Brighton Beach Memoirs*, Stanley returns home after a failed attempt to run away by enlisting in the armed services. His father, understanding the source of his son's pain, wisely tells him, "You go through life thinking I was perfect, you'll hate yourself for every mistake you make." If Stanley accepts this jeweled bit of wisdom, his life will be markedly easier.

Ideal fathers are ones who fail to pass this message on to their children. Instead they consciously or unconsciously maintain the illusion that they operate at an Olympian level above the plains of normal folk. The issue is not how well Dad performs, how successful he is, or how admirable he is. Many fathers are all of these. The ideal father prototype is the dad who sets himself up or allows himself to remain on a pedestal.

When fathers are known to achieve successes or demonstrate their competence, their children benefit from the positive role model and the source of pride this represents. It affirms that they are the son or daughter of someone who is special, which touches them with the wand of specialness by proxy. What is damaging to the child of the ideal father is not his successes, but the invisibility of how he achieves them and of his imperfections.

The physical and emotional distance with which fathers normally carried out their role meant that their children were cut off from seeing how they achieved success in whatever way they did. This success at a distance gives a magical quality to the father's achievements. The children do not see the degree of effort involved, the mistakes that are made, the help of peers, the points of discouragement, the near misses and the forgotten disasters. This all serves to elevate the father in the children's eyes. The greater the apparent ease with which the father has achieved success, the more he takes on the status of a superhero.

My father was not successful in terms of the status of his job as a carpenter. He did, however, seem like a master of his trade. Around home he seemed able to repair, rebuild, or gerrymander anything from a television to a door lock. His jack-of-all-trades handiness led me to believe he must be a highly skilled carpenter. Only as an adult, when I hired workmen myself, could I see that in comparison, my dad's workmanship was often crude. He got the job done but he was not an artisan.

There are many fathers whose achievements are by no means extraordinary who try to maintain an image of perfection. They do this out of their own need to prove and value themselves. Most do it with little inkling of how they might be creating difficulties for their children. Some do this by acting as though they always have the answers to every problem or are always right. Some do it by their intolerance for their children's mistakes, others by masking or stubbornly refusing to allow for their own errors.

Tina's father had been a sort of child prodigy. He entered college at sixteen and went on to become one of the youngest tenured faculty members at the same college. As a parent he seemed to need to maintain his standing as a prodigy. Around the dinner table, for example, he liked to toss out challenging questions for which only he would have the fully accurate answer. When Tina or her brother tested their intellectual mettle, he would lightly praise their attempt, while finding the weak spot in their thinking. Tina, who was one of the brightest young women I have known, was in graduate school before she began to believe she had an intellect.

The roots of ideal fathers' striving to maintain a highly positive image usually go back to their own fathers. Geoffrey Wolff wrote about his father's distorted attempts to be successful in *The Duke of Deception*. Wolff's effort to understand his father's career as a con artist took him back to his physician grandfather's unvarying focus with his own son on achieving the best of everything. Duke got the message. "Because he exhibited none of the superiority so precious to The Doctor, he pretended to it." The superiority of the grandfather in the Wolff family led to a legacy of deceit to hide the feelings of instilled inferiority. By the third generation Geoffrey was coping with the illusion of superiority, which was in its own way as damaging as the real thing.

It takes a long time for children to arrive at the understanding that their fathers' apparent flawlessness could be a problem in the father and not proof of their own imperfection. Fathers make it more difficult to gain perspective when they use their inherent power to suppress any exposure of their weaknesses. It only takes a penetrating, icy glare or a line like "Do you have any idea how long I've been doing this sort of thing?" for a father to ward off a child's questioning of his expertise.

One father who was a rather self-righteous school principal used the tactic of walking off in disgust whenever his children said or did something with which he didn't agree. His obvious disdain, together with the inability to even discuss the matter, left his children feeling that they had wronged him so badly they didn't deserve to be around their father at these times. In this way the father maintained his holier-than-thou status in the family. This father in actuality used a good offense as his own best defense. He was hiding some shameful behavior of his own by keeping the focus on his kids' behavior. For years he had been sneaking off after evening meetings in the community to seek out prostitutes. It took the family years to realize that his rejection was his way of abandoning them because he could not deal with his own shame.

The power of the ideal father has the effect of distorting the child's self-perception. Seeing the father as perfect enhances all that the father is and does and diminishes the child in his or her own eyes. The child feels minuscule and inadequate by comparison, though in this case the focus is on accomplishments rather than power. The child's idealized view of the father also blinds him or her to the ways the father may have failed even in basic ways as a parent.

Jim, the university professor in Missing Our Fathers, is an example of the way we can overlook a dad's shortcomings. Jim always felt his father had provided for all his needs. His reverence for his father allowed him to regard as minor flaws his father's lack of physical affection, guidance on social issues, and interaction on a feeling and intellectual level. Jim inferred what he needed from his father, but it was not delivered directly, and thus his father's way of parenting remained perfect and untainted in Jim's eyes.

When the ideal father remains aloof or too busy or does not successfully transfer some of his skills and success in life to his children, the children will not only be likely to feel like failures by comparison, but will doubt ever having the capacity to match the father. Without the reality check that comes with interaction and self-revelation, the children cannot see their fathers in perspective. The father's achievements serve to distinguish and elevate him, not unite him with his children. A standard is set that defines success by the manner in which the father has achieved it.

Despite a solidly respectable career of his own, one man, at age sixty, still felt like an outright failure in comparison to his father. He remarked to me, "My father was like a projector sending up on a screen the standard I was supposed to meet—and didn't."

Long after the projector stops running, the children of ideal fathers continue to see the standard on the screen. Even though they may not believe they can live up to that standard, they still feel tremendous pressure to try. It is as though their fathers are standing over them exhorting them to keep trying. If the standard cannot be met, the child can at least make the effort in following the father's example. Many try to fend off their despair at falling short of the father's success by working far harder than they saw their fathers work. This heroic effort is intended to substitute for reaching the father's level of achievement.

Amanda was in her mid-fifties, yet she still basked in the glow of remembering how she was her daddy's favorite. Her two older brothers had captured their mother's adulation. Whenever there were arguments, the mother sided with the boys. If there were chores to be done, Amanda got the worst job or the one that took the longest.

Amanda's dad was usually gone all week, either because his work took him out of town or because he simply worked long hours. When he was home, Amanda felt as if she had an ally and a protector. Because Amanda believed she was under the protective wing of her dad, it was natural for her to identify with him. His dedication to work and his exacting standard became hers as well.

One afternoon, as we discussed how safe and valued she felt around her father, Amanda flashed back to a Saturday in her early adolescence.

Her dad was home, sitting in the living room as she bounded down the staircase on her way to be with friends. He asked her if she had remembered to complete a chore for him. When she answered that she had not, a shadow of disappointment passed over her father's countenance. She knew she had let him down.

What was lost on Amanda in that brief encounter was the recognition that life with her father was not always safe. His disappointment over a small matter had pierced her heart. Her father's support was so crucial to Amanda that she could not bear to fail him. In order to be sure she would never see that look again, Amanda devoted herself to completing all that was expected of her. The pattern carried into adulthood, particularly in her work life. She was always the dependable staff member who worked longer and harder and who always got it right.

Unfortunately, Amanda could not take pride in her achievements or the praise she often received. The focus of her effort was on being invisible to others, never to see the look of disappointment. Her visibility, even in the most positive ways, only left her feeling more vulnerable, so she continually worked herself toward oblivion.

The stress experienced by these children of ideal fathers comes not only from how hard they push themselves, but, more important, from how hard they think they have to push themselves. Because they view their dads in idealized terms, the children assume that however hard they saw their father work, they need to work much harder to stay anywhere within the length of his shadow. If success seems to have come to the father with ease, without his apparently having ever broken into a sweat, the children must work until the perspiration flows.

The pressure is not only that of how hard they must labor. Living up to the image of the ideal father leaves the children without room to make mistakes in the process. These children typically have highly unrealistic images of how well things must be done, believing, for example, that any project must be totally error-free to be considered satisfactory. Anything less is a poor job. This distorted perspective leaves such offspring unable to relax as they perform, incapable of appreciating what they do accomplish, and fearful of exposure to others' judgments, wherein they feel sure they will be found lacking.

Gene always thought of his father as a Renaissance man. He was not only a skilled and highly respected surgeon, but he was a wonderful artist. He could fix virtually anything with the precision of an artisan, and all his family, friends, and relatives sought him out for his rabbinic wisdom. It wasn't enough that his father could do all this, he did it with a natural ease. Everything seemed to flow off his fingertips or his lips as though it required no forethought. Gene used to sit in awe for hours in his father's workroom, watching his father from a stool beside him.

One summer when Gene was away at camp, his father spent the whole summer constructing a new bedroom as a gift for his son's bar mitzvah. When Gene arrived home to the surprise, all he could think was, "It's just perfect." It was the best gift by the best father made in the best way possible. His father had thought of everything: the built-in bookcases, the headboard with lighting for nighttime reading, a place for his alarm clock and radio, air conditioning, closets designed with spaces for all his possessions. The bedroom was a labor of love and spoke the words his father rarely actually said. Gene felt like a prince living at the top of the castle.

His father always told Gene, "A thing worth doing is a thing worth doing well." He demonstrated that in all he did, but he didn't try to teach Gene how to do the things he did so well. He was a reserved man who never wanted to impose his own way of doing things on his son, so he only explained what he was asked. Gene rarely asked, because he was in such awe and didn't imagine he could do what his father did in any but the most laughable form.

Gene's father gave him the gift of perfection, of seeing what a naturally talented man could produce and of having that man as his own parent. The gift was also a curse, because the gift became the standard of performance for Gene and it was a standard he did not believe he was capable of attaining.

What made Gene most doubt his capacity to be like his father was the apparent naturalness with which his father did things. Gene had to work hard to achieve his successes. In college he did extremely well, but he studied all the time. Later, in business, he always felt he needed to put in longer hours than anyone else. He was caught in a vicious circle: out of his belief that he lacked the natural talent of his father, he overworked on everything he did, and because he put in so much effort, he devalued his accomplishments. Someone with real talent, for example, his father, could have done the same or better without all that effort.

In spite of his view that he wasn't gifted, or really because of it, Gene continued to drive himself to be perfect in everything he did. He was as hard on his subordinates as he was on himself, pushing them to do their best and ridiculing them or blowing up at any mediocre efforts.

Even on the golf course Gene could not let up. He hated losing, but often got beat by players who were clearly not as good. He took a lesson once and the pro was stunned. He told Gene he had the most perfect, natural swing of anyone with whom he had worked. His problem was not his ability or his form, it was how tightly he gripped the golf club! Out of believing he wasn't good enough, Gene held on too tightly and threw off his whole game. He couldn't imagine what a natural he really was.

It follows that if I feel diminished in comparison to my father, I will have a hard time believing in myself. Children of ideal fathers measure themselves by how far they feel they fall short of their fathers, not how well they measure up to others. In fact, their distorted self-view leads them commonly to believe others will more readily match their father's standard than they will. Moreover, they believe others will expect this same standard of them.

Mike had taken over his father's business and built it up extremely well. When his father had run the business it seemed that things operated very smoothly. His dad knew how to handle any problem that arose. Despite how demanding his father was, even with his customers, everyone respected him and responded to his directness. Mike's father had mellowed considerably in retirement and tried to be supportive of Mike in a way he had not been as his boss. He repeatedly voiced his pride in his son's performance. Yet Mike complained that he still felt intimidated whenever he called upon heads of companies. He viewed these people as truly successful, while he was merely his successful father's son. Mike was so caught up in trying to please his father and pouring all his energy into winning his father's praise that he could not understand that he was having his own success. As a result, he did not build confidence in himself. He approached each challenge as though for the first time and was unsure whether he could handle it.

When we do not internalize or take credit for our own abilities, we are insecure with each new test. We live in anxiety, waiting for the time when our true, until-now-hidden ineptitude will be exposed. This is not merely the anxiety that someone might observe a defect in our work, a spot on our clothes, so to speak. We fear being suddenly stark naked in front of a huge spotlight. The illusion of competence we have carefully woven will come unraveled by the pull on one loose thread. Mike talked of how he lost his boldness when he walked in to see a "successful" company president. He felt that all it would take was one sentence to wipe him out, to expose him as stupid and thus not worth giving the time of day.

The fear of exposure as a failure leads many children of ideal fathers to erect barriers between themselves and anyone who is a threat to their guarded vulnerability. Mike attempted to do that by working extra hard, but the veneer he managed to create was a thin one. Throwing themselves into work is a common way these children handle their insecurity. It not only serves as a way to compensate for shortcomings, it can put them at a remove from others. Out of their expectation and fear of being judged, they choose to put themselves out of reach on a feeling level. These are people who may act as if they are indifferent to others' opinions, reveal little or nothing of themselves to others, take no risks lest they be criticized. They attempt to have no blemishes simply by revealing none.

Children of ideal fathers tend to lack confidence in themselves, carry considerable anxiety, and fear exposure from others. These reactions occur not only because children feel inferior to their fathers, but often because the fathers have, in their preoccupation with sustaining their own image, neglected to validate their children. Because they regard their dads in such idyllic terms, these children have an intense desire to receive their love and approval. While they doubt their capacity to measure up to their fathers, it is only the fathers, because of their elevated status, who can reassure them. As one son lamented to me, "I was so hungry just to be able to go to him with something I'd done and have him say it was okay. That would've been so nice."

Children of ideal fathers generally do not blame their fathers for their lack of validation. Indeed, they may go to great lengths to protect their father's image—deflecting criticism and guarding them from exposure to negative judgments. To see dad's flaws is to see him as no longer perfect, which topples him from his pedestal. Instinctively the children may also understand that within this powerful man also lies the potential for unraveling. They need the illusion of his strength and success to lean on, to shore up their own feelings of weakness. They fear the loss of that in their lives and guard against it to preserve the structure of their own psyches as much as his.

As one young man told me, "The image I have is of him being big and me being small. If I surpassed him somehow, then it would be like looking at him through the other end of a telescope." Rather than risk this dramatic shrinking of his father's stature, he tended to hold himself back from developing his own considerable talents.

By protecting, sustaining, or simply buying into the image of their fathers as flawless, children of ideal fathers can take on a crushing emotional burden. They may end up seeing any of the ways they fall short of their fathers as signs of being deficient. In accepting the picture of themselves as failures in comparison to their fathers, they become entrenched in the pain of feeling unworthy. The huge disparity they believe exists between themselves and their fathers and their inability to hold their dads accountable leaves them caught in a vice of self-disparagement. They do not feel entitled to receive the love and approval they want and need from the fathers they idealize. Therefore, they believe they have no right to complain about not getting it. Yet without the fathers' validation they remain trapped in their negative self-image.

This outlook becomes fertile soil for depression to take root. It is not uncommon for children of ideal fathers to become depressed, because they carry such feelings of inadequacy and powerlessness. These feelings are coupled with the belief they are helpless to change their situation. If these children hold back or give up out of despair at ever being good enough for the father, then, of course, they have no chance of altering their self-concept.

Even without struggling against depression, children of ideal fathers have a difficult time developing confidence and a sense of self. It's like the old westerns where the town wasn't big enough for both gunfighters. The identity of the children is crowded out by the father, but the children are more likely to leave town with their heads low than to attempt a face-off.

Healing the Wounds From Ideal Fathers

The first step in healing for children of ideal fathers relates to the image they carry of the father. As long as we maintain our father on a pedestal, we remain awestruck peons. We look up to the wonderful qualities of the father and look down at or ignore our own qualities. We feel small and inept by comparison. It is often extremely difficult to alter this view, partly out of loyalty, partly out of not wanting to relinquish the aura of specialness attributed to the father, and partly because we are left to face the challenge of acting on our own potential.

Removing our father from the pedestal does not mean destroying his image, it simply requires seeing him in real terms. In many instances moving toward an honest appraisal of the father involves putting an end to a pattern of covering for or protecting him. Children of ideal fathers may be so focused on the father's aura of success they do not realize how engaged they are in helping to sustain this status.

Fred had focused on his father for several sessions in our therapy. He seemed quite clear about the ways in which his dad's judgmental nature and lack of support had undermined his concept of himself. One of his memories was of the time his dad was called to school after Fred had gotten hurt accidentally on the playground. The first words out of his father's mouth were, "You had better not have been misbehaving again!" His father's look was of mistrust, not caring. He did not notice the bright red patch on Fred's head that marked a still bleeding cut in need of stitches.

The story was in keeping with the general pattern of neglect Fred had experienced from his father. The postscript fit another pattern: Fred did not hesitate to add an explanation that absolved his father of wrong-doing. What came across as a blatant failure to nurture became, in Fred's view, an understandable oversight because his father likely had been interrupted in his demanding schedule at work.

When we stop filling in all the potential cracks in the character of the father, we can begin to make an objective appraisal. We need to review our father's strengths but also look for his foibles and for the ways he let us down. We need to examine how he may have failed to meet his own expectations or goals. Fred's dad, for example, was a professor of theater arts, but it never dawned on Fred that his father might have dreamed of being an actor himself at an earlier point in his life.

An extension of believing we do not measure up to the paternal standard of success is to project onto others the same standard and the same power to judge us. In working with my clients on this omnipresent vulnerability to the judgments of others I sometimes suggest they imagine they are carrying their father around with them perched on their shoulder. The point of this exercise is to exaggerate their tendency to feel their father observing and judging them. The exercise helps them realize that whether their insecurity comes from the perceived judgments of others or their own self-evaluation, its original source lies in what they experienced from their father.

The next step in healing is to be able to make the connection between our behavior and feelings and the inflated image we have allotted to our fathers. We need to see, for example, that our insecurity, anxiety, and fear of exposure are related to the one-sided validation that went in the direction of the father's ego and did not make its way back to our own. We need to recognize the destructiveness of behaviors intended, consciously or unconsciously, to compensate for our diminished self-view. Examples include the tendency to push ourselves too hard or the inverse behavior of being afraid to push ourselves, leaving no room for ourselves to make mistakes, and keeping ourselves at an emotional distance from others whose judgments we fear.

Being aware of the roots of these self-protective yet self-destructive behaviors helps to free us to overcome them. We can be more motivated and more hopeful about making such changes when we comprehend that we developed the behaviors for specific reasons that are no longer valid and may never have been necessary.

The key to making a transition toward healing ourselves is in coming to terms with how we have relied on the image of our father as all-competent and thus supplanted building a strong image of ourselves. Where sons especially are subject to having their identity measured through their dads, daughters, particularly those who were growing up prior to the psychological gains of the women's movement, have faced another complicated obstacle. The power of ideal fathers has been magnified by the patriarchal culture. The qualities of success that were ascribed to the father were reserved for men anyway. Thus, the daughter of an ideal dad has had to overcome the cultural message as well as the familial one to be able to honor her own worth.

Amanda, who had been so affected by the singular episode of disappointing her dad, had a metaphorical picture of herself as a vine. She was a beautiful vine, but always needed a post to grow around or toward. Without the post to center her or to offer a direction she became a shapeless ball of leaves. This metaphor proved to be a powerful catalyst for her growth, because it focused her on working toward becoming her own post as well as the vine. The realization that she had to do her own growing was scary, yet began to feel increasingly liberating.

She found she could appreciate her own beauty and strength when the responsibility for her shape was her own.

Building up our own self-image is not something we do wholesale upon ourselves. We get there by a series of long-practiced steps, beginning with the assumption of full responsibility for the transformation. We must be determined that no one, including our father, will define us. Forming ourselves from the inside requires listening to ourselves carefully each step of the way as we try to make changes, listening for what we believe is right for us. If we are patient with ourselves and take the time, we will hear a voice from within that expresses our true self-knowledge.

Listening to ourselves provides the right compass, but movement requires taking risks. We don't have to push ourselves in ways that are excessively uncomfortable, but if we don't attempt new behaviors that stretch us and thus feel somewhat unsettling, then we will not have accomplished anything significant enough to enhance our view of ourselves. These steps can be small in practical terms or degree of change, but large psychologically. For example, being the one to propose what the family or group of friends will do one night can be an act that makes us more visible with others and takes courage.

When we begin taking risks, we must concentrate on seeing ourselves and what we have managed to do rather than focusing on others viewing us differently. We need to take ownership for our accomplishments. As obvious as this sounds, it is a difficult task. Children of ideal fathers have been so used to trying to please others they feel invisible to themselves or they do not accept that it is their action that brought about an accomplishment. I often have to remind people: "That was you that did that!" Our tendency is to not value the achievement; since it doesn't count for much, we let it slide quickly out of mind.

The healing process for children of ideal fathers can be summed up in four stages: removing the father from his pedestal; recognizing what we have done to ourselves to keep him in an elevated position; developing our own compass and measuring stick to guide and evaluate ourselves; and becoming proactive about risking and owning changes. As we strengthen our own self-concept, we humanize and enrich rather than diminish our vision of our fathers. Ironically, we can see more about our fathers and about ourselves that we can genuinely appreciate when we relinquish our rose-colored glasses.

3

When Power Is Misused

Ideal fathers are overpowering because their children suffer in comparing themselves to them and because they fail to provide the feedback and connection that would allow their children to absorb and integrate their own strengths. The effect of ideal fathers is rather benign when contrasted with the malignant impact of autocratic or abusive fathers who overtly misuse their emotional or physical strength.

Autocratic Fathers

A father is autocratic when he consciously or unconsciously tries to exert too much influence over his child's behavior. This father would be described as controlling, domineering, intrusive. He fails to support and develop adequately the child's confidence and ability to make decisions. He responds with judgments while restricting his child's efforts to function independently. The father may subordinate the child's needs for growth to his own need to feel important. Furthermore, he may treat his child as a possessed object rather than a distinct and separate entity. He often justifies his domination through an inflated view of his own knowledge and experience, a deflated view of the child's, and a misguided desire to be protective of the child's well-being.

I recall a conversation my father had late in his life with the son of an old acquaintance. My father was trying to remember which of this man's uncles had died first. When the man told my father the correct sequence, my father persisted in disputing the accuracy of his memory. The man gently protested and reminded my father that he was indeed talking about his own family and had no doubt when each uncle had died. My father paused and begrudgingly said, "Well, maybe so."

The memory of this interaction makes me smile even today because of the brazen presumptuousness of my father. I am truthfully not sure, however, whether I was more taken aback at the time by my father arguing his absurd position or by his ultimate admission of fallibility. Such admissions were not a part of my experience of my dad in growing up. His cocksure belief in his own judgment and his willingness to extend his opinions into all aspects of life for me and my brothers were boundless.

When we argued politics, there could only be one correct outlook. My father's personal stake in the political correctness of his sons' views got me discharged from the dinner table on more than one occasion. He tried to tell me everything from how to dress or walk properly to how to study for tests in subjects he never took. I knew on some level that he truly wanted to bring out the best in me, but his efforts were so intrusive and smothering they led me to conceal as much of my life from him as I could. The only way I could find to end his domination was to remove everything from his purview.

In a sense the autocratic father is playing out the traditional expectations of a father without the appropriate boundaries that we now understand children need. The behaviors of the autocratic father are in keeping more with what men have routinely experienced in their work lives. The hierarchical structures and emphasis on accountability, competition, and domination that are central to so many work environments tend to condition men to focus on authority and operate out of top-down interactions. The father may have been treated this way himself or have treated his own employees in this fashion and then brought these same behaviors home. This authoritarian orientation is characteristic of fathers who believe they must meet the work world head-on with toughness in order not to be dominated themselves and in order to provide for their families successfully.

It seems all too logical that what appears to be effective at work should be at home as well. Fathers have not readily recognized how different the needs of family life are from those of work. There are some who would argue that men have been raised to work from the time they were children, so it should not be surprising that in turn they try to raise their children according to the code to which they have been most exposed. Moreover, their perspective was limited by their own experience in growing up, since most had fathers themselves who were little involved at home and principally played the role of provider.

Erik Erikson, in his ground-breaking psychohistorical analysis of Hitler's childhood, attempted to explain how the prototypical German middle-class father of that era might have affected his children. This was a father who demanded unwavering respect and equated respect with love. He was aloof, harsh, and domineering. Erikson's description of this stereotypical Germanic father suggests how consuming his effect was on family life: "When the Germanic father comes home from work, even the walls seem to pull themselves together. . . . The children hold their breath, for the father does not approve of 'nonsense'—that is, neither of the mother's feminine moods nor of the children's playfulness."

While we might like to believe that the Germans of that era cornered the market on authoritarianism, there was and continues to be ample orientation toward paternal domination among other cultures. The Erikson description, while an extreme example, reflects what is a widespread style of fathering—engendering fear and unquestioning obedience as a means of keeping order in the household. Order is the primary goal of autocratic fathers. These fathers are convinced that a "healthy" fear of them will serve their children well.

Jennifer's experience of being locked out by her dad when she lingered in the car on a date was not the only time she was the recipient of a harsh reaction from him for supposedly doing something wrong. The message was ingrained that "bad" behavior would elicit his anger, and his anger was deeply feared by Jennifer. The extent to which Jennifer dreaded any transgression that would ignite her father's wrath is illustrated by the time she made a crack in the garage door with the car. After painting over the crack to hide the accident from her dad, she spilled the paint on the driveway. She then bought more paint and painted the entire driveway black.

What is masked in a father's autocratic behavior are the needs being served for him. Having order makes the father's life easier, not necessarily the child's. After a day's work it's nice to have peace and quiet and little to deal with. For some fathers the idea that their home is their castle reflects an impenetrable place of rest or a place where one is the king, someone special. Often, however, it serves as a haven where the father feels at least some semblance of power over his life.

The father whose pride rests on this kind of authority at home is a man whose dominating behavior is used to hide his insecurity. In the 1982 movie *A Voyage Round My Father*, the father is blinded in an accidental fall when his son is a toddler, but goes through his entire life acting as though nothing has happened. In order to maintain that fiction he must also avoid talking about anything serious and remain in charge of the family's conversation at all times.

A father's controlling behavior can be a cover for a whole range of uncomfortable feelings about himself. The father who feels that he has been a failure in the work world or who struggles daily with doubts about his self-worth or ability or who feels that underneath his outer cloak of bravado is a weak, inept person may relish the feeling of power he can gain from his domination at home. It can be assumed that such men fear exposure of their weaknesses and flaws. Most men feel that they are expected to appear strong to others and therefore feel compelled to some degree to prevent others from seeing signs that would belie that invincible image. The more intimidating their controlling manner at home, the more they are likely to feel vulnerable inside themselves. Dominating behavior, however, may not only keep others off the scent, but allow these fathers to avoid experiencing their own vulnerability.

One Saturday morning as I was doing my routine of stretches, my daughter turned on the television and started watching a cartoon. I was doing my best to ignore the cacophony emanating from the set until I realized that the cartoon was actually about fathers and sons! A father duck was acting like a drill sergeant and trying to get his young duck son not to be a chicken (pun intended). The son initially tries to deceive his father, but finally confesses that he is still fearful. At this point, the father confesses that he was always a coward, too, and was only trying to get his son to do what he himself could not. The two go off arm in arm.

This cartoon tapped into a common caricature of fathers—the tough, demanding father who is, underneath it all, really a softy. Unfortunately, not many such fathers readily acknowledge their soft side to their children. They are more inclined to hold on to their appearance of toughness rigidly and be intolerant of displays of weakness in others. Philip Roth remarked of his father, "He could never understand that a capacity for renunciation and iron self-discipline like his own was extraordinary and not . . . shared by all."

In some sense, we admire this willfulness in our fathers. We regard it as part of their strength. Many families do sense that there is an illusion to this outward appearance, but, as with the emperor's clothes, they prefer to maintain the illusion rather than deal with the naked emperor. Roth's mother, in fact, was at one time thinking of divorce but couldn't confront his father, because "he couldn't take it. . . . He would crumble up. It would kill him." How many authoritarian fathers have been spared for this same reason, a reason which also protected his wife and children from facing his masked weakness.

Families of autocratic fathers frequently exist, then, within a paradoxical situation. The father's dominating behavior places him at the center of family dynamics and makes him a powerful force in the family. If the vulnerability the father maintains under cover should be exposed, though, the power structure that provides the family stability could crumble with the father.

Children and mothers often are intuitively aware of the father's hidden weakness even if they rarely if ever see it revealed. Yet this understanding of the father's true character is often carried by each family member as a dark secret, not to be openly acknowledged or tested. Instead, the family conspires, as they did in *Voyage Round My Father*, to protect the father's image. Thus, they end up in the role of protector for this seemingly strong father.

While on some level of emotional security children benefit from the sustained illusion of their father's image of authority, there are other levels at which emotional dilemmas are created. The child who wants to identify with a father's strength can feel caught in a quandary. If my father's power is a front, then can my own power be real? If he feels powerful and acts like it, but I know he's covering his weak side, what do I believe about authoritative behavior—when is it real and when is it a cover? What should I expect of myself—what he tells me to or what I feel, especially when my feelings are so confused? What should I do with my own feelings of vulnerability? Do I respect Dad for what he is or disdain him for what he isn't?

The burden for a child who accepts the role of image protector for a father is immense, and usually such youngsters become mirror images of their fathers. They try to appear to the outside world as competent, strong individuals and within themselves feel at least as insecure as their fathers must have felt. Protecting the father's image of strength does not breed strength in the children. Rather, it perpetuates the pattern of hiding any weakness.

Rita thought of her dad as another Captain Von Trapp from the film *Sound of Music*, not because he could sing, but because he was a widower with a large family and he was fiercely devoted to keeping the family together. He had remarried, and Rita's stepmother was a demanding, intolerant woman. Rita's father had always sided with his wife and supported the rigid rules she imposed on the kids. Rita became a perfectionist herself, but could never do enough to feel satisfied herself or seemingly to convince her father or stepmother of her worth. Rita was in her thirties before she began to see that her father's own rigidity and allegiance to his wife were self-protection to assure he would have a caretaker for his children and himself. Out of her own need for security and at her own emotional expense, she had honored his needs.

The autocratic father, whether or not his children see the cracks in his armor, does not breed confidence in his children. The father not only ends up controlling behavior, but distorts the children's view of their ability to act. Kafka contended he saw the entire capacity of fatherhood residing in his father. There was none left for him, as though there were only so much capability rationed to each family and his father had coveted and snared all of it.

Many children of these fathers take an all or nothing view of things, which is not surprising since that perception characterizes their fathers' rigid approach. In the face of their fathers' tight controls over their lives, they feel like nonentities. They perceive themselves as failures, for they cannot compare to their fathers. Their fathers actually are trying to achieve the opposite persona for their children. The natural consequence of controlling behavior, however, fails to support the children's independent growth.

Children of autocratic fathers must struggle with a frustrating set of dilemmas to overcome the destructive impact on their self-identity. The father's controlling nature does not leave adequate room for the child to make his or her own choices and take initiatives, which are the pathway to developing an identity. The paths open to the child are those either selected or approved by the father.

What children in fact need for healthy psychological growth is the support of the father to discover their own likes and dislikes. Instead, the controlling father is, in effect, constantly laying out conditions that must be met to win his approval. This leads the child to be watching his or her behavior constantly and to be drawn magnetically to function within the sphere of what will please this demanding man. It becomes a challenge to win him over, and, of course, this hard-to-get approval, following the law of supply and demand, is made all the more precious.

Conditional love and acceptance, however, is not satisfying. There is much anxiety attached to it, because one doesn't know for sure it will be there and when it may be withdrawn. Any affirmation from the father is attached to the fulfillment of his conditions and is not taken as a personal achievement. The child experiences much pressure to be what the father wants and does not feel accepted for who he or she is. The child is left feeling unknown, empty, and always under the threat of rejection.

If we could imagine the monologue that takes place on some preconscious level in such a child's mind as he or she agonizes over how to behave with an autocratic father, it might go like this:

"If I obey my father's rigid rules I stay out of trouble with him and in some ways feel that I am a good child. It leaves me feeling empty inside, however. I am not my own person. I feel weak and cowardly. If I disobey him, I feel stronger in some ways, as if I do have a mind of my own. I retain a spirit and an identity of my own. I feel more alive. But I also pay a price by getting punished or being rejected by him. I feel as if I'm being bad. Even though part of me knows I'm doing the right thing to not always listen or agree, the other part can't accept that it's okay, because he is my father and he thinks I'm bad."

The children of autocratic fathers want to retain the closeness they obviously need, which paradoxically gives them access to the approval of the father at the expense of believing in or valuing themselves. One way offspring try to resolve this dilemma is with a paradoxical response. Commonly children of such fathers try to "stay close" by keeping a distance. They do those things that will win approval, but often they do them less for approval and more to keep Dad off their backs. They go through the motions to please him, while hiding their true selves. They learn more and more to steer clear of their father in an attempt to avoid his judgments and restrictions. Some make themselves virtually invisible around him.

As the monologue reflects, regardless of a child's wish to avoid a father's control, there is too much ambivalence to remain outside the father's gravitational pull. The desire for more freedom and individuality is counterbalanced by that for approval and connection. Feelings of dislike and of not wanting to be like the father, which are a natural reaction to Dad's efforts to dominate, face off against the need to like and be like one's father.

Even when a child appears to have rejected his or her father blatantly, the father's influence will be at work. Autocratic fathers, by the intensity of their presence and intrusiveness, force themselves into their children's psyches. A child cannot spend twenty-odd years around a parent who is frequently imposing his will and remain unaffected.

Todd had crafted a life so opposite his corporate executive father's, dropping out of school, wearing his hair down to his shoulders, refusing to set a direction for his life, that he saw himself only in this oppositional stance. He came to me for help in understanding his judgmental, angry behavior with his girlfriend, behavior that felt out of character to him. He was shocked when I posed to him that his behavior was a mirror image of his father's.

Like many other children of autocratic fathers, Todd had purposefully tried to excise from his own personality the qualities he resented in his father. For Todd this meant not to appear demanding, judgmental, or angry. To behave this way, he was always amenable to what others wanted to do. He expressed no needs of his own. He was superficially as congenial a person as one might hope to meet.

Todd's tantrums with his girlfriend became the price they both paid for his efforts to be unlike his father. He carried into the relationship years of hunger for nurturing and acceptance brought on by his unyielding father and his own prized abstinence. That hunger needed to be filled somewhere, and whenever his mate let him down, Todd let her know about it, but without realizing the roots or true nature of what he was doing.

In a sense, the array of paradoxical choices which children of autocratic fathers face add up to one very difficult decision: how much do I resist my father's efforts to stay in control and risk his wrath and rejection and how much do I conform and risk my own? The more dictatorial the father, the more the child must either wholly conform or rebel.

At forty-five Renee was still trying to come to terms with the role her father had played in her life. She knew she carried tremendous anger and disdain for her father, but by living in a different city with a lifestyle that totally contradicted what her father wanted for her, she hoped to have established her freedom from him. It was not that simple.

Renee's father was the kind of autocratic father who truly knew no boundaries. He put his nose into every aspect of Renee's life. Even Renee's feelings were fair game for his intrusions, corrections, and hostility. If she was upset, he told her she ought not to be. If she was excited, he thought she should calm down. Renee felt like a puppet around him. In fact, he was always trying to get her to perform for friends and relatives.

As a young child, Renee was a Shirley Temple clone, in looks, but also in temperament. She could maintain her ebullience for others regardless of her inner state. In her early years being an actress became her way of coping with her father. She was on stage for him all the time, delivering the lines she thought would keep him satisfied. She knew just how to perform to avoid his irrational tirades. She kept her true feelings to herself.

By early adolescence Renee developed a new strategy for dealing with her father—escape. She would disappear for hours to be with her friends or hang out at a nearby park. She discovered by trial and error that her life was better when she didn't ask first, but just went ahead and did what she wanted. She often paid for her independence because her father would yell and lecture, but all the while she had the satisfaction of having done something she wanted. The other way, to seek his permission, brought irritation and lecturing and no permission.

Renee increasingly learned to stand apart, from her father and from anyone else who was a threat to her freedom, which felt like virtually everyone. She was so raw from her father's unrelenting commentary on her life that she could not bear to deal with conflicting needs or perspectives from others. She could not compromise for another soul. When she was with anyone but her closest friends, she could barely wait until these people were gone so she could feel free.

Renee created the distance she needed from others in part by making herself into a renegade. In every school and work situation she dressed and acted the part of an outsider. She was no one to be crossed either. She would bite the head off anyone who tried to cramp her style. At one job they called her "The Executioner," because of her adroitness at cutting people down with a single, snarling sarcasm.

Through psychotherapy Renee slowly began to understand what she had been doing to herself to avoid what her father was doing to her. She realized that her acerbic approach to others and her flamboyance were ways of keeping people at a distance; that she felt on guard all the time with others and had perfected an impenetrable shield with them; that while she had switched her persona from Shirley Temple to Bette Davis, she was still always acting and performing for others.

What helped Renee the most was realizing that in order to protect herself from her father's intrusiveness, she had become totally reactive to him and had disconnected from her own inner life. She did not know who she was; she did not feel her own feelings. This made her superb at being untouchable by others and at protecting herself, but what was she left protecting? She started to feel her aloneness and her emptiness. She became aware that for all her battling to be free, she had never made her own choices or taken her own steps.

Renee's capacity to block out her feelings and develop a hardened exterior allowed her to resist her father at least superficially and create an active life that did not depend upon his support or approval. Many children find this alternative overwhelming and frightening. They prefer to find a way to coexist with the father without rocking the boat.

It is easy to see why children prefer a safer route. Autocratic fathers can offer the illusion of a safe, stable existence. They tell you the rules, and if you follow them carefully you will get to where you are supposed to be, and Dad may even be there to pat you on the back. It is only deviations that cause trouble. The more controlling the father, the more clearly delineated the path and the less room to have to make difficult, scary choices.

The illusory part of the security for the children who play it safe comes to pass as they grow older. The later adolescent and adult lives of such children are inversely unstable in proportion to the controlled stability of their childhoods, because they do not know how to manage their own lives unless it is through someone else's eyes. Not unlike the children who choose to rebel, these adult children continue to have great difficulty being in touch with themselves. Many are blocked as well from being alive to their outer environment. As psychoanalyst Linda Leonard noted in *The Wounded Woman*, domineering, rigid fathers can squash a daughter's (or son's) sensitivity and spontaneity. The children lose a sense not only of their own boundaries but their own potential and perhaps never let themselves actually live their own lives.

The price tag for security with autocratic fathers is compliance. Often in the process of meeting the rigid demands of their fathers and trying to avoid disappointing or angering them, the children go overboard in the attempt to be "good." They may strive relentlessly for perfection, leave themselves little margin for error, feel guilt for not doing enough to satisfy their fathers, and experience shame for feeling unworthy of their fathers.

These children carry considerable tension and feel on guard much of the time because they are always concerned about not meeting their fathers' and others' expectations. Since autocratic fathers tend to get angry when their standards are not met, their children learn to expect angry responses to their efforts. Also, these children are inclined to have an inflated view of how important their actions are for others, because they are so used to being watched. Yet, ironically, they feel unimportant, empty, and invisible, because they have not been listened to and because what they did seemed far more important to their fathers than who they were. Sadly, they end up absorbing their fathers' critical attitude and become their own worst critics.

Ron was an example of such a child. His father was Mr. Precise. Everything had to be in its place; everything had to be done properly. Whatever Ron did, his dad readily spotted the defect in it, the part he hadn't done perfectly. If he cut the lawn, his father found the edge that wasn't straight. It always seemed to Ron that his father knew the right way to do everything and when he did anything, there were no mistakes.

It was impossible for Ron to argue with his father. It seemed futile, since his father would certainly be right. Also, when his dad was challenged, his temper reared up. The storm always passed quickly, but the aftermath was such a cold rejection that it was actually worse than the anger. Ron didn't fear that his father would hit him when he got angry; he feared being cut off, exiled. In fact, his father's favorite punishment was simply to send him to his room until he was ready to act properly or do the right thing.

It was in his state of exile that Ron learned how to have leverage with his father. He found that he could be as dogged about remaining in his room or pouting in a corner as his father could be about insisting on perfection. Ron knew he could never match his father in competence or in debate, so he would withdraw. He did make periodic efforts to please his father, laboring intensely to finally achieve the perfection in some way that his father would acknowledge. These efforts usually failed.

Increasingly, it was easier to refuse to be around his father unless he made a point of inviting Ron to do something with him. Ron put on a front at these times, acting in accord with what he knew his father wanted, at least as best he could. He soothed himself by thinking that the real Ron was someone his father would never know and that was his father's loss. He kept the "real Ron" hidden well below the surface. He kept his father at bay by rapidly flipping into his withdrawn pout when his father became critical of the surface Ron.

The insidious part of this pattern for Ron was that in his withdrawal he buried and rejected his true self. Nothing he did ever seemed good enough for him. He judged himself the way he felt judged by his father. He could not take satisfaction or pride in the successes he did have. Moreover, the hurt at never feeling acceptance and understanding embittered him and yet left him with a crying hunger for approval. He did not learn how to ask for this need to be met. Instead, he learned to be derisive with others, again the way his father was with him, whenever he felt let down or disapproved of by them. He applied the same pout used to ward off his father to life itself.

The path for children of autocratic fathers diverges at some point early in their development. Their lives become focused around either fear or aggression and dependency or domination, depending on how their spirits have been affected. The child who has consistently felt intimidated by a domineering father will be fearful around that father and likely in his or her interactions in the larger world.

Because their fathers still serve as role models and because they know they are expected to be strong, boys in particular will approach the outer world with an aggressive stance, while remaining timid with their fathers. Others respond to their fathers' attempts to rule them by rebelling against the father, usually at a point in adolescence or young adulthood when they are not so dependent. Sons may be freed to challenge their dads directly when they equal or surpass them in physical stature. The size and strength differential for daughters usually leads them to more indirect rebellion. For many, the act of rebelling or becoming aggressive is really a way to try to master the fear they have long harbored in reaction to their fathers.

As with aggressive behavior, boys are more likely than girls to take on a domineering style with others. When they do, they try to prove to themselves that they are not the weak, dependent person they feel like around their fathers. To be dominant with others is also a way of behaving of which they believe their fathers would approve, as long as it is not with them. These individuals are not likely, though, to feel free or genuinely in control of their own lives. They usually end up shadowboxing throughout their lives, not knowing how to be in control unless it is at someone else's expense or there is someone in authority to resist.

When a father's dominance crushes his child's capacity for independent action, that son or daughter will continue to act like a child into adulthood. I am certain many of you have experienced a shift in your behavior when you have returned for visits with your parents. There can be a powerful pull to behave the way you did as a child with each parent.

Lewis Yablonsky wrote in *Fathers and Sons* about how magnified this regressive behavior can be with some domineering fathers. He recalled working with a young man, Frank, who at twenty-five behaved like a guilty little boy in his father's company, giving no opinions of his own and going along with all his father's views. When Frank visited his father with his wife he would not even have sex and his voice would change into a teenager's squeak. Frank recognized on some level that he was still intimidated by his father and felt disdain for himself, but he displaced these feelings by getting angry at his wife. The idea of directly resisting his father's dominance was beyond his emotional capacity.

Daughters of autocratic fathers have strong incentives to play it safe and function as "good" daughters. This is the more culturally acceptable stance for females—we are still coming to terms as a society with what it means to have women be assertive. Girls perhaps take more of a psychological risk when they are rebellious. Boys can define their rebellion in terms of manliness, while girls may feel liberated but be treated as unfeminine.

Daughters often have a great deal of pressure from autocratic fathers to maintain a good-girl, prim and virginal image. In fact, many fathers who are not especially controlling about most issues will be controlling about sexual matters with daughters. As a result, the fathers' protectiveness regarding sexual activity leads to their daughters' difficulty being open with them about any sexual relationship. Those daughters who are sexually active live shrouded in guilt and secrecy, fearing their fathers' disapproval.

Fathers' attempts to stay in control of their daughters' sexuality lead to their being cut off from part of the communication around this vital, but unsettling, sphere of life. As an example, I have seen a significant number of daughters in my practice who went through abortions without ever telling their fathers. At a time when they needed the support of their fathers, they not only felt they had to forgo asking for it, but had to mask their emotional and even physical discomfort to avoid exposure. Moreover, having to act in secrecy inherently added an element of shame for most of these women. The shame in relation to the father was not necessarily about having an abortion, but that he would be disappointed if he knew his daughter had engaged in premarital sex or had an affair.

Healing the Wounds From Autocratic Fathers

Children of autocratic fathers, as with ideal fathers, have an inflated view of the father's knowledge and authority. Where ideal fathers are revered, however, autocratic fathers are regarded with considerable ambivalence. Instead of looking up to their fathers blindly, these children are conflicted, because their fathers' competence or judgment may not match their public displays of authority or because the manner in which they exercise authority is itself alienating.

Overcoming the image of the autocratic father is not as overwhelming, then, but undoing the destructive impact can be. These fathers have done direct damage to their children's self-esteem and typically have induced considerable insecurity and shame. The shame that these children carry is perhaps the greatest obstacle to healing. As one young man explained, "The shame is never far below the surface. I carry it in all that I do. It only takes a little reminder or criticism to throw me back into it."

The core task of healing is to learn to be our own person, to exercise the ability, intelligence, and judgment that have been suppressed by the father's domination. Before we can begin to assert that buried self, we must tackle the ways in which our confidence has been undermined and free ourselves from the entangling web of shame that makes progress so difficult.

Living in fear of the father and with feelings of failure often led these children to engage in behaviors that in turn created another layer of shame. Those who sought to avoid their dad's intrusions, anger, or judgments by acting obediently or passively were left with a blot on their concept of themselves. One individual bluntly explained, "I can't seem to forgive myself for never having stood up to him and told him what I really thought, or told him that I didn't agree with him and wouldn't go along with his plans for me. Here I am almost forty and I still feel like I'm a weak person for that."

For those children who were bold enough to act on their instinct to fight back or rebel, shame haunted them as well. They may in fact have done wrong things, like the minister's son who smoked pot in the basement of the church; or they felt that they acted badly because they internalized their fathers' judgments despite trying to resist them. Both the rebels and the compliant ones end up, then, feeling shame for the means by which they sought to avoid being shamed.

Overcoming shame requires an act of forgiveness for ourselves. In order to arrive at the point of absolving ourselves it helps greatly to gain perspective on the power differential between the child and father. We must understand from the child's vantage point and not that of the adult's hindsight how limited the child's options were. Obedience was most likely the only way to maintain security; rebellion may have been the path to holding on to a measure of self-worth. We did what we needed to do to survive the situation.

Allowing for the vulnerability of our childhood selves is not an end point in the healing process, but this forgiving perspective frees us to focus on what the adult self needs in order to establish or restore a strong identity. The core task for adult children of autocratic fathers is being one's own person. These individuals are not used to believing it is their right and responsibility to make their own decisions, let alone acting to do so. Even if we have struggled to attain the right to make our own choices, it is a frightening prospect to wield the responsibility.

Women working to be autonomous have been fortunate in that there is both cultural and personal support for such transformation as a result of the women's movement and the emergence of feminist thought and attitudes. Men have typically shielded themselves from recognizing their dependent side through their immersion in work and through the opportunities work affords one to appear decisive and independent. Men are often not decisive or autonomous with regard to their personal lives. They commonly find it quite difficult to state their preferences about simple things like the clothes they like or what they want to do socially. Unfortunately, there is little social support for men who want and need to develop their nonwork identities.

Children of autocratic fathers may have disconnected altogether from their internal selves out of the lack of freedom to express their own views and desires. They need to practice the art of listening to themselves. When we are accustomed to taking direction from others we do not give ourselves the opportunity to formulate our ideas. When we first try to practice doing so we may draw a blank and panic at the void, much the way people who struggle with writing fear the blank page. As with any transition to new behavior, we must practice repeatedly until the change begins to come naturally.

If we keep listening to ourselves, we will find that indeed we do have our own mind. No matter how we have been dominated or suppressed ourselves, we cannot lose the innate capacity to have our unique outlook on life. We need to trust in what emerges from that inner voice, believing that our own judgment is the best tool we have for making sense of life's demands.

We must then take the risk to make our own choices. Autonomy and healing from shame are achieved by the accumulation of decisions and actions that tell us in tangible fashion we can manage our lives and accomplish positive things. It is sufficient and probably necessary to begin with making minor choices. For some people it may be enough to express a preference for what restaurant they want to go to; for others it may require starting to buy their own clothes. Eventually, the level of independent action may require sizable risk and major change: leaving a job because of a demanding boss, moving out of town, changing careers to something we truly enjoy, getting a divorce. What is important with these decisions, large or small, in helping to develop our personhood is not the ultimate choice, but the source—whether it comes from inside ourselves or in response to the influence of others.

The degree to which we continue to be affected by the reactions of others limits our ability to function independently. A man who was a pipefitter found himself constantly off balance with himself and volatile with his family because of the daily barrage of taunting that went on among the male crew. He knew intellectually that the teasing was not meant personally, but it felt too close to the messages of his youth when his father made him feel he was stupid. His reticence to assert himself at work and his irritability at home left him trapped in his negative view of himself.

Just as we must free ourselves from our childhood shame, we must also overcome our hypersensitivity to what others think of us in order to be secure within ourselves. It can help to recognize that we are projecting our paternal experience on to others, but we must also practice standing our ground, risk putting forth our own beliefs, values, and feelings, and stretch our capacity to tolerate conflictual or angry responses.

Another aspect of healing for the children of autocratic fathers lies in how they function in the realm of power. Those who were accustomed to being submissive find it difficult to make use of the personal efficacy that comes with their emerging adult autonomy. Children who resisted their fathers' control may overreact to adults in positions of authority and may relate inappropriately to subordinates or people they hope to influence.

Learning to exercise power comfortably and effectively is fundamentally a matter of knowing that we are in charge of our own lives. Being clear about our boundaries with others, having the freedom and capacity to say no when necessary, or advocating for our needs allows us to use power for taking care of ourselves and not for dominating others. When we employ power in this way as an honoring of ourselves and not at the expense of others, we have indeed attained a secure identity.

4

Abusive Fathers

Abusive and autocratic fathers can seem alike. Autocratic fathers, though, are not necessarily abusive. There is naturally a continuum in how a father attempts to enforce rules and maintain control. Some autocratic fathers do not even use anger or any form of intimidation. They simply are consistent in their expectation that their rules will be adhered to. Commonly they do end up using anger or some degree of intimidation when they are not obeyed. The fathers who resort to extreme expressions of verbal anger (cursing, belittling, shouting) or physical anger are abusive.

Not all abusive fathers are autocratic. Often abusive fathers are quite erratic in their handling of rules and discipline. They may be loose and even indifferent about most of the child's behavior, but suddenly erupt with abuse for some minor indiscretion or a major transgression. The reactions of some abusive fathers are predictable. Abused children commonly reflect on how they used to await their dad's arrival home nervously to see what mood he was in, which would then dictate their behavior around him. The abuse itself may occur with regularity or there may be a consistency to what triggers the abusive response. Many abusive fathers are unpredictable in their reactions. This quality intensifies the sense of dread about them, because the child never knows when the abuse will occur.

Alcohol is a major contributor to abusive behavior in fathers. In his study of adult daughters of alcoholics, Robert Ackerman found that almost one-third had been physically abused and one-fifth sexually abused by an alcoholic parent. In 60 percent of these cases this parent was the father (in 20 percent of the cases both parents were alcoholic and the abusive parent was not specified). Almost 40 percent of these daughters witnessed spousal abuse in their families. These rates of abuse were three to four times higher than those for women raised in nonalcoholic families.

The 19 percent of daughters who were sexually abused is a shocking statistic. The pain and terror behind this abuse cannot readily be described. It is interesting, however, that even with the number of physically and sexually abused girls in the total group of daughters, the behavior most remembered was the verbal belligerence of the alcoholic parent. In part, this is true probably because children will repress traumatic events. This was the case with Philip Greven, author of *Spare the Child*, who could recall the events leading up to the one time he was harshly spanked, but could not recall the spanking itself.

Moreover, to survive the horror of abuse, a child will likely dissociate himself or herself from what is being done. A sexually abused child separates mind and spirit from what is happening to the body. This is why some incest victims do not recall the acts of incest for years, if at all. In the moment of abuse, their true selves were hidden deep in the recesses of their souls, guarded from consciousness by a trancelike state.

The verbal belligerence, though, is somehow harder to shut out and cuts through to the core of the child. How often parents remind children of the wishful epigram, "Sticks and stones can break my bones, but names can never hurt me." Nonsense. The names, the nastiness, the tone of hostility or disgust have a cumulative effect. They are like an emotional cancer eating the healthy cells of the child's self-esteem, leaving a core of shame. As Philip Greven poignantly declared in *Spare the Child*: "The feelings generated by the pain . . . are mostly repressed, forgotten, and denied, but they actually never disappear. Everything remains recorded in our innermost beings."

Greven also tells us that punishment can become so incorporated into our minds and bodies that we find it difficult to grasp what impact it has had. It is common to find that adults who experienced serious abuse as children do not think of that mistreatment as abuse. Abuse must be something far worse that happened to someone else who was less fortunate. Many will state that this is all they knew and thus it seemed normal. What is extraordinary becomes ordinary when it occurs frequently. We become blind to its consequences even though we are not immune to its impact. The patent psychological devices to which we resort in order to cope with abusive situations, like repression, dissociation, and denial, inherently leave us out of touch with the emotional consequences. Our feelings are damaged in ways that we may well not associate at all with the abusive treatment.

For example, many children of abusive fathers have so well repressed their feelings that they do not see themselves as angry. They believe either that they accepted their plight as normal and thus felt no anger about it or that they adapted to and insulated themselves from the abuse. It is common for these children to carry illusions about their feelings. There are those who fear getting angry themselves because they imagine if they did, they would act like their fathers. These children are deliberately gentle and absorb a great deal before fighting back. Because they repress their anger so well, they fool themselves into believing that they do not carry anger.

In families where a child is an observer of abuse of a sibling or mother and not the target, it is common for him or her to feel untouched by anger or to experience anger only for the victim and not for oneself. Again, there is fear of being like the father if one expresses anger. There are also feelings of guilt for being relatively unscathed and thus the child does not believe he or she has a good reason to be angry like the abused person does.

With those who are aware of their anger, many blame themselves for this feeling. They are ashamed of being angry, but attribute it to their being a bad person rather than to their father's mistreatment. This self-flagellation is the result of the devastating impact of abusive parenting on children's esteem. They are left feeling a deep sense of shame about themselves because they have understood their abuse through a child's logic; that is, they would not be so severely rejected if they were not indeed awful children. This shame-based reaction readily translates into feelings of rage that are inverted, turned against themselves. All these dynamics can be equally true when the abuse is emotional rather than physical.

The most revealing indicator of how damaged Cynthia had been by her hostile, name-calling father was her relationship with Brett. He was her first serious boyfriend since she began to live on her own. Brett conveyed wholesale disrespect for her: He wouldn't call when he was going to be late; he would interrupt her when she tried to make a point, scream at her when he got upset, and laugh derisively when she cried at his mistreatment. Despite how blatantly cruel Brett was to her, Cynthia kept checking with friends to see if they agreed that he was being mean. She didn't think she deserved his harshness, but she would continually seek to understand what she might have done to upset him. The relationship ended after two years when Brett decided he had enough.

Another way that abused children may distort the character of their feelings is to blame others. These are the people who blow up at the bank teller for taking too long or at the fast food cashier for giving the wrong change. They are relieving themselves of the powerlessness they experienced with their fathers and discharging their accumulated anger at a safe target. Usually they have no idea why they do this and despite their rationalizations for their behavior are left with a residue of shame.

Philip Greven expressed the belief in *Spare the Child* that anger is the key to understanding the long-term consequences of corporal punishment. As he put it, anger "is the central emotion that shapes our psyches long after the original pain has subsided and been forgotten or denied." To recognize the anger inside us is to see what has actually been done to us. It is to reluctantly see our fathers in a darkened light, which adds another layer to our pain.

Unfortunately, for those who do see their fathers' abuse as the source of their pain and anger, the pain is not necessarily lessened, it is only seen more clearly. This clarity may free them from some of their self-blame, but there is still inner confusion in trying to understand the shame that is experienced at this most fundamental of rejections.

Abused children frequently are more aware of their anxiety and fear than their anger, because anger can be so uncomfortable and risky a feeling to experience. Again, they may not directly link these feelings with the abuse itself. Being in situations where one risks criticism or hostile reactions will obviously trigger uneasiness in the person who has been abused. What is less obvious is how widely this concern can spread. Almost any social situation where we do not know the potential reaction of those with whom we are relating becomes a source of anxiety. Anyone who holds an element of authority over the abused person can induce fear far in disproportion to his or her actual power to harm that individual.

Whenever it was time for Paul's semiannual review at work, he noticed his skin condition would flare up. While he sat with his boss he would sweat profusely, and his heart felt like a bird flapping its wings in his chest. These physical symptoms, of course, were matched with intense dread. All of this discomfort occurred despite Paul's consistent track record as a productive, valued employee. Despite his promotion and his yearly above-average pay increases, he approached every evaluation as though he might well be fired.

The intensity and pervasiveness of this fear and anxiety have roots in how we experience an abusive parent. For Paul the trauma was anchored in the fact that his father's worst acts of abuse took place unexpectedly and in public places. Even when the abusive treatment is relatively predictable, a child will still live in fear of the hurt to be inflicted. It is the anticipation of pain that conditions the child to live in a state of dread.

The longer the delays between a potentially punishable act and the doling out of the discipline, the more tension and fear are evoked. The more unpredictable the abusive behavior, the more aware the child will be that the abuse may occur at any time for the slightest transgression. The result is that the child lives in a constant state of alert. His or her sensors for abusive reactions are set at a low frequency and the rush of fear is easily set off.

June's father had a way of being all too present for his daughter. He had a well-established pattern of stopping at the corner tavern every day after work at the factory. When he came home his mood was initially good, but somewhere along the way between his arrival and his ritual nap on the living room couch he would get belligerent with someone in the family. June hated being there when he came home and did her best not to be. When she was there, her tension level rose the longer he was home.

"I can still picture him lying there on that couch," she recalled. "I would tiptoe around the whole house for fear of waking him. It was like in a fairy tale where the heroine is afraid to awaken the sleeping monster. Sprawled out there on the couch, it seemed like his presence spread through the entire house." In practically every new situation well into adulthood, June still feared waking the monster in others. The anticipation of their anger was like waiting for her father to walk in the door.

June's fear of waking the monster made her a cautious person in new situations and led her to avoid circumstances where she did not know what to expect. She was so filled with fear that the bubbly, adventurous spirit that had characterized her as a young child seemed crushed. Her stance in the world became that of a passive person.

One way the abusive father damages the spirit of the child is by undermining his or her sense of control. The insecurity and anticipation surrounding the father's lack of control lead the child to be largely focused on the father's behavior and what might upset him. This concentration on the father promotes a generalized external focus that detracts not only from awareness of one's own feelings, goals, or needs, but also from the sense of having the freedom and capacity to even pursue them.

Philip Greven points out in *Spare the Child* that the parent who hurts a child as a way of imposing discipline teaches that child not only to be obedient, but to be indifferent to suffering. The child learns to distance himself or herself from hurt and will likely also avoid perceiving the feelings of others.

Abused children, then, often have difficulty being empathic with others. Their compliant behavior and numbing acceptance of their fate can leave them with an apathetic view of life. They learn to expect little, to have little hope, to want or need little. They are less likely to upset their fathers this way and less likely to be disappointed. They may extract the joy from their own lives before it can be stolen from them.

June's nightmare of the monster awakening was all too often Martin's experience during the first seven or eight years of his life. Martin's father deserted the family finally, but those early years were devastatingly frightening. Even Martin's bedroom was no refuge from his father, who periodically came home after Martin was asleep and in his drunken rage barged into Martin's room, hauled him out of bed, and dressed him down mercilessly for some concocted infraction.

Martin had two places of refuge that felt safe: the woods he could walk to about a half mile away and a place deep inside himself to which he could withdraw. Though the woods was a place where he could be at peace, he also did reckless, dangerous things there. A path in the woods took him to a waterfall, and Martin used to lose himself in the excitement of balancing on the slippery logs that formed a natural dam at the edge of the falls. He did this partly because he was not concerned for his own well-being and partly because these stunts made him feel as if he had some courage. Around his father he felt like a coward. The problem with his inward withdrawal was that he went into a deep depression and pulled away from everyone else.

Martin got into a fight once and lost his temper so violently that he had to be pulled off the other boy. He was told he was choking the boy, but had no memory of actually doing so. He was afraid after this incident of losing his temper again. It felt safer to absorb the taunts and blows of others in silence. Martin was dubbed a pushover by his classmates. Their mistreatment felt familiar, if not deserved, to Martin. Because he feared his own anger, yet expected to be abused, it felt safer not to try to make friends.

A curious quirk of fate put Martin in the hands of a baseball coach who had the same shaming, rough style that Martin's father had. His father had taught him to catch bare-handed and threw the ball to him harder each time he dropped it. The one difference with the coach was that he saw potential in Martin and responded positively when he did well. Martin became an all-star catcher in high school, which in turn became a meal ticket for college.

Martin ultimately became successful in all the conventional ways. He became a physician, perhaps because the trappings of the profession might insulate him from the rejection of others. He was a division head at a teaching hospital, earned an excellent income, and was well respected by his peers. He was often consulted by his fellow doctors about their difficult cases.

Yet whenever he presented cases at grand rounds or was questioned by anyone above him in the hospital hierarchy, he went into a panic. When he knew in advance that he would be giving a talk, he often went into a depression or became so moody that everyone knew to steer clear of him. He was so caught in the web of his own worries that he seemed insensitive to even those whom he trusted and felt close to, neglecting the basic amenities while being oblivious to their feelings.

Martin could well have gone on for years accepting his swings between anxiety and depression, panic and withdrawal. In a way they felt normal, what he had always felt growing up and thereafter. These mood swings were deserved in Martin's view of himself. He still could not imagine that others found him knowledgeable or competent or likable. His horrible battles with his feelings felt like punishment that he earned for being a misfit.

Neither Martin nor June regarded their fathers as abusive prior to being in therapy. When they could see themselves as having been abused, it put a great deal in perspective. While this realization brought pain, it also brought relief.

It still astonishes me, however, how insistently many abused children will defend their fathers' behavior, minimize it, explain it away—at least to others. No matter how often or how badly they have been mistreated, they retain or recoup their hope of finally winning over their dads. For some, the act of naming their fathers, calling them "abusive," is an executioner of their hope. The abuse may be their only source of connection or attention and therefore they cannot reject it. They prefer to go on defending their angry dads.

Philip Greven quotes Alice Miller's haunting description in her book *For Your Own Good* of a young drug addict whose father beat her regularly: "Her tolerance has no limits; she is always faithful and even proud that her father, who beats *her* brutally, never would do anything to hurt an animal; she is prepared to forgive him everything, always to take all the blame herself, not to hate him, to forget quickly everything that happens."

Miller notes that these repressed feelings do not simply disappear, but are directed at other targets to spare the father. Tragically, the most common and persistent target is the child himself or herself—no matter how old or how far away from the father.

When children of abusive fathers blame themselves for their fathers' wrath, they become trapped in an internal cycle that interferes with virtually all other levels of how they function. They need to repress their own anger and hurt because their shame takes away the right to feel justified in it. If they do not repress their anger, its expression leads to more shame. The shame, which translates into feeling undeserving and worthless, causes these children to expect bad consequences and thus to be filled with fear and anxiety. Because of their negative picture of themselves they feel they cannot be successful in relationships or get what they want from others. Their emotional and interpersonal isolation cuts them off from the kind of experiences and feedback that could promote an emergence from this dark maze.

Of course, whether the children see it or deny it, it is the abusive father who casts his shadow over his offspring's interaction with others and view of oneself. By his example, the abusive father has demonstrated all too vividly that people can hurt you deeply, even people you are supposed to be able to trust. These children are, then, conditioned to expect hurt. Their own self-protective device, their ability to anticipate abuse, prepares them to continue to look for it.

The mistrust and hypervigilance that characterize these children are most likely to be felt toward other men whether the abused child is a son or daughter. As Linda Leonard put it in *The Wounded Woman*, "When the father image is damaged, so is the image of men."

Sons will view other men with foreboding and therefore seek comfort only in the arms of women. Women, on the other hand, will avoid the arms of men. Men want the security of relationships, but they carry an unhealthy dependence and lack of trust into their interactions. Women may avoid relationships altogether or they may remain in relationships without risking intimate connection. They live with considerable tension about igniting conflict and therefore put much energy into averting situations that could elicit upset from their partners. Sadly, though, many women and men may repeat the abusive relationship they experienced with their fathers, choosing a pattern with which they are at least familiar out of their lack of self-worth and learned indifference to suffering.

The approach-avoidance pattern of relating to others common among these abused children is a projection of the often paralyzing ambivalence they carry toward their fathers. They hate them, but love them; reject them, yet still want their approval; avoid them, then seek them out; ally with and protect them and want to act on their rage and destroy them. Largely this ambivalence comes from being hurt and intimidated by someone whom we deeply want and need to love and nurture us. It also arises in part from the confusion of having so much overt power and yet disguised weakness in the same father. Abusive fathers reflect in extreme form the reality that power and weakness coexist in the same man, no matter how overpowering his image.

Healing the Wounds From Abusive Fathers

We cannot begin to heal from the trauma of abuse if we do not recognize cruel parenting for what it is. Many children of abusive fathers are adults before they realize that they were abused. When they see how their own spouse, their peers, or other adults respond to their children, they finally have a standard of comparison. Their own experience as a parent of having feelings of protectiveness and nurturing will frequently awaken them to what was missing with their fathers and to how distorted their punitive behavior was. Becoming a parent, thus having direct contact with the vulnerability, innocence, and basic needs of children, is perhaps the most powerful source of perspective on abuse.

What opened Martin's eyes to the impact of his father's malevolence was the simple act of reading fairy tales to his young son. One night when his son was frightened by one of the tales, Martin comforted him and told him he would always be there to protect him from any monsters. As he said these words, the memory of his father barging into his own bedroom flashed through his mind. His eyes filled with tears. He knew that his own child needed to feel protected. And he understood that the very person he had needed to protect him as a child was the source of danger. He had lived in the same house with the monster and that's why he could never feel safe.

In addition to not recognizing the paternal abuse they have encountered, these children tend to be indifferent to their own pain and discomfort. They are used to an extreme degree of physical or emotional harshness and to absorbing that kind of treatment. Thus they acquired a skewed scale for what is normal to put up with. Their immunity to pain is further distorted by the message from their fathers that they deserved the treatment they received.

An important aspect of healing requires doing for ourselves what the father did not do—separating the behavior from the person. Whatever mistakes or bad behavior we engaged in must be seen as part of normal childhood and not fundamental defects in our character. I often ask adult children of abuse to bring in pictures of their childhood or watch old family films in order to help them truly see the innocence in their faces or their behavior. When we can perceive the basic good in our childhood nature, we can understand that we were not deserving of abuse. If we were not deserving of mistreatment as children, we do not deserve it as adults. We can then begin to stand up for ourselves when we feel treated unkindly. Halting abuse from others sends a healing message to ourselves that we deserve better.

The revelation that we did not deserve our father's punitiveness may open the floodgates of anger. As with Martin, it is typical for abused children to fear both the anger of others and their own anger. I recall pointing out to one man how muted his speech was, as though he were reluctant to use his whole voice. He explained that he consciously kept his voice subdued so that he would not sound angry like his father and scare people.

Children of abusive fathers need to learn to express anger. Again, because of the extreme pattern they witnessed with their father's anger, they have a distorted picture of what it means to get angry. They need to understand that anger does not have to be hostile, ugly, and mean. Anger can be stated respectfully and even kindly. When it is put forward in this fashion, it allows us to take care of ourselves within relationships.

Getting in touch with the anger we feel toward our fathers serves a more constructive purpose than mere venting. Our anger is making the statement that we were not bad or deserving of cruelty, that our father was wrong. To feel indignation also affirms a demarcation between our father and ourselves. Our resentment makes clear that his behavior is something we disavow and therefore distinguishes us from him. Feeling this psychological separation helps alleviate the fear of being like our father with our anger and fosters greater objectivity toward what his own anger communicated. We become less susceptible, then, to believing we must have been that bad person he punished.

Learning that we can mobilize anger in a constructive way lays the foundation for the most critical step in healing from abusive fathers. Knowing that we can get angry in a firm, unyielding, yet appropriate manner assures us that we will set the limits we need for the protection of our integrity. When we believe that we are capable of countering or halting anyone's abusive behavior toward us and that we can prevent others' intrusions or excessive demands, we feel safe in our encounters and strong within ourselves.

When we can create our own safety with others, we can allow ourselves to be closer and more intimate in relationships. As one woman marveled, "Now that I feel like I don't need to walk around in armor, I'm more approachable to others and I'm more comfortable with them. I'm not as afraid and so I don't act like a porcupine ready to shoot my quills."

By being more socially accessible, we open the door to others truly knowing us. In turn, we are likely to receive positive feedback that contradicts the invectives of childhood. Ultimately, we undo the damage from our fathers' twisted use of power by discovering the strength we carry within ourselves and finding that we can comfortably use it to relate to others.

5

When Fathers Are Weak

If he had let me under his guard, I should have crept into his heart and found the wound there.

Daddy, We Hardly Knew You, Germaine Greer

In *The Wounded Woman*, Linda Leonard recounts a disturbing fairy tale from the Grimm Brothers, "The Handless Maiden." In this tale a father unknowingly gives away his daughter to the devil in exchange for unlimited wealth. He does so because he believes he has nothing of value and therefore nothing to lose. He has forgotten he has a daughter he can lose.

The devil has no power over the daughter as long as she has access to water to keep herself clean. The father obeys the devil's order to keep the daughter away from water, but her tears falling on her hands continue to prevent the devil from taking her. When the devil directs the father to cut off his daughter's hands so that she can be taken away, the father complies out of terror for his own life. The daughter's tears continue to stymie the devil and he gives up for the time being.

The father tries to make amends to his wounded daughter and suggests that they can live securely with the fortune from the devil. She refuses to stay with him, however. She sees his weakness and knows she cannot count on him to value or safeguard her in the face of a threat to him. Instead, she goes off on her own.

At some point in our lives we must come to terms with whatever weakness exists in our fathers. Sometimes we see that weakness readily and sometimes it takes years to perceive it. The weakness can be dramatic and represent an overt danger for children, as with the Handless Maiden. More often it is subtle or covert. The children may well ally with their fathers in covering over this behavior in order to sustain their own illusions. In the film *A Voyage Round My Father*, mentioned previously, the entire family conspired to accept the father's need to maintain the illusion of not being blind.

When I talk about weakness in fathers I do not necessarily mean it in a conventional way, like the scrawny man on the beach who gets sand kicked in his face and cannot defend his wife and children, like the father in the film *Back to the Future* whom only a son's passage through time could rescue from a legacy of sniveling. When a father's own psychological wounds prevent him from meeting his children's needs and lead his children to feel responsible for his emotional well-being, that is, in essence, when a father is weak.

The father may be unavailable to his children because he is powerless over an addiction or fearful of accepting adult responsibilities. He may be unable to show affection or listen to his children because he is too self-absorbed or perhaps filled with shame for some perceived failure. Instead of providing constructive limits and safe boundaries through the appropriate exercise of parental authority, he may manipulate his children with guilt for causing him problems. He may repeatedly threaten to abandon his children, yet blame them for making him feel this urge. All of these examples typify the behavior of weak fathers.

Away at work or in the larger world, fathers may well remain heroic in their children's eyes if they seem to negotiate those arenas confidently. They can appear strong just because they work hard or simply because it is easy to maintain illusions when we do not directly see how they function away from home. Ironically, it may well be in the home itself that fathers' weakness most clearly manifests itself. At home fathers may be seen as stoop-shouldered, sagging under the wear and tear of daily demands.

Even when fathers are given the power to discipline and to decide, children can see how their mothers wield power over many aspects of life. A father can appear surprisingly dependent when he has to fend for himself or the children. One man, faced with the threat of separation from his wife, bemoaned, "Who'll do the laundry?" a plea that revealed the level of dependence on which many men function.

When fathers are clearly not successful in the world outside of home, children are inclined to focus on the symptoms of weakness associated with their poor performance: a low-status job; being fired, especially more than once; not advancing in their careers; not completing formal education; being socially inept in situations involving their children's lives such as school meetings, weddings, or family gatherings; inability to join in common recreational activities; even speaking with an accent or being noticeably unfamiliar with or out of sync with community and cultural mores.

While any of these circumstances in themselves are not inherently manifestations of weakness, children may experience them this way because they believe they will be exposed to social ridicule. They want to be proud of their fathers in addition to having their fathers be proud of them.

The more extreme or visible the father's failures are, the more the children carry embarrassment about their father and shame about themselves for being connected to him. These external failures may dominate and blind the children to the more subtle ways in which the father's weakness keeps him from meeting their needs.

The weakness in fathers may emerge gradually over time. For Willy Loman in the play *Death of a Salesman*, the seeds were there and his weakness emerged with the unrelenting demands of life and the nature of his work. Willy's lack of adaptability or resilience led him to stop living—a case of staying in the same place leading to backward movement.

A father's weakness can emerge suddenly, too. One telling, fatal act can lead to a fall from grace in the children's eyes. This might be the case with the father who loses his job and never really recovers, or who has an affair and is exposed to the whole family, or who has a heart attack and is seen as physically vulnerable.

In the same family a father may fall suddenly in one child's view and never fall in another's. Willy Loman's son Happy remained blind to his father's collapse even to the end. Long before, his other son, Biff, had written him off as a complete phony after finding him with another woman on one of his road trips.

Geoffrey Wolff, the author of *The Duke of Deception*, did not have to see his dad totally disintegrate to understand how weak he was. His younger brother, Toby, though, who spent much less time around his father, did not overcome his fear of him until years in prison had left his dad a hollow shell. When the decline is more gradual it allows a child to use his defenses to cushion the fall or even to block it out altogether. We need stronger barriers to hide from the shock of sudden truth. The trauma from a father's sudden fall can be difficult to overcome.

Fathers who are aware of their weaknesses and how they interfere with their responsibilities to their children will try to mask their ineptness. Through their own forms of denial and often by putting emotional and physical barriers between themselves and their children they make it difficult for their youngsters to understand them.

Germaine Greer describes her prolonged struggle to discover who her father really was in *Daddy, We Hardly Knew You*. She is ultimately able to pierce the family mythology that her father remained distant from her all her life because he came back from World War II a broken man. Instead she found out that he had kept his distance because he had lied about so much of his earlier life, including his early discharge from the army due to emotional problems. He avoided her because he could not risk her scrutiny. She also came to understand he was unable to show love because he felt too much rather than too little.

Throughout this struggle Greer had to face a more demanding inner war to not succumb to her feelings of rejection. These are feelings that come with a father's failure to communicate his love and approval regardless of the cause. Children do not normally conclude that such behavior comes from a weakness in the father. They assume it's because something is deficient in them. If only they were better somehow, he would be more responsive.

A father's inability to validate his own children will manifest itself in different ways. For example, the beleaguered father in *Brighton Beach Memoirs* admits, "I forget to tell people how I feel." Or a father who believed his son was being shielded from the hard knocks of life by an overprotective mother chose to avoid confronting the mother over what he felt his son needed. Out of their lack of facility for expressing feelings or handling interpersonal exchanges that might be uncomfortable, many fathers hunker down in the recesses of family life.

Fathers may ignore their children's needs because they are too caught up in their own unmaterialized dreams. One father wanted desperately to own his own business and worked long hours to salt away as much money for it as he could. This man felt he couldn't take time off to see his daughter perform in the school play, so he ridiculed her efforts as a silly waste of time. His daughter was already in high school, but the dream couldn't be deferred a few hours to give support to his own daughter's dreams.

Another man spoke of his dad's weakness in direct, profound terms: "My father could never put me in front of him." This man carried in his mind a sacred image of his religious tradition where a father stands behind his son and places his hands upon the son's head and gives him a blessing. In some fashion he needed to have felt his father's hands on him and heard the spoken blessing that could send him forth in life as an anointed son. Unfortunately, his father could never put his own needs for attention or recognition behind his son's.

Fathers' own neediness may have led them to compete, usually covertly, with their children for the attention of their wives. Sons especially offer an easily disguised target in the battle for attention. How many fathers have chanted the refrain, "Don't fuss so much, you'll spoil him," at their wives in the belief that they were trying to keep their boys from being pampered and thus becoming too soft to face life's challenges? Yet how many of these men, just beneath the surface, had a crying hunger themselves for a soft touch and special attention?

Most of our fathers grew up within the tradition of male self-reliance. From an early age, they tended to pull away from their mothers, relinquishing much of the maternal nurturing they no doubt still needed. Few had accessible fathers who filled in the gap. This unmet need for nurturing was carried into married life and played out in an unconscious competitiveness with their children.

The Provider Role, Money and Insecurity

Perhaps the most obvious sign of weakness in a father revolves around his role as a provider. Children generally overlook a great deal about their fathers' inaccessibility in the name of their being hard workers. Since the provider role has been at the core of expectations regarding fathers, the sense of security a father brings to his family is readily attached to his determination about being a provider.

While children generally want their fathers to be successful economically, it is not low earnings in most instances that convey a sense of weakness about the father. To feel secure within the family, children need to know the father will have the strength and stamina to do what it takes to cover the basic living needs of the family, not necessarily become rich. Children do not really need the stoicism or driven behavior typical of many fathers. Rather, they simply need to feel the father will consistently put the well-being of his family ahead of all else if that well-being is under threat.

Some fathers lose their ability to provide adequately after some years of successfully doing so. They may be victims of layoffs, plant closings, stock market and other economic vicissitudes, or their own motivational collapse or stubborn pride. Other times it is the cumulative effect of an addiction that topples the father's ability to maintain his job or manage his money. Children can deal with these economic downturns if their fathers eventually deal with them. One young man, whose father had been unemployed for two years after being a high-level corporate executive, continued to revere his father because he was as aggressive in looking for work as he had been in carrying out his past positions.

Fathers can indeed be poor providers on a material level yet feel stable to their children, while others can amass considerable wealth without providing security. Children develop attitudes about money largely based on the attitudes they experienced from their fathers and not on how much money actually existed.

Typically fathers' fixation with money matters is tied to their family history with money. Growing up in the depression, experiencing a family's decline in financial standing, having lived in poverty or with parents who were themselves constantly fearful about making ends meet could all instill lasting anxiety about financial security. Some fathers became driven, working constantly to ward off insecurity, though not necessarily with success. Others were timid, perhaps remaining in underpaid jobs, afraid to risk change and whatever known security they had.

My own father was extremely money conscious. His first question about virtually any activity or purchase concerned its cost. In his mind

I am sure he was in part trying to teach us the value of money. To a large degree, he was also playing out his own years of insecurity as a child in war-torn Poland. The impact on me, however, was to infuse daily life with anxiety about whether we had enough money to live on and to narrow my world to the class of practical and justifiable expenditures. Life did not feel like something to be savored, but rather to be costed out.

The updated film version of *Father of the Bride* parodies this common preoccupation with expenses. In the end the father misses the special moments of his daughter's wedding reception because he skimped on parking assistants and was out parking cars. All too many father-child relationships have been sacrificed on the altar of money. As fathers struggle to maintain fiscal security, they may do it at the expense of the relationship. They may become so restricted in their own lives, they do not know how to give to their children in any form. They become nonentities for their children, shriveled up by their own tightness.

The singular focus on money is a way for fathers to control the major resource that they believe makes their families feel secure. When fathers fail to give their children the sense that this security exists, either because they are inadequate at providing or because they are unable to manage their own fears about being good providers, they inflict a pervasive insecurity on their offspring. Each new expense is laden with tension concerning Dad's reaction. The children ultimately incorporate the father's nagging worries into their own outlook.

Roz's dad was an accountant for a small midwestern firm. Her dad earned a modest salary, but with five children the available income was always stretched. It was her father's depression upbringing, however, more than actual dollars available that cast so much angst over money matters. Roz's grandfather had died during the depression and her father had quit high school to help support his family. The combination of sudden death and economic calamity during that period in his life had left her dad feeling highly susceptible to disaster. He had sufficient money for his family, but he always believed he needed more in case of an emergency.

Roz saw how hard her father worked and how carefully he watched each dollar spent. When Roz was a senior in high school and considering going to college, she got a lot of encouragement from her guidance counselor and teachers, but she could see how edgy it was making her dad. She was the oldest of the kids and was concerned about resources being left for their education as well.

When Roz decided to forgo attending college, neither of her parents balked, so she assumed that her choice was the right one for the family. Roz's plan was to work and save up enough money to pay for her own education. Twenty years later she had not yet done so. She had occasionally taken college courses or started a program, but her plans were always put on hold because of unexpected expenses or the needs of her own children. Even when she and her husband managed to amass some extra money for her to apply to her education, she could not bring herself to dip into the savings. The sense of security that their reserve funds afforded her carried more emotional weight than the old dream of a college degree.

Roz's example reflects not only the pattern of paternal insecurity being passed on to the children, but of the children assuming the responsibility for relieving their fathers' tension. Daughters especially have been subjected to being caretakers for fathers because of their socialized role of being responsible for relationships. The women's movement has unquestionably raised awareness about the arbitrariness, if not inequity, of this division of labor, but change has been incremental.

For daughters who grew up in the fifties and sixties, the expectations and conditioning for them to be protective and nurturing with others were quite explicit. In relation to the weakness of fathers, this caretaking was functional as a means of coping with the insecurity—allowing the daughter to help mask the weakness, making it easier for the father to function, or giving the daughter something constructive to do to sublimate her own insecurity. As adults, these daughters might continue in their familiar role, as Roz did, or they might be drawn to finding the stability they never had with their dad, either on their own or with a partner.

Unfortunately, as Roz learned, a father's weakness is a double-edged sword for his children. The children's own development is undermined because of the ways the father fails to perform his needed role. Yet these youngsters labor under the burden of feeling they must compensate for what the father could not be or do. This task is made all the more difficult because the children operate with their own insecurity. They carry a burning question somewhere within their consciousness:

"How much of his weakness is also in me?" They either assume that it is in them and feel weak themselves as a result or they feel vulnerable to the possibility that this weakness will emerge at some point, like invisible ink under the right light. This is a terrible burden to carry, and often it is borne in secrecy.

Because of their psychological identification with their fathers, boys acutely feel the danger of inheriting their fathers' negative traits, just as they hope they will be the beneficiaries of their positive ones (yet fear they will not be). As Robert Bly puts it in *Iron John*, they may fall into hopelessness and accept the belief that "I am the son of defective male material, and I'll probably be the same as he is."

In spite of this fear of being like their fathers, these children often feel responsible for making up for their fathers' weakness in the eyes of the world. Sons may regard this duty as part of their male familial legacy. Again, in Bly's words, "a son assigns himself the task of redeeming the dark father." The son tries to exorcise any shame he carries about being deficient himself and simultaneously tries to redeem the family name.

Sean became a successful attorney despite his father's mistrust for those with money. Sean liked to calculate what size nest egg he would need in order to survive if he ever lost his job. As he approached his own retirement his anxiety and the size of the necessary nest egg both kept growing. The irrationality of his tension was apparent, but the root of it only became clear when he reflected on how his father spent the last years of his own life living in a state of virtual poverty. Ironically, after his father's death, Sean discovered from his father's bank account that he was still putting away savings each month to the end of his life.

In actuality, Sean's insecurity about money began in his childhood. His dad had been openly very proud of his working-class standing. The homogeneity and camaraderie in the community where Sean grew up would normally have reinforced these feelings. Sean had always felt like an outsider in his own neighborhood, however, because his family was the only one without a car. In a community where virtually everyone worked in the same factory and earned close to the same income, for Sean this was a mark of failure. It also repeatedly exposed him to humiliation with his peers, because he always needed rides to go places with his friends.

Sean could never fathom why his dad did not buy a car. It may have been his irrational fear of not having enough money or a result of his drinking and gambling. While Sean's needs for food and shelter were otherwise adequately taken care of, this glaring omission planted a seed of insecurity that had a significant impact on Sean's later drive for success.

Life became centered for Sean on creating an impenetrable bulwark against insecurity. He fought a never-ending battle to feel that he had accumulated enough resources to not have to fear loss or humiliation ever again. Sean no doubt ended up with the same preoccupation about financial security that his father carried, but it manifested itself in a different form. He tried to earn a great deal, while his father spent as little as possible to insure his own security.

Sean used his income not only to assure a comfortable future, but to support his impeccable taste in clothes, food, wine, the arts, and travel. He wanted his life to reflect culture and quality and went to great pains to select the best in those categories. Sean's selectivity was more than a statement of his values; it distinguished him from the shameful public image of his father.

The Lack of Protectiveness

The security children need from their fathers is much broader than money. They want their fathers to look beyond the lights left on and the money spent on new clothing to a general atmosphere in the home that speaks of things being taken care of. They need to know that crises that inevitably arise will be handled carefully and thoughtfully; that smaller problems can be solved with rationality and sensitivity; that the family's interests will be protected with reasonable responses to the interferences or apparent injustices that others might inflict.

Children need to know their fathers will stand up for them or the family. The father who allows the pushy uncle to take over the family business or the schoolteacher to unfairly vilify his child or even the fan at the football game to take over the family seats undermines the sense of a protective shield that children know they can count on.

Without this shield, life in the family feels exposed and insecure. When fathers not only fail to provide stability and protectiveness, but instead seem to fall apart or become overwhelmed when faced with challenges, children tend to be left with a dual burden. They lack confidence and feel considerable anxiety because of the insecurity of the home atmosphere and the lack of a positive role model for coping with

life's stresses. They also feel compelled, however, to protect or bail out
the inept father.

Sylvia talked about her father as being another Chicken Little. He saw
possible calamity at every step into the unfamiliar. He was forever warning Sylvia about what could go wrong when she wanted to try a new
activity, like ballet, or started making new friends at school. Because her
mother was not much different and she was the oldest of her siblings,
Sylvia assumed the role of troubleshooter for the family. From the time
she was ten, Sylvia took the lead in directing the family through crises
and acting as its spokesperson.

Sylvia maintained an outward appearance of coolness and confidence
that belied her inner life. She recalled:

> I know that underneath my calm exterior I'm almost as fearful as
> my father. I anticipate the worst like he does. But I feel so alone with
> these fears. I have no one to fall back on, because I can just imagine
> how my father will freak out if I tell him I have a problem. Then I'll
> end up calming him down and still having to figure out what to do
> for myself. So I'm always on guard, always cautious about creating
> problems for myself that I can't solve entirely on my own. It's a des-
> perately lonely, scary way to live.

Because Sylvia was so focused on protecting her father and avoiding
any of her own problems spilling onto him, she did not recognize or
appreciate how able she had become at conducting her own life.

Fathers fail their children not only when they seem incapable of managing problems that come at them from the outside, but when they lack
control over their own behavior. My father's favorite words of advice
were: "Too much of anything is no good." He would expand on this
wisdom by adding that this meant "too much, too little, anything with
'too' in it." My father was certainly not moderate in my own mind in
many aspects of how he lived, but his attention to this value fostered a
vigilance in me about not tipping the scales too far in either direction
with whatever I did.

Fathers help to shape our internal structures of control through setting limits on our behavior and encouraging boundaries in relationships
with others. They teach us how to manage our lives when they provide
models of temperate behavior and through the cautions they proffer to

us as we grow. Too much control in a child's life, we have already noted, leads to rigidity, anxiety, and feeling constrained. Too little control is not the antidote. Children pay a price for this imbalance as well.

There are two opposing ways that fathers can show a lack of control: in an active sense by themselves living wildly, in extremes, uncontrollably; and in a passive manner by simply not exerting influence, setting no limits on the child, abdicating authority to the mother rather than sharing it. Such fathers may even turn over their responsibility to the child. Young children feel at the mercy of a father who acts in extreme fashion. Some children gradually learn how to influence such a parent. With humor, perhaps, or the right soothing words they find they can calm the out-of-control father.

Even with the acquisition of this social skill, however, children will live in a state of alert. A dad who gets out of control instills unpredictability in the child's life and thus a high level of anxiety. Children of such fathers constantly prepare themselves for the consequences of the next loss of control—physical harm, an emotional assault, socially embarrassing behavior, and so on.

Fathers may reserve their extreme behavior for home. They may rant and rave rather than attempt to assert appropriate limits or become problem solvers. They may be childish or reckless in their responses to even minor frustrations. They may behave without control because of alcohol or drug abuse, which adds a further element of predictable unpredictability to their children's lives.

The issue of a father's lack of control plays out painfully for children in social situations, either at home or in public. Children are acute barometers of social stigma. They become increasingly worried about fitting in with peers. When they fear how their fathers will act in front of others they are intensely affected. Fathers who behave embarrassingly with their children's friends or in public infuse their youngsters with feelings of shame.

The concern in these social situations is not simply decorum. Fathers are needed to help teach their children how and when to set limits with others and with themselves. Fathers who lack this ability themselves leave their children with the fundamental insecurity that comes with not knowing how to appropriately define and protect themselves with others. Out of not wanting to behave like their fathers, children may become timid about establishing limits and boundaries with others. They are left undelineated as individuals, not knowing where they begin and others leave off.

A woman whose dad used to become extremely anxious and critical when he had work or money problems described how she used to react:

> At first I would be annoyed with him. But when he kept up the barrage of blaming and kept spinning his wheels emotionally, I would start to feel more and more anxious myself. Pretty soon I would fall into thinking I must have done something wrong even though I knew I hadn't. By the time he calmed down, I was more worked up than he was and I felt about two inches tall.

Coping With Shame

It does not take much embarrassing behavior for a child to be on alert around a poorly controlled father—a school conference where the father loses his temper, an athletic event where the father is overly competitive, an important social event where the father is late. One man who knew his father had a tendency to mistreat waitresses and service people hated to be with his dad in public places. He would position himself as far from his father as possible in a restaurant and look the other way when the waitress was taking his father's order.

For a young, middle-class woman who grew up in a neighborhood where everyone kept their homes neat and tidy, it was her father's chaotic messes around their house and yard that mortified her. She believed that their home was the laughingstock of the community.

Children who are ashamed of their fathers often will try to escape from their shame by isolating themselves either from their parent or from the rest of society. They avoid people about whose judgments they cannot be sure, and this will be most people. Unfortunately, we cannot hide from our shame. It gets locked inside and we carry it with us. These feelings of shame regarding a parent are complicated. They turn in on themselves. Our shame about our fathers twists inside us and we become ashamed of our shame. Regardless of the enormity of our fathers' failure, we feel guilty of being disloyal for carrying our shame.

For Geoffrey Wolff, author of *The Duke of Deception*, the pain of his father's sociopathic behavior accumulated throughout his adolescence.

He lamented, "The more time I spent near my father the worse I stammered." He also became more and more like his father. He was caught in a terrible dilemma. He wanted to be close to and identify with his father, as any child would. Yet his father's repeated dishonesty increasingly steeped Geoffrey in shame.

For some time Geoffrey tried to resolve his dilemma, as children with shame-inducing fathers often will, by maintaining conflicting postures between his father and the world: "I was loyal to my father behind his back. I was a scourge to his face but I wouldn't hear a word said against him by anyone else." Ultimately, he could not sustain this duality and "orphaned" himself by cutting himself off from his father.

The option of severing connection with the father does not work for all children trying to cope with their dad's inability to demonstrate mature adult behavior. The more out of control the father is, the more the children may feel the need to step in and take charge. These are children who, like Sylvia, function as junior adults from a young age. They tackle responsibilities well beyond what is fitting for their age despite their own lack of confidence. Being responsible for the father becomes a means of trying to ward off the anxiety and the shame these children feel.

6

The Responsibility Trap

When fathers do not manage their lives because they are too passive, they elicit less dread in their children than an overtly out-of-control dad. Their offspring, however, may feel more responsible for filling in the void created by the paternal passivity. In the past, the traditional father regarded his breadwinner role as largely fulfilling his contribution to the family. As a result, he typically bowed out of participating in large and small decisions, from the social and vacation plans to birthday parties to college applications. It would fall then to the mother to move the family through the family's normal passages and demands. While fathers are certainly more involved today in general, they still too often abdicate their responsibility for daily family functioning.

Many fathers have been so unused to operating in the domestic realm that when their children leave home and call for routine contact, Dad turns the phone over to Mom. It is as though even social calls require her expertise and can only be meant for her.

When children see their fathers function so passively on the home front, they are deeply disappointed. They may try to prop up the father's image by writing off his passivity to the fatigue of long work hours or pressures. Many will blame their mothers, seeing them as overbearing or pushy rather than admitting their fathers may not be pulling their own weight.

I have often heard individuals complain that their mothers came between them and their fathers, saying "If only Mom had backed off a little more, I'm sure Dad would've been more involved." The simple notion that their fathers could have stood up for themselves and become more involved opens a Pandora's box of anger and pain. To blame it on work or Mom avoids the uncomfortable conclusion that Dad was not strong enough to meet all his demands.

In many households, however, the children, particularly older sons, were expected to shore up the areas where fathers abdicated. The children themselves may have observed their mothers' struggles and become frustrated with their fathers. Feeling the need to fill in the gap, they took on inordinate responsibilities for their age, for example, advising and comforting their mothers at times of crisis. One woman recalled how she stood by her mother's side after her grandfather died because her father stayed in the background and did nothing.

A man told me, "I could see such disappointment in my mother's eyes when she looked at my father. I didn't want her to feel like that and I knew I could do better for her. I tried to put a light where there was none."

These children are left with an overwhelming burden. Not only must they make up for their fathers' deficiencies and try to find success in their own lives without having their fathers as positive role models, but they feel they must function as substitute husbands as well. They are left understandably overwhelmed, but perhaps more tragically, they are not free to live their own lives.

As these individuals grow older, they are apt to take on too much responsibility for others as well, at work, in relationships, and in friendships. Just as they fell into a pattern of ignoring their childhood needs for the good of the father or the family, they do the same with their adult needs. These are people who in today's self-help vernacular are called codependent. They sacrifice their own integrity and wholeness for others.

Kyle functioned from the time he was twelve into adulthood as his father's assistant in their custom auto parts store. He didn't choose to go into the family business, he knew it was expected of him. By the time he had his driver's license he started making the deliveries. The bad news about this role in the family business was that Kyle's father repeatedly made promises about completing jobs that he simply could not keep. On his deliveries Kyle was the one who had to confront the angry complaints and looks of dismay. He developed a standard array of excuses and apologies, but the customers' dissatisfaction ate at his insides.

As he became more involved in sales and production, Kyle conducted a silent strategy to keep his father from dealing with the new requests for business. Kyle was determined not to let down other people, never to make promises he could not himself keep. As a result he delegated very little work and labored under the constant pressure of meeting everyone's expectations while keeping an eye trained on his father. Kyle did his best to shield his father from the antagonism his father induced in others. He hid the shame he felt for his father. At one point he told me: "I never used to tell my father about the times when I covered for him. I didn't want to embarrass him or give him the idea that I thought I was better than him. Actually, I didn't want to feel like I was better than him, because then there would be no one to look up to. I preferred to hold on to that illusion rather than face things alone."

Kyle had bailed out his father so many times that he essentially was more involved in running the business than his father. Because he operated under his father's shadow, however, he did not view his accomplishments as his own. He wanted to take over the business and free himself from the constant anxiety he carried about what his father might do next. Unfortunately, he didn't believe he could handle the business without his father.

Moreover, in trying so hard to cover for his father, Kyle "grew a crooked tree," as he put it, ignoring his own needs for nurturing and independence. He had many interests he could have followed: He loved the outdoors, read voraciously late at night when he had the opportunity, and probably could have been an artist. He buried these interests, again because he couldn't imagine he could survive on his own and because he didn't believe his father could survive without Kyle to cover his tracks. It was a symbiotic relationship in which Kyle sacrificed his future.

Kyle assumed another responsibility typical of children of weak fathers—he was overprotective of his mother. While on the one hand, he avoided confronting his father's irresponsibility, he understood that his mother could not depend on his father. He saw the unhappiness it caused her and it pained him. He tried to fill in the gap and be someone upon whom she could rely. Her sadness weighed upon him and prevented him from feeling comfortable with pursuing his own passions. If she could not be happy, how could he? This burden became another reason for Kyle to truncate his life.

Missing Guidance and Support

Kyle's inability to move forward was due not only to his father's unreliable behavior, but to the absence of a positive role model and source of encouragement. Children do not assume that it is part of their father's responsibility as a good parent to provide the guidance and support they need to develop their talents freely. As Kyle did, they will likely blame themselves for lacking the courage to try, while perhaps finding reasons to excuse the father's inability to help guide them.

A father may not be a good teacher or may lack high expectations for his own life. If he conveys positive expectations for his children's lives, however, it will help give them a sense of hope and direction. Unfortunately, when fathers can voice no expectations for their children having a better life, the youngsters get the message that they are not expected to achieve. Moreover, they may feel that their fathers do not believe in them. The father's weakness becomes transformed into a rejection and a devastatingly negative statement to the children.

Traditional fathers tried to give their children a role model to which they could look up. They did this typically through career or work. Since the children didn't usually directly observe their fathers at work and more often than not weren't taught their fathers' work skills, it was hard to gain confidence from their dad's modeling. Instead, they learned that work was consuming and a man's most worthwhile activity, not that they were equal to the task.

Children can feel lost and unsure of themselves when they have fathers who demonstrate strength in at least some significant ways, but do not guide them. With fathers who show neither strength nor sensitivity to their needs, the children will suffer feelings of self-doubt even more intensely. Out of their lack of confidence and direction in their lives, these young people are pulled and swayed by the views and enticements of others and find it difficult to make choices of their own about major and even minor issues.

These children will follow one of two patterns as adults: Either they live in fear and lack the resolve to take command of their own lives or they somehow possess the resolve, perhaps out of the determination not to be like their fathers, to take risks and forge a different kind of life. It is not as though these latter individuals are untouched by the lack of guidance, however. Underneath their resolve they will experience considerable anxiety, making their struggle to shape their lives an uphill battle shadowed by the fear of falling back down.

Matt's friends always used to tell him enthusiastically how much he and his father were alike, in their looks and in their behavior. They thought it was great because Matt's father was such a nice guy. It made Matt sad, though, because while he knew he looked and behaved super-ficially like his father, he felt as though he didn't really know his dad well. He did know that his father worked for the same company from the time he was sixteen until he retired. It was clear that his father bowled every Tuesday night and faithfully went to church on Sunday morning and to the monthly meeting of the church Ways and Means Committee.

What Matt didn't know was why his father never took the chance to go into business with his good buddy, how he felt when he went off to fight in the Korean War, why he didn't finish college, or what he thought about much of anything. Most of all Matt wondered how his dad got up day after day to trudge into work when he was apparently so unhappy with what he did.

Matt never saw his father make plans for or even talk about the future. Nothing ever seemed to change about his life unless it happened through someone else. Matt was determined not to let life pass him by this way. He seized every opportunity that came his way. But he ago-nized over each change he made, every promotion he took. He won-dered what his motives were, worried whether he was making a mistake, questioned whether he would be able to do what was expected. Ironically, despite the fact that Matt's life had much more color, excite-ment and variety than his dad's, his changes were the result of others seeking him out rather than his own initiative. He would take the risk, with considerable anguish, to meet a new challenge, but he still felt pas-sive, that he wasn't planning his own future.

Eventually Matt hit the top rung of his career ladder. With his suc-cess he encountered a knotty dilemma that prevented him from taking satisfaction in his accomplishment. When fathers have not achieved much in their own lives, it puts their children in a bind: At what point does my success diminish my father in his own eyes and perhaps even in mine? At what point may I hurt him by my own achievements? When Matt received his first year-end bonus he had trouble telling his father:

> I could feel my ambivalence come out. Part of me wanted him to know about this sizable amount and hear his pride. But then I also

thought of the years he had pinched pennies to be able to pass on an inheritance to me and how with a few months' work, in one fell swoop, I'd matched his lifetime of effort. I wanted him to know, but I wanted to control the meaning he would take from it, so it would give him pride, but no pain.

Children may want a better life than their fathers', but they are confused and troubled by what it means to surpass them. When Philip Roth went to college as a young man, he feared outdistancing his father, so he defined his task as being there to learn for his father, too. As he put it in his memoir, *Patrimony*, "It wasn't just I who was being educated but he whom I was delivering from ignorance as well." Roth understood that he was emotionally merged with his father at that point in his life.

Children of weak fathers find it painfully difficult to separate their own achievements from the father's reaction to them and their own reaction to how the relationship might be affected. They may be inclined to fear success and avoid it in order to elevate their fathers and sustain their higher status. One young professional described his quandary this way: "I'm damned no matter what I do. If I do better than he did, he may get angry and reject me, plus I'll lose my image of him as someone to look up to. To be at the same level as he was creates a problem. That's no good. And to do less well would just be worse." This man remained frozen in place for some time until he could achieve greater emotional separation from his father.

Fathers themselves may well fear being outdistanced by their children. They may feel their youngsters' achievements highlight their lack of success in life. Some react out of jealousy and seek to undercut their children. Others may look to their offspring to bolster their identities and vicariously fulfill their own potential. For these fathers, a son who becomes a football hero or a daughter a class president is a ticket to acclaim. Fathers, too, can be fused with their children. A young woman lawyer remarked: "I used to cringe when my father started to talk about me to his friends. He had a way of describing what I was doing with my life as though he was doing it, too. He didn't seem to make any distinction. It made me feel very uncomfortable."

The emotionally parasitic father blurs the sense of personal boundaries children need. Youngsters whose deeds are swallowed whole by the father do not experience accomplishments as self-generated. Their achievements, therefore, are not self-fulfilling. The pressure to satisfy the father's ego makes the children's actions take on an external focus. The deeds are done for the father, not for themselves. As a result the children do not develop confidence or the knowledge of how much to expect of themselves. This dynamic with a fused father produces another complicated emotional paradox. The children become ashamed that the father must feed off them for his identity, yet they also feel a weighty responsibility not to let the father down.

Weak fathers, even when they are not emotionally fused with their children, are likely to create a reversal in the normal pattern of a father validating his offspring. These fathers signal to their children that they themselves and not the youngsters need support. Often children react to their father's weakness by protecting the father so that his weaknesses are not revealed. They may also try to shore up the father in ways that might free him somehow to become more supportive himself. Children do not necessarily act without self-interest in protecting Dad.

Another common response is to relinquish opportunities for validation rather than risk exposure of a father's weaknesses. I still regret that I chose to convince my father not to attend my college graduation because I thought he would find it difficult to negotiate the travel and the social nuances and because I thought I would have to manage him through the process at a time when I wanted only to be responsible for myself. I tried to protect him from the discomfort I imagined he would feel and I shielded myself from my own discomfort. That he let me convince him confirmed me in my misbegotten mission.

Whatever the father's weakness, there are two fundamental responses that will not vary: The children will still want and need the approbation that is lacking and they will continue to put a great deal of energy into shaping themselves to try to get it. Paul Auster, in *The Invention of Solitude*, described his feelings about his withdrawn father this way:

> I mulishly went on hoping for something that was never given to me—or given to me so rarely and arbitrarily that it seemed to happen outside the range of normal experience. . . . It was not that I felt he disliked me. It was just that he seemed distracted. . . . And more than anything else, I wanted him to take notice of me.

Auster found himself as an adult tracking his father's attention to his grandson, as if this show of affection could stand indirectly for the long-sought-after recognition and affection he failed to receive. He understood, as we all need to, that "you do not stop hungering for your father's love."

Children are caught up in conflicting emotions with these weak fathers. They resent the lack of validation and whatever interferes with giving it, yet long to feel connected to the father. They need somehow to secure the assurance that they have a meaningful bond with the father in order to overcome the feeling of rejection associated with his unresponsiveness. One common, though frequently unconscious, way to play out this paradox is to pattern oneself after the father, despite rejecting his weak behavior. Geoffrey Wolff wrote in *The Duke of Deception*, "As I liked him less and less I became more and more like him." Children who vociferously voice their disgust or hatred for their fathers' actions almost invariably behave in just these ways themselves to a shocking degree.

In time, when fathers persistently fail to meet their children's needs, the children begin to act as though validation is not important or not something one can reasonably count on from a father. One woman who had been unable to hug her father for years out of disgust for his behavior in the home finally came to an acceptance of his limitations. As she was leaving him one day, she felt an urge to hug him and acted on it. It was not until later that day, with the prompting of a friend, that she realized her father had just stood there and never hugged her back. She didn't notice because she never expected it.

William Appleton notes in *Fathers and Daughters*, a book about the influence of fathers on the lives of women, that daughters of distant fathers learn not to expect much in general from the males in their lives. As a result they try to toughen themselves, to be independent and not have to count on a man. As adults they may seek out men they believe will be strong enough to compensate for what their fathers lacked.

Daughters with mothers who offer guidance, support, and a strong role model for coping with life are less affected by the weakness in fathers. Their psychological need is to identify with their mothers, so the mothers' strength gives them even less need to look to their fathers. Daughters will still fear being like their fathers in the specific ways they are weak, but mothers can provide a counterweight and core identity to draw on.

Sons are in a different position. It is critical for their masculine identity to see themselves overcome the weakness they have seen in their father if the father does not overcome it himself. Sons continue to need their fathers to be strong because they are the primary source of their male identity. A competent mother cannot substitute for the father's fortitude without ambivalence arising in the son. Her ability serves to highlight the father's weakness. Sons certainly need and benefit from a mother's strength, but when the father does not carry his own weight as a role model, the son's comfort at identifying with either parent is compromised.

Sons and daughters, then, are left with a complicated, burdensome legacy when their fathers are dominated by weaknesses. Recently a client was reflecting with me about her awareness of how much responsibility she bore for both her parents. She understood that she was filled with emotions she had absorbed from her parents.

We did a guided imagery exercise together in which she pictured herself on a hike up a mountain carrying a knapsack. The knapsack was filled with the feelings she had taken on for her parents. Included in the sack were a huge rock that symbolized her father's sadness about the direction his life had taken and smaller rocks for his financial insecurity, his resentment toward others for his fate, and his anger, of which she was often the target. As part of the exercise I asked her to sit under a tree on her imaginary walk, open the sack, and one by one remove each rock. She then filled the sack with nourishing food for herself and continued on her hike.

While unloading the burdens we have assumed from our father's unresolved problems cannot be done so easily, this daughter was in fact helped considerably by formulating an image of what she needed to do to help herself. She began to feel lighter and to give herself permission not to be responsible for anyone else's emotions or lot in life. Becoming clear about how she had been feeling so responsible and how weighed down she had been was an important aspect of her transition.

Much of the task of recovering from the imposition of a father's weakness involves gaining awareness of the load we have taken on and learning to set that burden down. As we continue to explore some of the common ways fathers manifest their weakness, we will see more clearly the nature of the inappropriate responsibility we assume and how to open our knapsacks to finally discard the rocks and other refuse that do not rightfully belong to us.

7

Overburdened, Troubled, and Silent Fathers

Gene, whose surgeon-artist dad was included in the section on ideal fathers in "The Power of Fathers," staunchly resisted the idea that a father as special as his could possibly have affected him negatively in any way. He could acknowledge that while his father enjoyed having Gene watch him craft or fix things, his dad never taught him how to do these tasks. I pointed out that this meant Gene's father was inept in at least one major aspect of his paternal role—he didn't pass much of his knowledge on to his son.

Clearly, all fathers are weak in some ways. There are some fathers, however, whose overall pattern is to function out of their weakness. Their difficulty coping with stress, managing their emotions, or giving of themselves to others, or their dependence on people, alcohol, or drugs, dominates their lives.

Three common patterns of weakness are presented in this chapter: fathers who always appear weighted down or overburdened by life's responsibilities; those who suffer from emotional or addiction problems; and fathers who are excessively passive and emotionally removed. Each pattern has its own insidious impact on the children.

The Overburdened Father

The father in *Brighton Beach Memoirs* is an example of the overburdened father. He always looks worried and preoccupied. His shoulders sag under the weight of his sack of responsibilities. His brow is forever furrowed. He listens every night to the evening news, not only to hear the latest about the inexorable war unfolding in Europe, but to know whether his relatives there are safe and whether they might need to come to the United States to stay with him. He works two jobs to support the family. The adults in his extended family turn to him for advice and solace. His children are afraid to bother him with their problems, lest they tip a delicate balance and provoke another heart attack.

Indeed, heart problems represent a concrete, dramatic warning sign that a father has a limited capacity for absorbing more responsibilities. Without such an ominous signal, children are nevertheless sensitive to the cues that a father is overwhelmed by his obligations. Mothers typically act as buffers, trying to ward off problems and potential worries in order not to overtax their husbands' limited capacity to cope. The children themselves will adjust their expectations and will either bring their needs for support to the mother or some other significant adult or stifle them.

Children of overburdened fathers may go beyond trying not to add to their fathers' load by attempting to be perfectly good. In this way they try to avert any risk of getting into trouble or creating a problem that might spill over to their fathers. They function as if walking on eggshells and thus live in a state of perpetual tension. They give themselves unrealistically narrow margins for making mistakes because they feel so responsible for their fathers.

These children may even believe that their fathers' well-being rests with their own ability to manage their lives independently. They regard their fathers as so weighted down that any added problem may be the straw that breaks the camel's back. In situations where they actually have reason to fear that stress will endanger the father's life or where they have constructed this picture of their father's frailty, they feel overpowering guilt for any mishap or transgression that comes to their dad's attention. A man whose father had recovered from a prolonged illness and then started a new business remembered:

> My dad came home exhausted every night. He was working practically seven days a week. We were all worried he would get sick again or just plain drop dead. One time I got in trouble at school. I begged my mother not to tell Dad because I was so afraid he would

be upset. She did tell him and I went around for days in a cold sweat praying nothing would happen to him.

The focus on how their fathers manage may leave these children so preoccupied they are inattentive to their own needs. They will sooner do something for their fathers than for themselves. The nurturing role that daughters have been socialized into makes them particularly susceptible to this type of caretaking.

Moreover, this exaggerated paternal focus is likely to sow the seeds of codependence, of trying to please others and worrying about others' well-being at the expense of one's own needs. Overburdened fathers may seek to draw their emotional sustenance from their children as well as rely too much on them. The children can become so fused with the father emotionally in their effort to care for him that they do not recognize their own competence as a helper. They act as though they are an appendage of their dad. When left to do something for themselves, these children may be paralyzed with doubt, not believing that they are capable of functioning on their own despite how much responsibility they have taken on to ease their fathers' burdens.

Leslie's dad was a sensitive man. His pain about the death of his wife when Leslie was still a toddler had been nearly unbearable for him. He was overwhelmed by the responsibility of raising a daughter on his own and was fearful that with how awful he felt most of the time, he would not be able to manage.

In a couple of her dad's weaker moments, when Leslie displayed the willfulness or voiced the need for attention that one would expect from a toddler, he slipped into some dramatic self-pity and warned Leslie that he could die, too, if he didn't get relief from the pressure he was under. Though Leslie only heard this frightful message a couple of times, she was profoundly affected by it. She recalled that after hearing her father signal that dreadful warning she stopped making any demands on him if she could help it.

Leslie was adroit at taking care of herself by the time she started kindergarten. She made her bed immediately after getting out of it in the morning. Her toys and belongings were always put away. By age six or seven she was making breakfast for herself and her father. When she came home from school she straightened up the house to be sure it was in order before he came home. Well before adolescence she became a sounding board for his troubles, a cheerleader for his efforts, and a soother of his bouts with despair.

Whatever energy Leslie's father had for his own life prior to his wife's death had left him. He lived like someone who had lost the wind to his sails. He had started out as a rising star with the company for which he worked, but he stopped putting in much effort and was passed over for promotions. His job always seemed on the line when the company was laying off people. He never resumed a social life, didn't date, and didn't cultivate friendships.

Leslie understood that her dad's sole joy in life was in observing her. The responsibility attendant with this role was magnified by the lingering fear that her father was so fragile he couldn't handle another major disappointment. Leslie's father, in the meantime, fawned over her every accomplishment, but also glamorized her life. While she struggled as a student and then as a young professional to keep her head above water practically and emotionally, he would go on about what a wonderful, exciting time she must be having.

Leslie was angered by her father's inability to see her life for what it was and appreciate the hardship she endured. She also felt extreme pressure to perform well so that in the end she wouldn't let him down. She was carrying the burden of achieving for both of them, but with her father on her back, Leslie's focus was more on his feelings. She could not take satisfaction or even feel that what she was doing was for herself.

Despite managing almost everything at home but the bill-paying throughout her teen years, putting herself through college and law school, and being one of the brightest in her classes and a student leader, too, Leslie never believed a word of praise from anyone. She lived in constant fear that something would go wrong for her and that it would be her own fault. Her dad's warning clearly reverberated through the unconscious chambers of her being. She had no faith in her intelligence, her competence, her social skills. She did know that she could keep a neat apartment.

Sadly, she was so used to serving as the leaning post for her father, she could not imagine that anyone could be there to give her support. Her friendships and her love relationships always put her in a caretaker role, or she clung to that familiar role because of the comfort it gave her. She was like Groucho Marx, not trusting any club that would want her as a member.

The Troubled Father

Children of overburdened fathers often try to bolster their dad until he can manage better or until some of the burden is lifted. The troubled father is not simply weighted down, he has been knocked off track in his capacity to function in his parent role. This may occur because he has an addiction or is disturbed emotionally or has a distorted view of himself, others, or life in general.

When Kyle's dad forgot about a deadline he had promised to meet or showed up at the office two hours after a scheduled appointment, his son never connected this behavior with his drinking. Kyle found it easier to think of his father as irresponsible or even eccentric than as an alcoholic, which seemed far more shameful to Kyle.

Chemically dependent fathers may function well enough to hide their problem for years. At some point, however, their weakness will seep through, often in pathetic ways. As with Kyle's father, they become increasingly erratic emotionally and unreliable. To be dependent on them is to live with perpetual insecurity. Their behavior is often inconsistent: They may be socially charming one minute and a ghastly embarrassment the next; a glowing success one month and fired the next; a great provider one week and broke the next; a go-getter, then a sagging, whimpering child. Their capacity to support their children can be as unpredictable as their emotions. Their ability to show love and approval comes and goes.

When fathers' behavior is impaired by emotional problems, the outcomes may be similar to those caused by the overburdened father or, depending on the nature of the problem, by the addicted father. Fathers who suffer from depression or high levels of anxiety appear weighed down or overwhelmed by their circumstances. Leslie's father could probably best be described as walking the edge between being overburdened and being depressed. He was virtually always the former and at times crossed over to the latter. When the emotional disturbance is more pronounced, the child usually knows he or she is living with a dysfunctional father. Consequently, the transfer of responsibility is much more complete and consuming for the child.

With problems that are more extreme, such as manic-depressive fathers who alternate between deep depression and hyperintensity, or fathers who become psychotic, the impact is similar to that of a chemically dependent father. The fits of anger and bizarre or out-of-control behavior associated with these illnesses present the same kind of unpredictability, fear, and shame as chemically dependent patterns. With any of these illnesses the child is subject to an anxiety-provoking environment and the lack of fundamental fathering. At worst, the child lives in a terror-ridden home and perhaps has to be a stand-in adult to replace the father.

Often children with disturbed fathers will find ways to wall themselves off from the father's behavior. They may do so by developing a life outside the home that is busy enough to keep them away most of the time. They may develop an intricate, detached internal life that allows them to withdraw into a private, predictable world.

Disturbed fathers, however, do not necessarily allow their children the freedom to escape. Geoffrey Wolff's father, described in *The Duke of Deception*, uprooted his son constantly despite Geoffrey's best efforts to avoid the repercussions of his father's con games. Later, his father was constantly turning to his son to bail him out of financial or legal jams. Geoffrey always felt the burden of trying to help no matter how futile the effort and despite knowing he was providing only a momentary solution until the next crisis.

A manically-depressed father who periodically took to bed for days at a time had enmeshed his son, Alex, in the role of rescuer by the time he was a young teen. His father found Alex to have a sympathetic ear and would call upon him when he felt ready to emerge from his depressed state. Alex, with the encouragement of his father, accepted the belief that he was the only one capable of getting his father back on his feet. Since the father sometimes threatened suicide and at other times was clearly risking his job by missing so much work, Alex felt as though he carried his father's fate in his hands. Not surprisingly, his heart pounded every morning as he walked past his parents' bedroom and checked to see if his father was still in bed.

Severe depression, chemical dependency, and psychosis are often chronic conditions. Children may well adapt in a manner that seems admirable for such adverse circumstances. In some ways they are strengthened by their adaptability, developing skills they might not otherwise have acquired and perhaps becoming more independent.

Children of dysfunctional fathers can be fooled by their seeming resilience into believing they have been unaffected by their father's inability to manage his life. They want to think they were able simply to pick up the pieces, glue them back together, and move on with their own lives. In reality, these children lose a sense of their own identities because they expend so much energy on keeping their fathers' problems from being exposed or on remedying the aftereffects.

A father does not have to be emotionally disturbed or chemically dependent to come across as troubled. An outlook that is consistently negative or bleak, a mentality that defines oneself as a victim or always finds fault with others are ways that fathers can be troubled in less dramatic or overt fashion. These attitudes do not generally inculcate the levels of anxiety, shame, and overresponsibility that the more disturbed patterns do. Nevertheless, they leave children shortchanged because these fathers are unable to function as their children need them to.

Anthropologist Gregory Bateson once wrote: "The fathers have eaten bitter fruit and the children's teeth are set on edge." A father's bitterness or negativity shapes his children's views of life. The children then lack the guidance to feel confident and positive about establishing their own life direction. Brooding, self-pitying fathers will also likely miss the mark in terms of the other basic paternal functions: They are too passive and self-absorbed to meet the minimum requirements for protecting and nurturing their offspring. Nor do they provide constructive role models.

Ultimately, regardless of what diverts or prevents the father from carrying out his role effectively, children are left with having to make up the deficits on their own. They must do this, however, in a double jeopardy: They lack the adult backing from the father for their own challenges, and they labor with self-doubt and fear of further embarrassment. They also dread that the father's troubles will be rooted in them as well. They tend to carry the awful weight of feeling somehow responsible for both of them for what isn't working. One fellow recounted Sunday evenings with his father: "I'd sit in the background watching him with his head in his hands and looking so blue and so worried. It was the only time all week we had in the house together. I'd keep asking myself, 'What did I do wrong?' And I'd wrack my brains to figure out a way to help him."

These children's fear they will have inherited their father's problems confounds their ability to handle their own feelings. Children of such fathers may lump all displays of intense feeling into the same category with their father's, regarding these feelings as inappropriate, as barriers to success in worldly affairs and perhaps frightening. They may then avoid showing their own emotions in the mistaken idea that burying their feelings preserves their resolve to be strong.

Those who identify with their fathers rather than believing they do not have to follow their fate feel vulnerable about effectively meeting life's demands. They struggle against the fear that they will succumb to the same problems their fathers did when faced with a crisis or difficult challenge.

Marjorie had been married fifteen years before she began to get the idea that she was trying too hard to keep everything in her life in order. She had married a competent, stable, successful, and reliable man. When her husband went on his frequent business trips she needed the itinerary laid out in explicit detail, and she remained uneasy until he was back at home. When her son and two daughters hit rocky moments emotionally or were under a lot of pressure at school or facing a disappointment, she became a worrywart, mother hen, and psychoanalyst all at once.

It was a revelation when Marjorie came to realize in therapy that all her efforts to anticipate danger for her family came from her years as a child feeling frightened and confused by her father's behavior. Marjorie's father was ultimately diagnosed as a schizophrenic and spent years in and out of psychiatric hospitals. The unpredictability of his coming and going was behind her need for all the details on her husband's travel plans. Eventually Marjorie's father stopped coming home, which created an even deeper fear of abandonment. She was terrified that someday someone in her family would inexplicably leave again permanently and that person's abandonment would leave her with the same empty horror experienced with her father.

While Marjorie worried that she could end up like her father, she displaced a lot of this fear onto her children also. She hovered over them, wanting them to be appropriate in their appearance and judicious in their behavior. She hated it when her kids or her husband somehow stood out in public. It wasn't only an issue of propriety for Marjorie, but rather that she viewed any extreme behavior as a possible sign her own youngsters might lose control altogether, like her father. Every six months or so her father had seemed to go through one of his psychotic sideshows. Once the local police had to pull him off a neighbor's car roof where he was wildly directing a cattle drive through a blizzard in the Rockies.

Marjorie never understood why her father had these episodes, but she always assumed that when the pressures in his life built up he would reach a breaking point. That was how her mother explained it to her as a child. Before she had her own family she wasn't so careful about doing things in moderation. As a parent, however, she watched her children closely, meticulously monitoring the activities they took on. She watched her husband, too. She particularly was anxious about how her family dealt with their feelings. She got upset when they became upset, because she feared their emotional eruption was only the tip of the iceberg. Maybe this door-slamming or that tantrum would prove to be the turning point and her father's dreaded schizophrenia would sprout again.

For Marjorie the real turning point came as she approached the same age when her father was first hospitalized. Not surprisingly, she entered therapy at that time, because her own fears of being like her father were ballooning. She began to see how her fears were blinding her to the ways she wasn't like her father. The signs were right there inside her that she didn't have to follow the same path, if only she would read them.

The Silent Father

The actor Gary Cooper was a heroic role model for men in our culture because he displayed quiet strength. He did what he was called upon to do without having to yap about it. A man of few words is a man who seemingly knows what he's about and doesn't have to brag, obsess, or complain about it. His actions and demeanor speak for him. His silence conveys his capacity to unyieldingly absorb what is expected of him and take responsibility for it.

There is something admirable about the kind of reliability and unspoken fortitude exemplified by Cooper and adopted by many men. But while this stoicism can function well for a man who has to face a difficult challenge, including the day-in, day-out responsibility of carrying out his provider role, it doesn't work well as a parental way of functioning. The silence in relation to one's children may come across as indifference. Rather than appearing to be a stoic approach to life, it can feel uncaring to a child. In addition, it may mask the father's own sense of weakness or inadequacy.

A father's silence is not simply a matter of the words he speaks. It reflects his emotional involvement as well. The silent father may be one who feels his involvement is unimportant and who therefore cuts himself off from others. Commonly he is ensconced on the couch watching television or reading the newspaper rather than interacting. He usually seems preoccupied or self-absorbed rather than vacant. But living in the recesses of his own mind means he lives in isolation—from the family and from himself.

Silent fathers are often oblivious to their children's lives. Their uninvolvement leads them to be unattuned. They end up not knowing their children's friends, their teachers' names, what they're doing in their favorite activities, their ages, or, worse yet, who they are as people.

When a father is cut off in this way it effectively means he cannot meet his basic obligations at home. The silent father, with his aura of inner strength, restraint, and self-discipline, may do well as the provider, the protector, and even the disciplinarian on occasion. His lack of voice on the home front, however, creates multiple problems. One pertains to the boundaries between family members and the division of responsibilities.

The father's detachment can result in the mother feeling undue pressure to exert influence and make decisions for the family on her own. Caught in this bind, she may become the dominant controlling force in the family to offset the father's failure to participate actively. The father's lack of involvement, in some instances, leaves the child without a buffer between himself or herself and a mother who comes on too strong while trying to compensate for the father.

For boys, with their psychological need to identify with their fathers, this passivity is especially damaging. Guy Corneau notes in *Absent Fathers, Lost Sons* that when fathers are absent, sons end up identifying with their mothers, while still struggling to find ways to identify with the father. This is true for the absence that comes with silence as well. Even if they try to see their fathers as strong, silent hero types, it is difficult to feel connected to or guided by them.

One day in therapy Dan remembered the first time he came home visibly drunk:

> I was surprised and relieved at first because my father didn't give the customary stern lecture I expected. He helped me get cleaned up, offered a few soothing words about how bad it must feel, and put me to bed. It was only later that I started to wonder why he never said

anything about being drunk at age sixteen. Did it mean it was really okay to do that? I was probably already on shaky ground with alcohol at that point and his complete avoidance of dealing with my drinking didn't help. I didn't really have a sense of how far I could go before it was too far. I really wanted him to say something to help give me bearings, but it didn't feel right to ask.

Like many others in the same position, Dan leaned heavily on his mother for advice and bolstering. He received lots of support from his mother and felt that he was special to her, but he did not carry that feeling into the larger world. He did not feel strong enough in his own right to make decisions and set a direction for his life. He waited for others' cues and for someone to be there to back him up. It was only after his father's death that Dan realized how much he longed to have heard more of his father's voice.

Fathers cannot maintain silence or a stance of neutrality and expect to convey a sense of direction to their children. They may do their jobs faithfully and believe they are setting a good example. But examples are like road signs without a map, offering a destination without the means to get there if you happen to be unsure about where you are. The silent father may indeed accomplish a great deal and perform in an exemplary fashion, but not value his own efforts. His children may not know what he has done, or they may know the facts but not the substance. As a result, they are deprived of the opportunity to look up to that father or to learn from his achievements.

As an adult, Matt heard stories from relatives about his father that he wished he had been told as a child. He was informed that his father had written for the school newspaper and quit when he was unfairly passed over for sports editor. If Matt had known about this he felt certain that it would have given him permission to stand up for himself in some situations where he believed he was unjustly treated.

Matt also had found some old sports stories when rummaging through the attic that were written by his father and published in the city paper. Apparently his dad had covered some of the high school football games as a freelancer. Matt was excited to see tangible evidence of a talent in his father of which he was wholly unaware. He himself liked to write, and he finally saw a connection between them he could honor.

This discovery of his dad's writing was tinged with sadness, though, because Matt regretted not hearing about it directly from his father. He could have discussed what this had meant to his father and how his father felt at the time. It would have given him a new perspective on his father that might also have offered encouragement about his own potential as a writer.

While Matt was deprived of seeing his father in a better light by his dad's silence, the reverse can be true as well. Sometimes a father's silence disguises real weakness. For example, fathers who are engaged in addictive behavior usually make efforts to conceal their drinking, gambling, or womanizing. Unless their behavior is exposed, their excuses or self-pitying ways can make them look put upon or oppressed.

Mothers who sense that things are amiss and push for answers or changed behavior can appear unsupportive. The father can actually come off looking saintly. His children may think: "Poor Dad. He works all day and comes home exhausted, just needing some peace and quiet. And what he gets is nagging and prodding from Mom. Yet he remains so patient and undemanding in spite of her."

Janet's father came home promptly at 6:00 P.M. every night from the office. He made himself one double martini and settled into his easy chair to read the paper cover to cover. Janet and her sister always found him warm and affectionate, though he only allowed brief interruptions from his reading. It seemed as though their mom resented his need to relax. She would routinely try to enlist him in discussing one problem or another. He would resist and they would frequently end up arguing.

Friday night was Dad's poker night. By the time Janet was in high school, those poker fests were lasting into the early morning hours and occasionally all night. For many months Janet and her sister regarded these Friday nights as their dad's need to blow off steam from his job pressures and to catch a break from their mom's demands. These were the excuses he used to defend himself when they started questioning him out of their growing concern.

One Saturday morning, after another all-night escapade, Janet used the car to run an errand. She found a woman's scarf that she knew did not belong to her mother. Her dad denied any wrongdoing when confronted with the scarf and for the next several months continued to give explanations for the girls' suspicions. Finally, after a family friend saw him with another woman at a bar on a Friday night, he admitted his affair. Janet's parents then divorced.

Janet remembered all too painfully how traumatic that period of her life was. For Janet, one of the most disturbing aspects of her father's betrayal of the family related to the length of time he had been having his affair. She realized that for years her father's unwillingness to invest in family life was entwined with his secret life. He didn't spend more time with them or engage in working out problems with their mother because his interests lay elsewhere. His image of an exhausted, brow-beaten husband was largely a decoy that shielded the family from knowing where he was truly putting his energy.

The most critical effect silent fathers have on their children is their lack of validation. Most children believe that their fathers love them on some level even when they do not hear it. With silent fathers, naturally, the children have to infer the love or approval they believe is there. There are nonverbal cues that reinforce this belief. It is astonishing, though, how many men and women claim that they never or rarely ever heard their fathers actually say they loved them or openly demonstrate how much they valued them.

There is a significant emotional difference between knowing you are loved and hearing it expressed directly. Maybe it's like the difference between being an unofficial winner of an award and being officially declared the winner and actually receiving the award. Having to infer validation can only pale against the feelings that come with directly experiencing it. It is a distinction that, out of self-protection, many children do not choose to belabor.

When children do not receive clear messages of validation from their father, they are inevitably left with self-doubt. They wonder if his approval or affection would be more overt if somehow they did things better, if only they were good enough. Paul Auster in *The Invention of Solitude* noted that he would find himself talking too much in an attempt to secure his father's attention or at least obtain a response from him. More than just getting his attention, he wanted, as all children want, to win direct approval from his father.

Auster said he had "a desire to do something extraordinary, to impress him with an act of heroic proportions. The more aloof he was, the higher the stakes became for me." So many children become caught up in trying to be heroes because they think their fathers will finally respond to them as a result.

Eleanor had six siblings. She fell in the middle, with two brothers and a sister on either side of her. Eleanor's dad worked a second sales job to keep the family going, so he was away most of the work week, including Saturdays.

His philosophy for relating to the demands of his sizable clan was ostensibly to treat his kids as though they were all equal. If he couldn't praise them all, he felt it was better not to single out any of the kids for special attention. This strategy fit well with his reserved demeanor and limited time and energy for life at home.

There were inconsistencies, however, in his policy of neutrality. All of Eleanor's siblings had some position in the family or special need that seemed to attract notice. There was a firstborn son and daughter, a "baby" boy and girl, a son who was a star athlete, and another son who had heart problems from a genetic defect. Eleanor's uniqueness lay in what a good child she was. She excelled in school, was always respectful and polite, and did her chores without complaining.

The irony in Eleanor's decided efforts to gain attention by being a model child was that she made it easy for her father to heed his other children because she seemed to be doing so well on her own. Eleanor was close to her mother and felt her mom's appreciation for her achievements in school and her help at home. But her mom was a simple woman who raised her children, kept the house in order, and volunteered at church. Eleanor had dreams of becoming a doctor. She believed her dad could value her drive to succeed more than her mom could. Besides, she would need a great deal of financial assistance from her father and that meant he would have to recognize her potential for a career that superseded those of her siblings.

When it was time to apply to college, Eleanor had to pass up her hopes of attending an Ivy League school because her father would only support her going to a state college like the one her only older brother who went on for higher education attended. Even though Eleanor scored well on her medical aptitude test and probably would have gained admission to medical school, her father again disappointed her. He not only refused to help her financially but discouraged her aspirations, telling her that medical school was no place for a woman. He took no interest at all in her studies or activities at college.

Eleanor was not deterred from her drive to achieve. After working for several years, she saved the money to put herself through medical school and secured admission to proceed with her dream.

Throughout her adult life Eleanor had many achievements that made her stand out among her peers as well as among her siblings. No matter what commendation she won in her professional life, Eleanor always thought first of telling her dad about it. He responded unfailingly with a modest acknowledgment and changed the subject to some mundane accomplishment of one of her brothers or sisters. Eleanor would be silently crushed. Despite knowing intellectually that she had made quite a success of her life, in her heart she still felt as though she could never be good enough for her dad to consider her special.

There is another struggle, perhaps deeper and more confusing, with the silence of a father—the struggle to know this man, to understand who he really is. We need to make sense of our connection to this person who is so important to us, yet wreathed in mystery. Not knowing him on this deeper level leaves us feeling deprived, even cheated, of our patrimony. Auster captures some of the bewildering intensity of this struggle: "One could not believe there was such a man—who lacked feeling, who wanted so little of others. And if there was not such a man, that means there was another man, a man hidden inside the man who was not there, and the trick of it, then, is to find him. On the condition that he is there to be found."

The children take on the responsibility to find the father or to coax him out of hiding. They do so by being good or by being bad; by having important achievements or obvious needs or maybe just the right look on their faces. They are constantly attending to what might draw him out.

A client who had weathered a traumatic year after a divorce he had not wanted arrived at something of an epiphany. He had for months held on to the belief that he was to blame for the failure of his marriage. He came to the realization that this was a way to avoid feeling hopeless. If he was to blame, then maybe there was still something he could do to change himself and save the marriage. It gave him a feeling of control where otherwise he would have none and could see only an abyss before him.

This is also the way many children of silent fathers react. They remain caught in a web of self-flagellation, because despite the terrible pain, they have a glimmer of hope. Children can remain enmeshed for years in the view they must do something for the father instead of seeing how the father may have failed them.

8

Healing the Wounds
From Weak Fathers

There are painful paradoxes, then, surrounding weak fathers. We boost, bolster, and do things for them, at times to save ourselves and them from embarrassment, but also to try to earn the approval they seem so unable to give. We may carry shame, but we feel a commensurate need to defend. We also feel responsible to assist and protect them, to help them make it through challenges we believe they cannot meet on their own. We anticipate and we worry. We remain on edge about when the next failure might occur or when we might be called upon to come to the rescue.

Inherent in our psychological connection to our parents and our understanding of their role is the belief that we are invested with much of their same qualities. Thus, we find it difficult to escape the fear of becoming like our fathers when they are weak, even as we hope to have their strength. We continue, therefore, to do our best to infuse them with the illusion of what we need them to be. We hope they will rise to the occasion or respond to our efforts and demonstrate the strength and positive qualities for which we long.

The first step in healing from the weakness in fathers is to see them without blinders. On the one hand, this means recognizing or acknowledging their true limitations. Dad may have been overburdened because he did not cope well with pressures and not only because of how much responsibility he carried or the number of problems he faced.

Our father's silence and withdrawal were more than likely part of his style of operating—neither indifference nor a reflection of strength.

Men tend to remain insular as they approach problems because they want to mask feeling anxious or overwhelmed. They do not hide their emotions because they are competent, calm, or courageous, but because they have been socialized to maintain the appearance of invulnerability.

We are much more aware today of the patterns of behavior associated with addictions and mental illness. We can apply these insights to an understanding of the troubled father. To look back on the father's outbursts or seeming incompetence and understand that he may have had a problem with alcohol or been depressed offers a perspective that alters our childhood interpretations of his behavior.

Knowing about the nature of our father's problems and also about the context of his life helps us to realize that his inability to show his love, approval, or validation was his difficulty and not our shortcoming. We can use this perspective to help erase the sense of rejection associated with weak fathers. Germaine Greer in *Daddy, We Hardly Knew You* admitted feeling embittered and cheated when she uncovered her father's secret past of poverty, an adoptive family, and lies about his war service. She also understood why he had kept her at a distance.

Besides seeing our father's weakness clearly, we need to discern what our level of responsibility should be for him. We need to recognize the inappropriateness of a father relying too heavily on his children to care for him or to substitute for his role in the family. We need to allow for helping a father without being responsible for him.

Leslie, whose father put his life on hold after her mother died, had to stop being her father's companion for social events and had to set aside her guilt about leaving him on Saturday nights when she was old enough to date. She had to come to terms with the fact that it was not her duty to make her father happy or prevent him from being lonely.

Even when a father has serious emotional problems, the child cannot be therapist to the parent. He or she must maintain expectations that the father will do his part to seek professional help and to reach out to peers so that he is not leaning too heavily on his children.

The dependence or incompetence of the father makes it difficult not to feel guilty at setting limits. Without drawing lines, however, the children will not discover the father's capabilities. Often our exposure to the father's flawed functioning primes us to expect the worst, but left to his own devices Dad will likely find his own solutions.

I remember after my father lost his wife of thirteen years in his early eighties I feared that he would not be able to handle living alone. Since he lived in Florida our contact was by telephone. For weeks he sounded pathetic and hopeless. Every suggestion I made was met with pessimism and then dismissed. I pictured my father sitting alone for days at a time sinking into complete paralysis.

Suddenly one Sunday morning my regular call was greeted by a different person. He was cheerful and eager to tell me about his girlfriend! Not only did he now have a new relationship, but he had been going to social events and even dating for some time.

Even with silent fathers, as one man expressed it, "I told myself I no longer have to fill in the blanks." He used to try to compensate for his father in social situations by virtually talking for him, attributing his own beliefs to his dad so it would appear he was contributing to the conversation.

An important benefit of circumscribing our caretaking for the father is that it reminds us that we have our own needs and deserve to be valued, too. We do not exist only to meet his needs. Moreover, when we learn to uphold our boundaries with our fathers, we feel stronger. Being subsumed by obligations to our father obliterates our sense of individuality. We become invisible to ourselves. Refusing to accept unreasonable demands on our lives assures us that we can stand up for ourselves.

Jackie, whose father was a hypochondriac, was continually faced with decisions about how to manage his health care. She was the only adult child available to respond to his crisis calls. Her father frequently wanted her to rush over to attend to him, but he would refuse to go to the hospital or at times to follow through with doctor appointments.

Finally, Jackie started telling her father that if his problem was an emergency he would have to call 911. Otherwise, she would make an appointment for him with the doctor and he could decide whether to go or not. Jackie felt tremendous guilt initially and almost could not maintain her resolve. When she persisted, though, she found that her father's emergencies waned dramatically. The result for Jackie was not only reduced demands and greater freedom in her life, but the conviction that after many years of being manipulated by her dad, she was finally in the driver's seat.

Children of weak fathers may avoid closeness with others out of the expectation they will be unduly leaned upon or they cannot count on others. They may end up being caretakers in their relationships, playing out their familiar role. Developing the ability to set limits with their fathers helps these individuals maintain balance in their friendships and with mates. Inversely, practicing reciprocity in social relationships bolsters our capacity to restore healthy boundaries with our fathers.

Limiting our responsibility for our fathers also serves to remind us that we are separate individuals. The perception of our separateness aids us in overcoming the fear that we will suffer the same dysfunction as our father. If we can alter the pattern of our paternal relationship, we feel less subject to the same fate as our fathers.

An exercise I use with children of troubled fathers, who are particularly subject to anxiety about ending up like their dads, is to have them make a list of the ways in which they are like their fathers and in which they are different. The differences are virtually always pronounced enough to reassure these individuals that they are capable of keeping their lives on a course distinct from their fathers.

Children of overburdened and especially of troubled fathers are prone to fearing their own emotions. They have often observed their fathers not being able to manage stress or anxiety. They must learn that feelings do not arise only in extreme fashion and that even intense emotion can be expressed constructively and with modulation. There were reasons their fathers may not have been in control of their feelings, such as alcohol abuse or their lack of guidance in their own lives for managing problems. Rarely was the flaw the emotions themselves.

Overcoming the fear of their own feelings gives these children the knowledge that they can cope where their fathers could not. They feel reassured and more whole as individuals. They also are better able to risk challenges they have avoided because being aware of and expressing feelings helps maintain perspective in anxiety-provoking situations.

Children of silent fathers also need to learn how to talk about their affective lives. Their fathers have been poor role models for revealing interior life. Sons especially may be profoundly impaired in being able to relate feelings because they view their father's silence as part of the prototype of manly behavior. If they understand how the emotional detachment of their fathers truncated their relationships, they may be motivated to practice the language of affect that seems so foreign.

Another dimension of growth that comes with disentangling our identity from the father's weakness is in how we approach our own accomplishments. With silent fathers the children may struggle to achieve with the impact on their fathers in mind, trying to win approval more than satisfy their own goals. With overburdened, troubled, or otherwise unsuccessful fathers, the children may have difficulty reacting to their own accomplishments apart from the effect on their father, the way Matt in "The Responsibility Trap" was concerned about his dad's reaction to his large bonus. These children may hold themselves back out of the concern they will look better than their fathers and diminish their self-image.

Part of ceasing to take responsibility for the father and establishing our separateness is to have our achievements arise from our own personal goals instead of from the effect they might have on the father. The same is true of our actions and our efforts to support others, including our father. We need an internally oriented compass, not an externally oriented one. We must choose to do what feels right to us and recognize it as a choice rather than an obligation.

As with learning to express emotions, if we have not had a role model for doing so, it is difficult to make the transition to focusing on our own goals and choices. We must literally practice listening to ourselves. When we do, however, we further strengthen our identities and build the assurance that we will not succumb to our own weaknesses.

In order to progress toward self-generated goals we must relinquish the expectation of receiving the validation and support we have desired from our dads. Weak fathers do offer varying degrees of affirmation and encouragement. Therefore, we should make a realistic appraisal of what we can depend on our fathers for, but we need to concentrate on developing our capacity to bolster and value ourselves.

Adult children of weak fathers may seek to compensate for what was missing from their fathers through looking to their children or their mates for support. Such dependence on others will accentuate rather than overcome the shortfall from their fathers. There is a manner, however, in which looking to others is constructive.

Children of weak fathers often believe they cannot count on others. They may well have many friends, because people find them competent and willing to help, but they tend to be emotional loners. They are uncomfortable asking for assistance, partly because they do not expect it will be offered, but also because they find it alien to rely on outsiders. Allowing themselves to reach out to others and build a supportive network of people in their lives brings their healing process full circle. Having learned to count on themselves, they become free to count on others.

9

When Fathers Are Absent

I doubt that many men would quarrel with the statement, "No man ever went to his grave regretting that he didn't spend more time at the office." Yet how many children have grown up with the lament that their fathers just weren't around much and so they didn't know them very well?

Maybe distance is the "curse of fatherhood" as psychologist Sam Osherson, author of *Finding Our Fathers*, says. Maybe it's the price fathers, mothers, and children are bound to pay in a society that seems to value work more than family. In some ways there are even positive sides to the trade-off. The distance of fathers, as Osherson notes, harkens us to a larger world. We are drawn to exploring that larger world as we look to find out what our fathers saw in it and where they went. Their time away could give them standing of mythological proportions, though it could also leave us ignorant of their human ones.

As we grew up, many of us came to expect that our fathers would be away a lot. We convinced ourselves that this was par for the course, and we adapted because that was all there was to do. We are now beginning to understand that all along we were paying a price for a way of life that largely cordoned off a father's role as parent to what he did outside the home and to a narrow definition of provider and protector.

Research done in the last decade on father involvement shows that when fathers are highly involved with raising their children, the children feel more in control of their lives and their intellectual functioning is enhanced. These effects seem to be equally true for girls as well as boys. When fathers are not much involved, their offspring are more likely to have lower self-esteem, difficulty handling frustration, poorer intellectual skills, and less success in relating socially. The indications are rather clear that when fathers are positively involved their children have a stronger sense of themselves and function better in the world. The opposite is true when fathers are not involved.

The absence of fathers, then, doesn't equate with "out of sight, out of mind." Certainly not psychologically. When fathers are not involved the effect is damaging not only because of their lack of input, but also because of the way children interpret it. They tend to rationalize the father's absence in terms of his motivation, but then feel somehow responsible themselves for his not being there.

Commonly a father's physical absence is associated with his work. When a father is gone all day and comes home looking preoccupied, tired, and wanting to be away from the family's demands, children assume he's been working hard. This is true even if he doesn't travel or work weekends or come home late. He might actually have been stopping off at the local tavern for an hour or two and that's why he headed for the couch first thing. Whether he worked long hours or his hours at work seemed long, children credit him with shouldering this burden for the welfare of the family. Therefore they excuse his absence, whether he is physically present or not, as inherent in his paternal duties. Unfortunately, while they may be largely forgiving of their father, children may feel guilty themselves because they believe he is sacrificing his life to make their lives better. With this perspective, fathers become martyrs and the children become their obligations. They may feel more like problems for their fathers than sources of joy. One woman described how she came to have such feelings: "Whenever I came to my father with a request, he would sigh and look put upon. Often he would be angry. These weren't usually anything major, but I thought I was doing something wrong. I felt like a burden to him. I still struggle at forty years old not to feel that way around him."

Another common way children react to their fathers' absence is to interpret it as rejection. Whatever the real demands on the father's time and energy, the children may not distinguish necessity from volition. Somehow he would make more time to be around if he saw that as an attractive option. His absence is tantamount to not loving or at least not prizing his children. Children are more likely to extend this thinking toward self-blame than toward blaming their fathers. They tend to assume that they could have done more or done better and then their fathers would have been more interested in them. The pattern is much like that with silent fathers, the absence being taken as a more overt form of silence.

When children do not understand their fathers' absence, and most do not, they can be consumed by their fear of rejection. For Germaine Greer it was summed up this way in *Daddy, We Hardly Knew You*: "I clung to the faith that he was not genuinely indifferent to me and did not really find me repulsive, although I never quite succeeded in banishing the fear of such a thing."

The younger the children are, the harder it is for them to understand. Even as they mature, the child that feels rejected remains with them, shadowing their view of their fathers with a primal feeling of hurt.

Guy Corneau, author of *Absent Fathers, Lost Sons*, related a story of a young boy who had never met his father. The boy had been aggressive and felt out of control to his mother, so she brought him into therapy. Corneau recommended encouraging the boy to draw when he acted aggressively. For his first attempt the boy drew a picture of a family with a father. He then cut out the father and buried him in the backyard. When the mother asked him why he buried the picture, the boy replied, "He wanted to kill me. He's not here because he does not want me to exist." The boy later dug up the picture and glued it back together. His mother arranged for him to meet the father and the aggressive behavior eventually stopped.

The story of this boy captures more than one child's dreaded fear. It's what is beneath our worst fears as we try to come to terms with the paradox of a father's love and his absence. Children do tell themselves and believe on some level that the father does love them despite his busyness. There is still a part of them, however, often unconscious, that concludes their father does not want them.

Unfortunately, the drama doesn't end simply with the father's appearance. I am sure this young boy felt a significant easing of pain just by knowing his father cared enough to re-enter his life. The notion that "he does not want me to exist" has an internal counterpart as well, however, "Maybe then I don't deserve to exist." This internalized message comes in different forms or levels of intensity: "I know he's right and so I don't deserve to exist," or "Maybe he's right and maybe I don't deserve to exist," or even "What if he's right?" Regardless of the specific message, a significant degree of self-doubt comes with it.

In addition, when you take into account the obvious fact that absent fathers are not there to guide their children, it is clear that children of absent fathers will suffer from self-esteem problems. These youngsters find it difficult to validate themselves and are unsure how to get validation from others. Validation is foreign to them, and their self-rejection makes them unreceptive to and disbelieving of others' praise.

The combination of not believing in themselves and the lack of a father's role model leaves children with no sense of direction. They continue to search outside themselves for the validation they fail to receive from their fathers. As a result they don't learn to formulate their identity from within, which they could do if they experienced being accepted and valued. Without this capacity they cannot develop self-confidence; the external feedback has nothing to latch on to to make it stick.

On the other hand, without self-confidence these individuals do not initiate or assume ownership for activities or accomplishments through which they could build self-esteem. They are so focused on doing what will secure others' approval, they have no sense of being the initiators of their own achievements. Because they are vulnerable to losing whatever approval they do get, they feel as if they are always starting from scratch with each new venture.

While some of these children eagerly pursue external validation, others remain passive. Either way they are trying to cover the emptiness they feel. Those who are passive may be silently waiting and hoping someone will find them and give them the direction and validation they need, or they may remain withdrawn to avoid getting the rejection they expect.

The rejection that comes directly from the father's absence does not require physical absence. Fathers can be absent even when they are present. In an old *M.A.S.H.* episode I recently saw, Hawkeye laments that he is twelve-thousand miles from home when his father is about to have surgery. His companion responds, "My father could be twelve-thousand miles away when he was in the same room with me."

The silent fathers described in the previous chapter can be absent, but silence does not necessarily equate with absence. Absent fathers are often silent and withdrawn. They can just as easily, however, be fathers who communicate normally but function all too often at a remove from the family, for example, spending much of their time in a work room or doing chores.

They can also be fathers who make their physical presence known, but are not present in spirit. Fathers may sit in the same room with the family but be absorbed in television or the newspaper; they may sit at the dinner table but be at the office in their heads; they may go on vacation with the family but be far away. Children know the glazed look and the unknowing nod or smile that tells them their father has not been taking in their words. If this is a consistent pattern, they feel abandoned by this hollow presence probably as much as they do by a father being physically gone.

Jane brought a picture into therapy one day of herself and her father. At first glance, it just looked like a picture taken at an ordinary moment when perhaps everyone was a bit tired and therefore not very responsive. A closer examination revealed that her father was looking neither at Jane nor at whoever was taking the picture. He had his arm around his daughter, but he wasn't holding her or showing affection. In fact, he had as little contact with Jane as a person could possibly have while sitting next to someone with an arm around her.

"He's there, but he's not there," Jane explained. "It was always like that. He always had that faraway look in his eyes. He was preoccupied and he didn't even seem to want to be wherever he was."

Jane's mother, as mothers often do when fathers are disappointing in their behavior, tried to fill in the gap: "Of course he loves you. That's just the way he is. He has a lot on his mind. You have to understand." It took Jane about forty years, but she finally gave up trying to understand.

A father's absence does not make the heart grow fonder. It puts offspring in a quandary, confuses them, makes them feel pained and neglected, forces them to cling or hide or be on a constant search mission. This is true whether that absence is a constant in a child's life and the expected norm or occurs as a shocking interruption to an otherwise close connection. It is also true with fathers who slip away gradually, perhaps into an addiction or an affair or the escalating demands of work.

When separation from the father comes as a sudden jolt, it carries devastatingly raw and immediate pain and long-term aftershocks. While the pain of a gradual distancing is less shocking and perhaps less apparent, however, it is not necessarily less destructive.

Whatever the timing of the separation, the trauma can be softened if the child is given reasons for the absence that seem legitimate. Some degree of effort by the absent father to keep connected also helps. Children are incredibly forgiving if only they have a little something on which to hang that desire to forgive. It is the sense of hopelessness about the lost connection, the fear or reality of permanence, that can make it truly crushing. A youngster can feel hopeless when there does not seem to be a necessary reason for the separation. The child feels too unimportant to matter and therefore powerless to change the father's pattern.

There are three common ways that children become cut off from their fathers: through the fathers' excessive absorption in work, through divorce, and through death. These all involve tangible separations. Each form of separation can be explained to a child logically. But each leaves in its wake a potentially devastating path of emotional destruction if the child is left believing he or she didn't really matter enough.

The Workaholic Father

The Indian writer R. K. Narayan, in a painfully moving short story called "Forty-five a Month," captures the dilemma in which so many men find themselves trapped. A clerk, who is the father of a young daughter, knows that he neglects his wife and daughter. But the demands of his job keep him at the office late so that he gets home night after night when his daughter is already asleep. He finally determines that no matter what his boss says, even if he has to resign, his child's happiness is not worth sacrificing for the forty rupees a month he receives. He promises to come home early one night, actually on time, so he can take his daughter to the movies.

Sure enough, new demands arise at the last minute and the man's supervisor balks at letting him go. When he hears that he has been recommended for a five-rupee-a-month pay raise he meekly crumples up his shakily written letter of resignation. When he returns home he finds his little daughter asleep, but still "in her pink frock, hair combed and face powdered, dressed and ready to be taken out." His heart breaks.

We see in this story the deep yearning of the daughter for time with her father. She is prepared hours ahead of time for their date and is too excited to eat. The father, too, is eager to be with her, though partially out of guilt. In the end he succumbs to what is expected of him at work rather than what he wants for himself at home.

Some men are acutely aware of what they sacrifice in relation to their children. But whether consciously or unconsciously, most men end up being defined first and foremost by work.

Our fathers grew up with the social and familial message that what counts for boys is what they do, not how sensitive they are to others or how they express feelings. Even today, with the prevalence of career-oriented women, men believe they are measured by the work they do. Work is the path to success and is critical to the self-sufficiency men expect of themselves. The core of a man's identity is his work.

Work is not only at the center of a man's personal identity, it is entwined with his social identity as well, particularly in relation to his familial role. Our fathers saw their work as a means of winning over and keeping a woman in their lives. Work was the principal vehicle for performing family responsibilities—to put food on the table and a roof overhead. Despite the fact that so many women are working today and almost one quarter of them earn more than their husbands, men still tend to believe their provider role is their chief duty. Work substitutes for and takes precedence over time spent directly with the family.

Our work environments don't give men much reason to think differently either. Few places of employment recognize the need for fathers to have more time with their families. Work is not the place to get support for one's paternal desires.

For our fathers, as for the present generation of young adult men, work dominated their lives and became a way of being. Fathers were prepared to explain to their children why work forced them to be away from home and the family, but they were ill-prepared for the inverse rationalization: why they weren't there for their children. When they had to choose between work and children, it was usually no contest. The choice was so clear because they could tell themselves that being at work was still a way, if not the best way, to take care of their children.

In general, most of these fathers did not understand that they were wanted at home, that their children needed to be around them, to experience them, to be guided and taught by them. They generally regarded the raising of children as "women's work." They believed they could take care of their parenting role through the responsible example they set and by offering a sprinkling of wise adages in a "Father Knows Best" style. They did not know that their *being* was important and not just their *doing*. Besides, work was familiar behavior and therefore comfortable. Being with their children for many fathers was uncomfortable and only got more so over time as they invested themselves in work and became further estranged from their children.

Work has been an insidious force in the lives of families. Lots of fathers did not enjoy what they did or were not wedded to their work, yet work was still an enormous wedge between them and their children. Many were drained by the demands of the normal routine and even without spending long hours on the job still came home with little left to give to their families. Without necessarily wanting to do so, they gave the better part of themselves to their work. As Robert Bly pointedly notes in *Iron John*: "When a father, absent during the day, returns home at six, his children receive only his temperament, and not his teaching."

When a man does not experience satisfying, meaningful work at a humane pace, going to his job day after day takes a great deal out of his soul and leaves less of him as a father. Children do not quite understand how work can have this effect until they work for a living themselves. They may, however, see a hollow look in their father's eyes and feel his deadened spirit. They are left with a longing for who he might otherwise be.

There are also those fathers whose jobs keep their juices flowing. For too many men, work has a way of inexorably gaining more and more of the emotional territory of their lives. Because the rewards are tangible and the role familiar, and because it marks them as manly and successful in our culture, they become invested in work at the expense of the other dimensions of their lives. They may not even enjoy their work, but they are consumed by it. These men do not appreciate, because they are blinded by their workaholism, what their distorted priorities are doing to their children. When fathers do not keep a reasonable balance in their work lives, here are some of the consequences:

1. *Irritability.*   If the requirements of the regular work day have fathers coming home with little left to give, the father who cannot set limits on his work comes home with even less. He is distracted and has difficulty unwinding from thoughts about the job. He lacks patience and is short-tempered. He has difficulty extending himself to do things for and with his children because he resents having no time for himself. The equating of time and money endemic to the work environment car-

ries over to home, so father snaps at the little things that cost him money and keep him working so hard, like lights left on or clothing not treated carefully. The children feel they are themselves to blame because their dad works so hard and they cause him displeasure when he returns home. They feel they are the albatross around his neck.

2. *Distorted View of Work.* When fathers give over so much of themselves to work and have only crumbs left for their children, it gives the distinct message that work is more important than anything else, more important than people and fun and health. Children are either frightened off by this message or adopt it as a guide for their own behavior. Those who are frightened lose their motivation for work. They may become procrastinators, putting off doing things because they fear being consumed themselves. They may avoid being successful so they do not have expectations of performing the way their fathers did placed upon them. They may become drifters, steering clear of any traditional pattern in which they might become trapped like their fathers.

Those who model themselves after their fathers have considerable difficulty achieving balance in their lives. Not only do they lack guidance and an example in their father of how to take care of themselves and build pleasure and relaxation into their lifestyles, they do not question whether their overworking is unhealthy. Their identification with their father leads them to believe that being consumed by the job is the right way to live.

3. *Difficulty in Relating.* Our parents give us our first lessons in how to relate socially and how to be intimate. When fathers are overly absorbed in their work, their relationship with their children is truncated. The children, then, do not experience enough time with their fathers to feel comfortable with them. They may never learn how to relax and be open with their fathers. As a result, they may enter their peer relationships without the experience of being able to relate comfortably and intimately with a male.

Girls may carry a great deal of discomfort into their interactions with boys or even have the expectation that intimacy is not possible with males. Many daughters, even as adults, relate to their fathers in parallel fashion, like the way toddlers play. Stephen Minot in his story "The Tide and Isaac Bates" describes this pattern in a father and his adult daughter struggling to learn to be together: "The two of them never talked much about their inner feelings. They got along best just sharing chores. . . . If anything bothered her, she didn't feel obliged to tell him, and in return he didn't burden her with his own worries."

Boys, too, are left with a limited view about relating to males. Following the example of their fathers, they will tend to devalue social relationships and center their contact with males around activity and later around work. Intimate connection will be reserved for females, if it is engaged in at all. With other men it will feel foreign. Of course, this pattern is characteristic of many males anyway, but the sons of workaholic fathers will be among those men for whom difficulty with intimate male connection will tend to be exaggerated.

Sons who work side by side with their workaholic fathers in a family business can be particularly crippled socially. Often these sons become equally absorbed in the family business and are cut off from normal patterns of peer friendship at an early age. Virtually all of their social relating occurs in the context of work and may be with a father who cannot be intimate. Whatever they may gain in terms of an inferred closeness with their fathers is lost in the price they pay socially.

4. *Hunger for the Father.* Robert Bly and others have talked about the "father hunger" that comes with the absence of fathers. When fathers are lost to work, children have a large hole to fill. They will see only the shadow of their fathers and yearn to know and have more of them. They will feel jealous of those who have time with their fathers, probably imagining others knowing and having far more of their fathers than anyone else actually does.

5. *Feelings of Inadequacy.* Children of workaholic fathers will feel diminished because they view themselves as not worthy of their hard-working fathers. Whether they have been frightened off from working like their fathers or whether they work just like them, they will feel that they do not do enough and yearn to be somehow more than they are. This is the way they understand the father's absence and the path to somehow gain a better relationship with him.

In time, when fathers remain consistently immersed in work and unavailable, the hunger for connection becomes suppressed for most children. They start to accept that their fathers' absence is part of life. Work defines their fathers, and the children stop expecting more from them, regardless of the continued pain underneath. Paul Auster started to write his memoir about his father in an effort to connect to him after his death in a way he could not connect with him in life. Auster wrote: "Even before his death he had been absent, and long ago the people closest to him had learned to accept this absence, to treat it as the fundamental quality of his being."

We can become so inured to our father's absence due to work it becomes difficult to feel the loss if something happens to remove him from the family physically. A woman was divorcing her husband, who had long shortchanged his children by excessive devotion to his job. She wanted to ease the impact of the divorce on her children, and she took her ten-year-old daughter to a therapist. After a few sessions the therapist seemed somewhat perplexed. She told the mother, "I'm really surprised. Your daughter doesn't act as though she's really had a loss when she talks about her father."

No doubt this young girl felt deep pain because her father was leaving, but her sense of loss had obviously begun long ago. By the time the divorce took place she had already adapted to her dad's absence.

Not only do children stop expecting more from their workaholic fathers, but daughters in particular may also be primed for getting little from their relationships with men. Sally's experience with her father, who sold insurance, illustrates this pattern. He never knew how to say no to a customer. He believed the extra service he offered gave him an advantage over other agents. If there was a choice between mailing a policy that needed a signature or driving forty-five minutes out of the way to get it there in person, he would head for the car. As a result, he was quite successful in his job, but was home very little, even in the evenings and on weekends.

Sally's father wasn't around much, but when he was there, he liked to have things the way he wanted them. Dinner at seven. No noisy kids around. No unexpected bills or problems to distract him. If things weren't as expected, he often blew up at Sally's mother.

He didn't yell at Sally very often. In fact, she was his favorite. She had learned to anticipate how he would want things and did them that way as often as she could. Sally was so attached to her father and he was around so little, she hated to disappoint him. She also feared his anger, even though she wasn't on the receiving end of it very often. If he did yell at her, it meant to her that she had disappointed him. That left her believing she would lose the little relationship she had with him She would feel terribly alone at those times.

From the time she began dating, Sally got into relationships in which she was clearly the secondary partner. She was clingy with boyfriends and didn't sense it when they started to lose interest in her. Her marriage ended in divorce and the one serious relationship she had afterward fell apart. In each case, not only did work come first with these men, but eventually so did another woman in the form of an affair.

Sally was slow each time to speak up. She endured a lot of mistreatment during the affairs, taking the brunt of the tension these men felt for their guilt, deceit, and indecision about the relationship. Sally chose in these instances to hang in there, since she felt she was better off having part of a man than having to look for another. She worried that she would end up alone if she gave up the man she was with.

It is hard for many children of workaholic fathers to comprehend how they have been affected by their dad's unavailability. Our expectation as children was that our fathers would be heavily involved with their work, so their absence was readily excused as well as anticipated. The problems that emerge for the children are not easily connected with the father's absence or overinvestment in work. This lack of insight makes the task of healing ourselves more difficult, particularly because we are not attuned to the distortions that developed in our expectations for ourselves.

Healing the Wounds From Workaholic Fathers

After Sally's boyfriend left her, she started to wonder why she got herself into such imbalanced relationships. She decided that she didn't take enough time to get to know the men she was with, but then again, the men she spent time with were hard to get to know. It became clear to her that she was used to having only a fraction of a man. That was what she had with her father, and it had always felt like enough to count on. When he was there for her the rest of the world melted away. It was enough for her mother, too, and she seemed to get less attention than Sally.

It never occurred to Sally that accepting a fraction of a man made her into a fraction of a woman. She realized she had for too long been used to sacrificing herself to keep a man for the emotional scraps he might feed her. When she finally faced life without a male relationship she began to experience whole new dimensions in herself, along with the freedom to pursue them.

For Sally, being out of a love relationship helped make it clear that she deserved more from the men in her life. The critical learning, though, was certainly not about the need to be out of a relationship, but perceiving what is appropriate to expect from others. This understanding begins with recognizing how our sense of social equity has been distorted. Children of workaholic fathers tend to lose the capacity to ask for their own needs to be met. They are too concerned about burdening their dads or triggering an intolerant response.

A turning point came in Sally's growth when she decided to have her parents over for Thanksgiving dinner. She had not invited them for a holiday meal since before her divorce. Her father got on the phone and lobbied, initially to have the dinner at their home, then to change the time. Sally mustered her courage and calmly told her father that she wanted to host the dinner and that the time she offered was best for her. She was shocked when he backed down. Though she continued to be anxious about how her dad would react on the day itself, she had learned that she could stand up for herself without dire consequences.

Fundamentally, keeping our relationships with fathers and others in balance is about asserting our own value as people. Regardless of how many demands others experience due to their work schedules, we must insist on being treated as equally worthwhile. We have a right to our own agenda and needs. Workaholic fathers often act as though the world revolves around their schedules. They are frequently late for dinners and events related to home life. Part of establishing our self-worth is requiring that others respect our timetables and requirements.

Another dimension of caring for ourselves is to refuse to be mistreated because of another person's pressures in life. Workaholic fathers were often excused by mothers or the children for behavior that should have been deemed unacceptable. Allowing a pattern of inconsideration or unkindness because we understand the circumstances devalues ourselves and encourages the other person to continue these behaviors.

Gloria had a male friend who lived out of town. He had a demanding job for a computer company. She accepted that keeping up contact would require that she make most of the calls. He would eventually get back to her. She planned a trip to visit him and at the last minute, when she called to confirm their plans, he told her he would be tied up most of the weekend.

Gloria canceled the trip and spent several days fuming about this fellow's selfishness. She realized finally that she was wasting a great deal of energy on this man. Though she had had hopes of this relationship eventually becoming a romantic one, she wrote him that she would no longer make efforts to contact him unless he took the initiative and showed the relationship mattered to him. While Gloria never heard from him, she strengthened her resolve to not be taken for granted by others.

Another critical aspect of healing from workaholic fathers involves not taking ourselves for granted in our own work life. The offspring of these fathers frequently end up having trouble curbing their own commitment to work.

I have a client who took over his father's business. The father had always worked terribly long hours, and he managed to create a modestly successful business. The son was better at business than the father, and the company grew exponentially under his leadership. He never felt as though he was working hard enough, however, if he didn't bring home work to do in the evening and on weekends as he had seen his father do. This young man would repeatedly work himself to a state of exhaustion or illness before he could temporarily put on the brakes to his needless overexertion.

Prior to the last twenty-five years, it was sons who primarily inherited their fathers' work orientation. As the first generation of daughters influenced by the women's movement moved into the work world, it was still their fathers most often who provided the model for operating in the world of work. Many men and women today struggle with maintaining balance between their work and personal lives. The children of workaholic fathers may not realize the extent of the imbalance until they pay a price with their health, their marriage, or their happiness.

Altering the legacy of workaholism requires a changed orientation toward oneself. The message from our fathers, both indirectly by their behavior and directly by their stated attitudes, was that our personal measure of success in life is determined by work. As long as we rely on work as the standard, we will feel compelled to keep overworking. "I work, therefore I am" is the belief, which readily extends to: "If I work harder, I am better."

The determination to keep a more balanced existence requires that we value our health, families, avocations, and personal lives as much as our job. We must act on the belief that all of these dimensions are important and part of who we are.

Setting limits with work is akin to expecting equity in our social relationships. If we do not recognize that we deserve better treatment, we will not maintain firm boundaries with regard to the excessive demands of employers. Those who have been intimidated by their father's work habits and found their motivation to achieve impeded must discover that they can work at their own pace and define for themselves the role of work in their lives.

To say no to job requirements that cause our lives to be imbalanced can risk income, promotions, and job security. To take such risks we must feel our own worth independent of work. Without risking we will not break the cycle passed down by our fathers.

10

The Impact of Divorce
and Death

Never mind that you always were larger than life
and may be more with us after leaving
than when you were alive
we have but to let it in
to make space in the quiet and solitude
to be with the shadow that cannot be seen
but is always there.

You are dancing in my shadows
please stay.

"Untitled," Mark Silverberg

The pattern of absence and loss with workaholic fathers is not typically
the result of a sudden disruption. When children are separated from
their fathers by divorce or death, even when circumstances give them
time to prepare emotionally, the physical loss and the tangible fractur-
ing of the family can seem harshly abrupt. The impact of a father's
absence due to divorce or death will clearly be more intense and pervasive than when that absence is the result of a father's work habits.

Children expect their fathers to work a great deal, but they also want to believe they will always be part of life at home.

The Divorced Father

Unfortunately, divorce goes on around us all the time. No one is untouched by it. We are all either ourselves divorced or have relatives or close friends who are or will be. These days children start fearing that their parents will get divorced as soon as they are old enough to know what divorce is and have heard their parents quarrel. Wondering if parents may choose at some point to divorce adds a major element of uncertainty to a child's existence. The actuality of divorce permanently changes a child's outlook on life. Divorce exposes a child to the temporary nature of even the most sacred of relationships. It immerses the child in insecurity and gives him or her a crash course in the unpredictability of the life we lead.

All too often what happens with fathers as a result of divorce intensifies the pain, confusion, insecurity, and trauma. To begin with, usually it is the father who either leaves the family or is ousted from home when a divorce occurs. Commonly this has been done in order to maintain the most stable, nurturing environment for the children, traditionally the preserve of the mother.

When fathers leave they generally try to reassure their children that they will continue to be part of their lives and try to minimize how much things will change. The children normally want this to be the case as well, since the father's leave-taking in itself is difficult enough. Unfortunately, regardless of the intentions with which fathers exit the home, their track record on staying involved has been poor. There are certainly many fathers who remain close to their children after divorce and those who become even more actively involved. The number who do neither, however, is rather shocking.

Judith Wallerstein conducted a ground-breaking outcome study of divorce, from 1971 to 1981 in California. In Wallerstein's book, *Second Chances*, she relates that one national study of divorce found that 40 percent of children were not visited by their fathers. In Wallerstein's own study, she found that more than a third of the children were seeing their fathers at least once a month ten years after the divorce. These children were mostly teens or young adults by this follow-up, and thus this level of contact seemed relatively high. Nevertheless, it means almost two-thirds of the children saw their fathers less than once a month.

Wallerstein's important study found that regardless of the frequency of contact, most of the children of divorce felt rejected. This feeling of rejection occurred despite the fact that most of the fathers thought they had done a reasonably good job fulfilling their obligations. Some of this discrepancy is an unavoidable outcome inherent in divorce. It also comes with the way many fathers approach the time with their children. There is an obvious difference for children between contact out of obligation and contact out of a desire to be together. The children who felt rejected experienced their fathers as "present in body but not in spirit."

Children lose whether they actually see their father regularly or not if they do not feel valued by their dad. There are many reasons why some divorced fathers do not spend time with their children. Lack of desire to see them is probably low on this list. Larry Feldman in his chapter on "Fathers and Fathering" in *Men in Therapy* reports that 90 percent of the time where fathers are the noncustodial parent, hostility and conflict between the parents is a major block to their being involved. Other major barriers include the way many men allow themselves to be consumed by their jobs and the failure of employers to provide flexibility in work schedules.

In the end, perhaps the most significant impediment for many fathers is the discomfort they feel in their one-to-one contact with their children. The difficulty some men have in allowing themselves to conduct relationships on a personal, emotional level instead of a functional one comes out in the new structure of interaction posed by divorce. They may have been minimally involved all along and become used to the routine distractions of life at home that prevented them from being intimate with their children. Also, many men feel lost without their wives there to guide their parenting. Most divorced men lack a supportive network that could provide role models for this new stage of fathering.

As a result, many divorced fathers behave in ways that reflect their ambivalence. They want to be good fathers and have their children feel appreciated, but they also are inclined to avoid situations that make them feel uncomfortable. Out of their ambivalence, then, these fathers move in and out of their children's lives. They keep their visits short, they fail to call at important times, or they do not follow through with their promises. They act as if they care one minute, but then they're off in their own world the next. Maybe another woman has come into the picture or they get a job transfer. They let other things come in between or seem more important.

These dads are unaware that their demeanor is hurtful to their young-sters, but then they may well have been unaware of the emotional side of things all their lives. Many fathers do not realize that they are needed and that nothing fills the vacuum that is left by their departure. They act as though being out of the home makes their contact with their children less, rather than more, important.

Their level of contact with their children is not the only source of confusion divorcing fathers may inflict as their youngsters attempt to hold on to their positive feelings. Those fathers who end up in divorce because they have been involved with another woman or who have been aggressive or violent in the marriage, for example, leave their children with conflicted emotional reactions. The children become ambivalent about the father who departs for tainted reasons. The father's behavior has cheapened his image, and the children feel ashamed of their dad and perhaps for themselves by association.

They must now cope with a father who has caused them deep hurt, yet whom they still miss and/or to whom they still feel an intense oblig-ation. The struggle to untangle their own obligation is confounded by feeling unsure about how sincere or committed the father is about his. The children wonder how important they could be to a father who will not stop behavior that tears apart the family.

One daughter handled her ambivalence by seeing her father only when he called and invited her to do something. Calling him seemed a betrayal of her mother and might be taken as a message that everything was normal and forgiven. To not see him at all was too cruel. If he had to call, therefore, he demonstrated some interest on his part. By her Dad having to initiate the contact she felt she was holding him accountable in some fashion and then felt less guilty about her mother.

The economic concerns surrounding divorce commonly become another emotional wedge between fathers and children. During and after the divorce, fathers may shock their children with their readiness to relinquish what had been considered basic responsibilities. Many fathers, either because they want to protect their own financial situation or because of a perverse form of vengeance or plain indifference, are willing to allow their children to suffer economic hardships even when they are still legally responsible for them.

One man recalled to me with bitterness how his father's unwillingness to provide adequate child support had forced his mother to move the family from their tidy, middle-class home to a public housing project. He felt "discarded onto the garbage heap of society" by his father's indifference to their plight.

Of course, fathers, too, may suffer economic hardships as a result of divorce, but more often these difficulties prove temporary, while their families' are longer term. Many divorced fathers maintain their commitment to care for their children. Those who do not keep up their commitment create insecurity about money and threaten to destroy the integrity of their bond with their children. In fact, relationship commitments in general are likely to feel temporary and breakable if fathers refuse to honor theirs.

Children who feel cast aside by their fathers' behavior surrounding the divorce may want to disown them in retaliation. Moreover, they see themselves as deprived, second-class human beings, either because of how they have been made secondary in their fathers' lives or because their fathers now seem shameful. They also may become caught in a paradox of guilt: guilt for still loving this man who has humiliated them and guilt when they do not feel this love.

A woman whose husband left her and her two daughters for another woman painfully observed that her children "walked a tightrope with their father. They didn't feel they could say no to his requests to be with them. It wasn't okay to have other plans or to just not want to be with him. But when they came home, they started bad-mouthing him from the second they walked in the door."

Despite the fact that virtually one out of two marriages now ends in divorce, many children still feel some degree of shame simply for being the product of a divorced family. As one young girl put it, "It feels like you come from something that's broken." For adult children of divorces the feeling of shame that occurred, regardless of the particulars, was more pronounced. There was more stigma attached to divorce in the 1950s and 1960s in part because it was less common. To be the first or only child in the neighborhood whose parents were divorced proved traumatic, apart from the disruption and loss felt within the family. Having no father in the home was the typical manifestation of the divorce and was, therefore, integral to the stigma felt by the child.

In order to restabilize their lives without a father in the home, children generally act in one of two way: they convince themselves that they do not need the father there anyway, or they idealize him. When children deny the importance of their dads they are trying to block out their pain about his absence. Some children try to sustain the importance of their father in their lives by keeping him on a pedestal. They may lack contact with him, but at least they have a father who is special. Distorting the image of the father in a positive way can serve the same ultimate purpose as denying that he is needed. Both idealization and dismissal offer protection against the hurt and feeling of rejection.

Susan understood why her father divorced her disturbed mother. Life for him was one fight after another or complete chaos. She regarded him as the stable parent on whom she could count. Even though he was a highly critical man and quite self-centered, it was easier for Susan to ignore those qualities and just try to please him. The thought of being left with only her mother in her life was a frightening prospect. She was not about to start blaming her dad for leaving her behind.

Children can create believable excuses for the father's lack of involvement under the guise of a romanticized view: "Dad really cares, but he's just so overloaded in his job." Or, "He'll make up for missing my birthday with an even bigger present." Some children will resort to outright lies to protect this icon they have conjured up. I remember a teenage boy who was so hurt by his father's inaccessibility that he used to make up whole weekends of activities with his father that never took place.

Some youngsters maintain their illusions because they cannot afford to carry a negative attitude toward the father for fear he will withdraw even further—emotionally or financially. When fathers do not demonstrate their continued commitment to their children, their youngsters feel highly vulnerable to further loss, both from the father and from life generally. The reality all too frequently reinforces their fears, because fathers tend to become less available and less supportive over time.

As an example, in Judith Wallerstein's divorce study, *Second Chances*, among fathers who could afford to help their children with college, almost two-thirds did not assist them at all. When financial support is withdrawn because it is not legally required, which commonly occurs for children who reach eighteen, it reduces the father-child relationship to an obligation. The personal commitment and not just the financial one is called into question. The child wonders if he or she was loved or valued all along.

Being treated as an obligation or with an "out of sight, out of mind" attitude hurts and angers children when they let the feeling in. But letting the feeling out is another matter. It is frightening to think about voicing anger or displeasure toward someone whose presence is so important, yet with whom the connection may seem threadbare. Therefore, the anger is not usually expressed, directly at least, and may be buried altogether.

Serious consequences occur when no channel exists for dealing with the anger and hurt that are an inherent part of the father's separation. Many youngsters turn the anger inward. These children may remain stuck in a chronic depression, feeling helpless and powerless. Often they cannot associate their feeling low with the loss they have experienced. Wallerstein makes the following observation: "I am continually surprised at how passive these young people are in the face of disappointment from their father. Instead of getting angry, they conclude that they are powerless and undeserving. Not feeling the right or power to get angry, they do not complain."

Self-blame is the critical element behind these responses. These children of divorce are afraid to relinquish their fathers. Rather than acknowledge that their fathers do not deserve such unabiding loyalty or that their fathers' commitment to them is less than it should be, they take on the responsibility for the father leaving or for his distance. Again, as noted at the end of "Overburdened, Troubled, and Silent Fathers," blaming oneself at least gives a semblance of control: "I can change me, but I can't count on changing someone who is elusive and distant."

Whatever illusion of control the children gain with this self-condemnation they lose on all other emotional fronts. A cohort of negative feelings accompanies the view of themselves that they have somehow failed to be good enough for their father: low self-esteem, lack of confidence, the feeling of being unlovable, lack of motivation or ambition. These children see themselves as they believe their fathers view them. When they are passive it is because they do not believe in themselves and are missing the guidance and validation that they normally would get from their fathers.

Adolescents are especially hard-hit by divorce and the lack of contact with their fathers. Even with children who went through divorce at a younger age, adolescence brings with it an intensified longing for their fathers.

These children are looking not only for reunion but for the role model they need from a father as they formulate their pre-adult identity. The absence of the father at this juncture leaves sons without a visible prototype for being a man. Daughters miss the experience of safe, mature male contact at a point when they are likely beginning to experiment with and form romantic relationships with boys.

The sense of inadequacy that comes when boys feel abandoned by their fathers erodes their masculinity as well as their identity in general. They may doubt their ability to win over a girl, and they may feel inordinate pressure to hold on to relationships they do have. If their fathers appeared to have been rejected by their mothers, these boys will tend to anticipate rejection by girls and later by women.

If it is the father who has left the mother, these boys end up with a confused picture of how to relate to women. On the one hand, seeing their mothers hurt will foster protective feelings about women. On the other, they may find it difficult to commit to a relationship fully after seeing that their fathers could not.

Not only do these males lack experience with sustained commitment, but they have themselves felt the pain of a broken commitment and fear facing it again. For the same reason, the fear of deep involvement in a relationship may carry over to relating to other males.

Daughters, too, are left feeling vulnerable to rejection and timid about committing to relationships. They may feel unsure of their acceptability to males and of the adequacy of their feminine qualities, particularly when it is the father who initiated the divorce. Again, these are the feelings of self-blame and responsibility at work in the child, who looks to her own inadequacies to explain the divorce. The daughter's identification with a mother who has been rejected makes her feel potentially subject to the same fate.

Many teenagers go through a bitter period of rejecting their fathers. Then they begin to make renewed efforts to connect with and know their dads, often at the expense of mothers. Youngsters who have lived with their mothers may seek a change of custody or experiment in living with their fathers. Adolescent daughters often engage in conflict with their mothers in their efforts to establish an independent identity. They may then naively regard the father as an ally or someone who will better understand their desire for more freedom.

Sons may direct their frustration and hurt at the loss of the father toward their mother. These feelings may come in the form of anger because it is easier for them to express than other emotions.

One sixteen-year-old who had been a particularly gentle and sensitive boy turned his outrage toward his mother when his father moved out. His behavior was clearly a caricature of his father's—calling his mother names, drinking heavily, and avoiding any accountability. He was blaming his mother for the departure he could not somehow prevent himself. His extreme behavior allowed him to identify with his father while simultaneously attempting to maintain his ties to him. If his mother couldn't control him, his father, who would normally be preoccupied with work, might have to step in.

Of course, many children of divorce continue to aim their anger directly or indirectly at their fathers, especially if their efforts to reunite fail or they continue to feel abandoned. They may become hostile or antisocial or get into trouble with the law as they lash out with their hurt at some tangible target that seems more accessible than the father.

They are, in effect, saying: "You didn't give a damn about me, so why should I give a damn what I do?" They may unconsciously be attempting to get back at the father by embarrassing him through their misbehavior.

Teenage victims of divorce particularly may be daring and angry enough to be more direct with their anger. They may refuse to have contact with their father for prolonged periods and may openly spew out their resentment. Many may conjure up this scenario, but fear the consequent reaction too much to act it out. In reality, probably the most common pattern for children of divorced fathers is to be so knotted up with their efforts to control their pain that they turn it inward and outward at different times and in different ways. This was the case with John.

All John could remember about his father from before the divorce was that he displayed a lot of trophies from his various athletic achievements on shelves. His father used to talk about those trophies when company came to visit. Though he looked embarrassed, he could not hide a big grin. John was six when the divorce was final, but he's pretty certain that by the time he started kindergarten his father was no longer living at home. A couple of years earlier John's mother and sister had been seriously hurt in a car accident when John's father was driving. Somehow things never seemed the same after that.

John's mother used to complain for years about how "that man only seemed to know two things—his work and his damned athletics." When it came to making any decisions at all, he faded into the woodwork. He was apparently a large, foreboding, determined-looking man, with handsome, dark features, but eyes that fell into a blank stare when you asked him his opinion about anything. He continued to have sporadic contact with John over the years after the divorce, but periodically he would vanish for months at a time. During John's adolescence, his father faded from the scene altogether for about three years.

It was perfectly clear to John that his father meant about as much to him as his appendix. He liked the guy, but he had learned early on not to expect anything from him. Once John suffered a concussion in a football game and was carried from the field on a stretcher. His father stopped at the hospital where John had been taken and apparently checked with the doctor to make sure he was all right. John never personally saw his father there or heard from him later about the incident.

John saw his mother as strong enough to handle the parenting responsibility single-handedly. He didn't need his father or want anything from him. He tried thinking of him as a friendly, distant uncle. He would never ask him for advice or money or to come to an event in which he was involved. He was surprised that his father even came to his wedding.

It was, in fact, his marriage that gave a backdrop for John to begin to see himself more clearly in relation to his father. The things his wife started complaining about were strangely familiar: He worked too much, he didn't seem to want to participate in family decisions, he was passive about everything except his job and sports, he couldn't make a decision. It was painful for John to hear these criticisms, but he accepted them as the price he had to pay for having that kind of role model.

John found it harder to accept that he was a bitter, angry person and that that had something to do with his father also. He didn't like hearing from his wife that he was always critical and that there was a bitter edge to him when he didn't get what he wanted (though what he had wanted wouldn't come out until much later and after a protracted fight). John used his barbed wit to put down almost everybody. He trusted only a very select group of old, lifelong buddies, and even from those friends he would never openly seek support. He distrusted people in positions of authority who tried to control him in any way.

John needed to admit to himself that he kept others at a distance so that he would not be hurt again like his father hurt him; that he was bitter because his father had never really supported him and had used the divorce to allow himself permission to slip out of John's life. To be angry and bitter about his father's absence and rejection meant that John cared about his dad after all. To face his caring meant he had to confront more unacknowledged pain than he was prepared to do. It was easier to remain numb to his real feelings and retreat from people who might break through his protective shield.

The Dead Father

Guy Corneau observed in *Absent Fathers, Lost Sons* that boys whose fathers died showed fewer adaptation problems than those whose fathers were gone for other reasons. He thought this might be true because of the positive image of deceased fathers that is likely to be sustained. After all, to think ill of a father who has died seems almost unconscionable. Moreover, negative memories tend to fade over time in the face of the loss of the man himself and, of course, there are no new experiences to contradict the old. Also, death is not normally associated with conflict and anger as divorce often is, so children are less likely to be consumed with contradictory feelings about the loss of the father. On the surface, at least, death seems like a cleaner, clearer sort of loss and therefore less psychologically confusing.

When we compare the impact of loss by death to loss by divorce there are significant similarities and differences. Divorce gets experienced as a kind of death. No matter how often a child sees his or her father, there is a death to the familiar, intact family.

The endings a child faces with divorce, however, are not as final. The father can still be or become more a part of the child's life. Unfortunately, since so much latitude exists a child can be terribly confused if the divorced father chooses not to be involved. The lack of absolute finality in divorce has its curse, but is largely a blessing.

With death, its unequivocal finality has its blessing of sorts, too. There can be no false hopes, no confusing messages, no shattering disappointments from unkept visits or broken promises. The curse of death is that it leaves a child without the option to ever again connect or ask the unasked question or replay a missed opportunity. There is no way to resolve whatever has been left unsettled, to heal open wounds directly.

Death leaves us feeling this way, but the reality is that the finality is not as total as we think. On a rational level it seems final, but on an emotional level we do not close the books easily. We continue to search for the father who is missed as children of divorced fathers do, but the search is more inward. We try to see the ways we are like the father and thus, carry on his legacy. We try to find where he lives within us. We do this because it helps us to know who we are and because it is our way to still connect with our fathers. In this way we keep our dads alive indefinitely.

I recently read an article about a high school football player whose father died when he was two. The boy kept a newspaper clipping of his father taped to the inside of his locker for inspiration. Because his father had been a revered football coach, his son could see a memorial plaque in front of the school stadium where he had coached. On one occasion when the son was playing there, the boy knelt at the plaque and said a prayer. It made him feel that his father was with him that night.

Lewis Yablonsky in *Fathers and Sons* quotes a fifty-year-old man whose father died when he was eight: "It's becoming more and more evident to me that I'm not separate from him. It's a little scary, because he's been dead forty-two years now, and as we're talking I feel as if he's right here with me now."

This man recognized that he never really accepted the fact that his father died. He maintained an idealized image of his father for years, imagining that he was working for the FBI or fighting Hitler and would someday return.

Children often attempt to hold on to a positive image of a deceased father, but then can also be plagued by negative distortions about the death. When children at any age, though particularly when they are young, lack a sophisticated context for dealing with death and do not have the opportunity to share their emotional loss with the dying parent, they may experience the death as a rejection. In a touching letter to his son, community organizer Lou Becker wrote: "When I was a little boy, as you are now, my daddy—your grandpa—died. For a long, long time I thought that he had done that on purpose, and I guess I thought that he did it just to get away from me. I didn't know why he wanted to, but that's the only reason I could think of for him leaving me."

No matter how irrational it is, when we feel abandoned, we experience not only the void from a loss, but confusion, pain, and anger at the inexplicable nature of the leave-taking. The loss seems unnecessary and as if it should somehow be reversible, regardless of the absolute, clear reality of mortality. When a loss does not have to occur, we are hurt by it and resentful of it. With divorce it is more obvious that we might react this way. I think we do not understand death much better. Becker went on to write, "I missed him a lot, but I was also very angry at him for going away forever." Children can adapt and forgive so much, but a permanent loss is beyond their ability to absorb.

A young child may fear he or she is somehow responsible for the death. Little children think magically and narcissistically, as though the world revolves around them. If they have had angry thoughts or been "bad" (and what child has not?), they may believe these thoughts or misdeeds have caused the death or made their father so angry he has gone away forever.

As we get older we do not altogether lose this childlike thinking. Regardless of the obvious causes of the death, children at any age can question their involvement: "Could I have done more to take care of him?" or "Did I cause him to have added stress or worry?" or "Should I have spent more time with him before he was ill [or after]?" These feelings are tantamount to self-blame.

Feeling responsible to any extent carries with it a painful burden of guilt and shame. The guilt comes with the sense of having contributed to the father's demise or even his discomfort while he was dying. The guilt readily becomes attached to shame, which is what we feel about ourselves for being the kind of person who would commit this hurtful act. It feels shameful to believe we contributed to a father's death. Even feeling anger at that father or focusing on our own feelings of loss can elicit shame.

Kathy had the misfortune as a ten-year-old of discovering her father unconscious upon her return from a Girl Scout meeting. She called her

mother immediately to get help for her father and in doing so temporarily saved his life. Her father survived his massive heart attack for
only a few weeks. During the time he was in the hospital Kathy feared
going to visit him because he looked so awful and the tubes and mon-
itors were frightening to her. She saw her dad only a couple of times
before he passed away.

Two thoughts plagued Kathy about the loss of her father. She kept
playing out in her mind what would have happened if she had not gone
to her scout meeting or if she had been quicker about walking home.
Despite being told repeatedly by relatives that her father's heart attack
was so sudden and severe she could not have saved him, Kathy held on
to her doubts and a degree of guilt.

The more uncomfortable reaction for Kathy, though, was her fear
about seeing her father in the hospital. She could not forgive herself for
her perceived weakness and how she may have hurt her dad in his last
days. She was so consumed by her shame over the years, it never
occurred to her that at her age her mother or other adult relatives would
have determined when she visited the hospital. Her fear was only part
of the picture.

There is a very different set of emotional responses to the loss of the
father that comes with the existential impact of death, especially with
such a central figure in a child's life. Any death for a child brings home
the frightening reality of one's mortality. Death leaves a child with a
sense of vulnerability to sudden calamity that can permeate his or her
entire outlook on life. Death shatters the sense of control and security
which we rely on fathers to provide. A father's fulfillment of our basic
needs means that his death intensifies our naked exposure, our unpro-
tectedness in the world. We are ourselves vulnerable and so are all the
people who are important to us.

Children respond in different ways to this loss of security and the
vulnerability that goes with it. Some become rigid about trying to establish dominion over all facets of life. They are unable to cope with risk
or uncertainty. Their need to control may take the form of obsessing
over points of order, such as keeping the house neat or paying the bills
on time, since the larger events—in line with the death of the father—
seem beyond control.

Others may feel defeated by the overpowering message of death and
as a result function in a passive or guarded way. This caution may lead
to the avoidance of certain activities or situations out of fear of another

tragedy. It may also operate within relationships in the form of the fear of being hurt again. Lou Becker explained to his son: "So when I grew up, I thought that it was a good idea to try to be a person who didn't love other people a lot, because if you love someone a lot and he or she goes away forever, it hurts so much."

Roberta's sense of hurt and loss surrounding her father began well before his death when she was eighteen. Her dad had been an alcoholic when she was little and caused Roberta's older sister to be badly burned in an accident that occurred while he was drinking. As a result Roberta's dad seemed to avoid any situation where he would be alone with her or her sister.

As a young adult Roberta dated a great deal, but she refused to get serious with anyone. She would find a reason to stop going out with any boy who wanted to get "too close." As she approached her thirtieth birthday Roberta started to question her behavior.

Initially she blamed her difficulties with males on her father's emotional distance. As she explored her feelings more deeply, it became apparent that she knew on some level she had held back from him as well out of not feeling safe. When he died she interpreted it as a punishment for her lack of trust in him. She believed she didn't deserve any closeness after that. But she also feared that if she let herself risk a serious relationship, she would be bound to lose it.

Some children attempt to deal with the scariness of life without a father by stifling their feelings altogether, perhaps mimicking the stoicism of their fathers. In *Growing Up*, Russell Baker's Pulitzer prize–winning autobiography of his early years, Baker wrote that after his father's death, when he was five years old: "I never cried again with any real conviction, nor expected much of anyone's God except indifference, nor loved deeply without fear that it would cost me dearly in pain."

Both sons and daughters, virtually regardless of age, are drawn to become instant adults. Daughters become their mother's guardian. Bonnie was the child of immigrant parents. Her father operated a dry cleaning establishment. After her dad's death when Bonnie was fourteen, her mother took over running the business. Bonnie assumed the responsibilities of managing the home. She did most of the cooking and cleaning, and basically became the parent of her younger sister and brother.

It was as though her mother filled in for her father and she stepped in as the substitute mother. She also was protective of her mother—over her health, but also over her business dealings. Bonnie feared her mother would be taken advantage of because she did not speak English as well as her father had. She made sure she was at her mother's side at meetings with the accountant, the lawyer, or sales representatives. Her mother dubbed her "the watchdog."

Boys tend to believe that as males it falls to them to substitute for the father's male strength in the home. They, of course, lack perspective on what they are attempting to force upon themselves. Baker reflected: "The making of a man, even when the raw material was as pliable as I, often seemed brutally hard without the help of a father to handle the rougher passages."

In Baker's case, his mother believed she could help him prepare for manhood by using occasional doses of corporal punishment to toughen him up. Mothers play a significant role in how children adapt to a father's death, not only by how they take on the dual parenting responsibilities, but by being the best available lens through which a child can know his or her father.

When a father dies prematurely, his children are deprived of the opportunity to learn from his example about how to live a life. Mothers can only fill in so much for the absent father, especially for boys, who need to have continuity with their fathers to feel complete as men. With the death, the children simply do not have the opportunity to see enough of how their fathers lived. For one woman whose father died just as she was graduating from college and starting her first job, the timing was devastating. She felt that she was deserted at the precise point in her life when she had most needed her father to be available.

A man already in his thirties when his father died lamented: "I can't get my bearings. I feel like I'm lost in the woods and have no compass. My father was the one who'd talk to me about working too hard or not taking care of myself, or doing too much for others. He helped keep me within safe boundaries for myself."

This man reflected the important role fathers often play in helping their children learn to set limits and feel in control of their lives. The loss of the father leaves many children, again boys particularly, without direction and the guide upon whom they have relied.

The struggle to find direction in one's own life without the father's guidance is made much more difficult because of the idealized image children often carry about a father who has died when he was still young. That inflated status makes it all the harder to believe one can possibly measure up to the father. It also makes it hard to let go of him. The sense of loss is intensified by the idyllic view of the father, and it becomes all the more right to emulate this wonderful man the child fears he cannot do without. No matter how much the father validated the child through love and approval while he was alive, a dread may persist that one is still falling short of the father's example. Daniel's story illustrates how consuming this fear can be.

Daniel's father had been like the secular rabbi of the neighborhood. From Friday evenings throughout the weekend neighbors called, most of them to bask in the pearls of wisdom and good humor that emanated from Daniel's father. People flocked to his hardware store all week, too, as much for his sage advice as his wares. Though he had not gone to college, he was considered a genuine scholar by those who knew him. He could surely have become a highly successful doctor or lawyer, but Daniel was born so soon after he returned from World War II that he considered it an imperative to earn money immediately. With all his love of learning and his devotion to his friends and the community, his family still came first. In Daniel's mind his father's sacrificing nature led to a massive heart attack at forty-seven. There was no question he died for his family.

Daniel was sixteen when his father passed away. Daniel's passage through high school was like meandering in a fog. His college years demonstrated a concerted noneffort. He had a refined capacity for doing the bare minimum required. Daniel left college with no direction or goals he could call his own. He took a job in an insurance agency operated by a friend of his father's and settled into a comfortable, though insular, existence.

In his father's friend, Daniel was fortunate to have found a mentor to guide him. His boss was a pale version of what his father would have been, but the relationship gave a quiet stability to Daniel. Through his boss, Daniel was directed in how to invest his money, and after some years of blind luck and increasing savvy, he built a huge nest egg that allowed him to quit his job and live off his investments.

Daniel's intention was to enjoy his life before it was too late. It had always been his expectation that he would not live past fifty. Apart from expecting to have heart problems like his father, he didn't believe he deserved a life span longer than his father had. Daniel felt undeserving largely because he had not lived up to the example of his father: work hard, do your best, give 100 percent to all you do, but don't expect to live to reap the rewards of an exemplary life.

Daniel had chosen to resolve this paradoxical message by avoiding the stress that might cut short his life. Unfortunately, the path he chose backfired in two ways. He remained fearful of dying young, and by not making the effort to do his best, he felt further diminished in comparison with his father. Moreover, he had not earned his wealth in keeping with the way his father had struggled to provide for the family. Therefore, he deserved neither the money he had amassed nor the right to take pleasure in spending it.

Daniel stagnated amid feelings of self-recrimination and dysphoria. He wavered between finding life meaningless and bemoaning how he was missing out on it. His energy went into worrying about petty things. He constantly quarreled with his wife over the cleanliness of the house or how much she spent on groceries. Unconsciously, he had apparently found the way to resolve his conflict over not being like his father: He, too, would not get to enjoy the fruits of his life.

If Daniel had been able to communicate with his dad, his father might well have tried to pass on the wisdom that his son could construct a meaningful life on his own terms and yet be true to his father. With the father's death, however, obviously comes an end to the direct receipt of his guidance and affirmation. Perhaps the most powerful longing we have is to hear again, or for the first time, the father's affirming words. We want to be reassured that we were loved or that we fulfilled his expectations or that he can smile upon the path in life we have taken.

In the face of the emotional and physical void, we consciously and unconsciously try to hold on to the father. We compare ourselves to him, we look for his traits in ourselves and accentuate them. Those who were young when their father died will search within to feel the emotions or activate the lost memories that will confirm a connectedness.

One woman maintained her avid love of sports as the only identifiable bond she could retain with the father about whom she had such little knowledge. One of the few facts she knew about her dad was that he loved to watch one of the local college football teams, so she adopted that team as her favorite and went to as many of its games as she could.

In effect, we try to make up for the lack of physical connection by finding tangible evidence that we were connected in some way. We may latch on to his way of walking, his temper, his drinking, his love of football. The connection may be thin. It may even be self-destructive. But we want to find that lost father somewhere.

11

Healing the Wounds From Divorced and Dead Fathers

Fathers who die or get divorced represent the whole gamut of paternal types. A father's misuse of power or his failure to overcome his weaknesses or his persistent absence could all lead to divorce. Deceased fathers may be idealized; they certainly fall silent. Their legacy can be marred by any of the flaws that made them less connected or effective as parents when they were alive.

For the children of these dads, then, healing may involve any of the issues surrounding the type of father he was. Whatever these issues are, however, will have the overlay of two complex and confusing themes that dominate the lives of children of divorced or deceased fathers: vulnerability and responsibility.

The vulnerability of these children is due to their traumatic loss. The consequence of a father's death is not only to create immediate loss and insecurity, but to leave the child with the irrefutable knowledge that our lives can be tragically altered at any moment. The shadow of mortality is cast over the child as well as everyone that child cares about.

The challenge for these children, then, is to face the transience of life proactively. When a father dies prematurely, the child may feel resigned to a shortened life. Some individuals respond by living recklessly, with the attitude that they have nothing to lose. Others may live passively or timidly, attempting to preserve their well-being.

One client, Jamie, who entered therapy because of the high level of stress in his life, realized that he was trying to do too much because he expected to die young like his father. Children like Jamie need to care for their health rather than treat themselves as if they may die any minute. They must strike a balance that allows them to live fully and savor the preciousness of life without trying to compensate every minute for the possibility of a shortened lifespan. Jamie found himself more relaxed and enjoying his life far more when he began jogging and eating healthily than when he was driving himself to exhaustion.

The task is essentially the same for dealing with the mortality of others. Those individuals like Roberta from "The Impact of Divorce and Death," who avoid getting close to others for fear of losing them, discover that they do not really feel protected; they feel lonely, unhappy, and cheated. By choosing to care about others we can expect that the pain of any future loss will be mediated by the fulfilling contact we have had and the knowledge that we have helped make others' lives and our own more full.

The vulnerability that comes with divorce is about the fragility of bonds. Our capacity to trust and feel safe within any relationship is undermined when we discover that our parents' commitment to each other was only temporary. Rebuilding the capacity to trust requires the risk of allowing relationships to develop. Children of divorced fathers, however, may be impeded in this endeavor by a knot of conflicting emotions.

Loving others has become entwined with the fear of rejection and feelings of inadequacy, anger, and self-blame. Every new relationship is regarded as having the potential to send one into a tailspin of these emotions. These children must deal with how these feelings were linked to specific aspects of their father's behavior before, during, and after the divorce. In this way they can disentangle their painful feelings from relationships in general and determine what steps they can take to overcome them.

When John's marriage was starting to unravel because of his barrage of anger and criticism, he preferred to believe that his wife was the problem—another person letting him down. When he could begin to look at the connection between his behavior and his father's lack of contact after the divorce, he could see that his disappointment was not with the whole world. He realized that pushing others away only served to trap him in the old feelings of abandonment.

John began to face his feelings about his dad and simultaneously to take responsibility for his destructive behavior. He gradually became aware that like his dad he had a problem with alcohol, which in turn was a major factor in his negative attitude and treatment of others. He resumed contact with his father after several years of ignoring the relationship. His dad was still not a satisfying person to spend time with, but at least John could be frustrated with the right person for the right reasons.

The guilt and shame in which Kathy from "The Impact of Divorce and Death," was caught surrounding her father's death was part of a different emotional quagmire. She was inappropriately assuming responsibility for what was beyond her control and yet not allowing herself to have feelings that were in fact appropriate to the situation.

In attempting to help free Kathy from her self-imposed trap I pointed out to her that her father was probably too ill and too medicated to be focused much on how often she visited him as he lay dying. I also suggested that he probably would have wanted to spare her the trauma of seeing him in such bad shape and that the hospital itself might have restricted her from visiting at her age. I was offering her some perspective on the burden she was carrying that she could not give herself.

Children of divorced or dead fathers often are ensnared in an inflated sense of responsibility. To a degree, the loss of the father unquestionably places real additional duties on children. In the early stages of recovering from these traumas mothers need additional support and may have difficulty coping. These are certainly not times for youngsters to be self-centered. Over time, though, their own recovery depends on their ability to delineate fitting levels of responsibility concerning each parent.

Bonnie was still calling her mother at least once a day for thirty years after her father died. The daily calls went on for so long they began to make sense again because of her mother's aging. But for too long they reflected Bonnie's overprotectiveness of her mother. Bonnie felt the need to watch over her mother because of her limited social skills as an immigrant, but also because her mother never resumed a social life of her own.

Children such as Bonnie are faced with an onerous choice about how much to continue supporting a mother who maintains a truncated and perhaps dependent life. The divorce or death remains an open wound as long as the child is still faced with helping to pick up the pieces. There is a point at which it becomes necessary to accept that the mother has chosen whatever life works best for her. The children must recenter their lives around their own goals and needs.

Children of divorced fathers may end up in a caretaking role for them as well. More often, the dilemma the children face is over how much effort to make with a man who may not be carrying his fair share of the relationship or who has left a residue of feelings in the wake of his departure. Children need to find the ground between pure obligation and practiced indifference, so whatever contact they are having is their own choice and yet allows for the father to demonstrate his honest commitment.

June was too angry to see or talk with her father for months after his affair was exposed and her parents separated. When she resumed seeing him there were several years of rocky, unpleasant interactions. She decided to stop having contact with him until she could actually feel that she wanted to be with him. For almost a decade her communication with him was mostly through holiday and birthday cards, with an occasional phone call. Eventually she saw signs in her dad of a kind of caring and interest she had not experienced since she was little. At this point she began to have a genuine desire to see him and to allow him once again to be a father.

Of course, the problem when fathers die is the exact opposite—we cannot choose when to see them, whether out of desire or obligation. The responsibility we feel is more likely centered around meeting the expectations we believe they had for us or carrying on their legacy. When we idealize their memory as part of our holding on to them, we make the job of honoring them all the more arduous.

Moving forward with our lives requires a strong enough sense of self to supplant the vision we believe our fathers had for us with one of our own. One path to developing our own direction is to make use of a mentor to provide the guidance we yearn for from the father. A supportive network of peers will also help us gain the security to make our own mark.

Daniel, despite his years of floundering, was helped considerably by his father's friend. In time, he found that he was most comfortable and able to take on business challenges when he had a mature partner who had some expertise in a particular venture and could offer some guidance in its initial stages.

What we are seeking in trying to carry on our father's legacy or in striking out on our own is the affirmation that in our dad's eyes, we are indeed good enough. In the end, though, the validation that we seek from a deceased father is found far more in what we carry internally. When we discover within ourselves those qualities in him that we value—his courage, generosity, love of learning, determination—we know he continues to be part of us. That is the connection we most need. That is what gives us validation to the degree we can receive it without hearing his words or seeing his nod.

Whether we have been disconnected from our fathers because of their physical absence, because we were stifled or abused by their power, or because we need to steer clear of their weakness, there is a part of all of us that wants to re-establish connection. We want to be able to internalize, to find within ourselves those things we can respect, value, and love about our fathers.

We cannot feel comfortable, however, with possessing this internal father if we do not feel at peace with the quality of the external relationship with him. All too often we remain blocked from finding the pathway to heal this relationship by the physical and emotional obstacles we perceive. We remain cut off, then, not only from our fathers, but from some of the most essential and vital parts of ourselves. Part II of *Your Father, Your Self* describes how to work actively on rebuilding the ties to our fathers.

Part II

Journey to Our Fathers:
Healing the Relationship

12

The Desire to Reconcile

Sooner or later, we have to deal again with that side of the father
who hit us with an ax.

from an African tale, *Iron John*, Robert Bly

It is a wise child that knows her own father. I knew as I held my
father's old hand in my own, its exact replica, and watched my own
skull emerging through his transparent skin, that I am my father's
daughter. Now that he can be hurt no more, it is time to find out
what that means.

Daddy, We Hardly Knew You, Germaine Greer

The dad on the popular show from several years ago, *The Wonder Years*,
is a realistic and quite human father figure, unlike the fathers in most sit-
coms on television. At different times he is autocratic, ideal, overburdened, silent, and absent either emotionally or due to work. Through his
bullishness and his difficulty expressing himself we see a man who is
devoted to his family and cares deeply about the well-being of each of
his children. We can observe an ebb and flow in his relationship with his
kids as he contends with the inexorable distance that comes with their
aging and his demeanor.

In one episode he is bewildered by his daughter's rebellion. On the eve of her eighteenth birthday and departure for college she appears to be rejecting everything he wants for her. In an effort to give her something of himself that can bridge the gap between them, he offers her his World War II duffel bag and dog tags. Both are moved to near tears, and she grips his hand as she gives him back the dog tags to keep for himself.

Here is the father as hero and antihero simultaneously: a father who is able to reach into his own depths and arrive at the wisdom to show his acceptance of his child as she struggles to separate from home; a father strong enough to bend toward his daughter as she strives to establish her own identity. This is a father perhaps universal in his feelings and attitudes but who does beyond what a traditional father might well do. He enacts what so many fathers and daughters and sons wish for. All too often, however, the bridges aren't built, the risks not taken.

Too many of us remain emotionally and physically cut off from our fathers. This occurs in conscious self-defense and unconscious self-preservation. It takes the form of superficial relationships as well as bitter or estranged ones. While the pain of this separation often is denied or repressed, over the years the state of the relationship remains a powerful influence on our feelings and actions. Eventually, often in our thirties or forties, the hurt that is buried finds its way into our consciousness. We are forced to look at our fathers with new eyes.

Sometimes we are awakened by the shock of a father's death. The unsatisfying closure of death leads us to want a deeper understanding of the relationship and a better resolution than infinite silence. Author Geoffrey Wolff's memoir of his father, *The Duke of Deception*, begins with his gratitude that his father's troubled life has come to an end. The memoir carries Wolff on an emotional roller coaster until he arrives at an understanding of his reaction, which he has learned is rather basic: "I had been estranged from my father by my apprehension of other people's opinion of him, and by a compulsion to be free of his chaos and destructions. I had forgotten I loved him mostly, and mostly now I missed him. I miss him."

In Wolff's case, his father's death released him from the trauma and burden of seeing his father self-destruct through his fraudulent behavior over a period of years. Wolff was freed then to examine his father's life and his relationship to him in ways he could not do when his father was alive.

For some, it is the recognition of the father's aging and signs of his mortality that lead to a desire to reassess this man and our relationship with him. Ron was finally moved to approach his father about his long-buried hurts because, he said, "I don't want him to die first." Ron was reluctant to take the risk of talking honestly to his father about his feelings, but the awareness that he could be deprived of ever having the opportunity if he waited too long gave him second thoughts.

Changes in our own lives can make us want to reconcile with a father who has too long kept a distance or played his own part in a disharmonious relationship. Becoming a parent ourselves is perhaps the most powerful such catalyst. This experience gives us new perspective on our fathers, teaching us the real demands of parenting as well as its joys. We may be more sympathetic to the father's impatience or ineptitude. Or we may have renewed upset at his lapses because we observe our own commitment to parenting.

We may feel we can bridge some of the distance with our fathers because we can picture them at a parallel point in their own lives. Comparing their own parenting with their father's is a particularly intense experience for sons, who want a model for their role as fathers. For both sons and daughters, becoming a parent puts us in touch with our own needs for guidance and desire to be parented ourselves. Old yearnings may then come to the foreground.

Usually the changes in our lives put us in touch with our father's humanity. Perceiving our fathers in more human dimensions makes them seem more accessible—either by taking them off a pedestal or letting them out of the doghouse. We are able to see through some of our father's defenses to what the man underneath might really be like. Events such as getting into a work situation that parallels that of our father, having a comparable failure, getting divorced, or contracting a similar illness are examples of life experiences that might give insight into the father's emotional makeup and perspective on what he may have known.

A backlog of unexamined feelings and desires can be kindled by these realizations. We may start knowing that something was and is still missing. We may fear that the relationship will never change, but we start wanting more.

- Sean was turning fifty, going through a divorce, and trying to deal with an estranged son. He felt overwhelmed. Sean had basically believed that he had gone on with his life and learned not to expect anything from his father. If he felt anything for this irrelevant man, it was a residue of anger. I asked Sean to write a letter to his deceased father telling him what he wished his father had understood about him. Sean himself was surprised with the opening line of his letter, written with no forethought: "I'm sorry I never got to know you better."

- At a workshop about men, Ruth found herself in tears at some of the references and stories about fathers. She started questioning whether the succession of poor relationships she had had with men was related to her father. She had always had a superficial relationship with him, right up to his death. She suspected that she didn't know how to get close to a man and avoided doing so out of fear. She recognized that the grief she started to feel about her father was for much more than his death.

- When Matt was given a major promotion at work, his father had been only quietly supportive. He seemed pleased, but said and asked little. Matt wanted something more from his father with this promotion. He believed his father had a wisdom about life that he didn't share with anyone, and Matt felt cheated he wasn't receiving any of it. He could see how he had played the game the same way everyone else in the family had done—never to challenge his dad to be more connected. He told me: "I think I always assumed this is how a son relates to a father. We're supposed to dance around each other and not admit we want to be closer. But I'm tired of it. I feel like I'd understand myself better if I knew him better."

- Dick took his kids on a visit home to his father's place on the east coast. He carefully observed how his father related to his grandchildren. He had always felt his parents had provided a happy home, but he was shocked to see how little love his father showed those kids. As he told me about his visit he started to cry. Initially he thought his tears were for his children's experience with their grandfather, but then it became obvious he was crying for the child Dick, who had also missed out on affection from his father.

All of these individuals yearned to connect with their fathers in a way they never had before. But it was more complex than this. They wanted to understand the impact their fathers had on their emotional lives. They all grew as they struggled with their own pain. They had reached the point, however, where in order to complete the healing process, they had to face the sense of loss they had avoided or blocked out.

In order to come into harmony with themselves, they had to find harmony in their relationships with their fathers. They could only accomplish this end by working through their feelings to the point where they could understand and accept the relationship for what it was. They had to move from ignoring and suppressing their hurt to the hard work of seeking reconciliation and resolution.

To truly heal ourselves and to have the hope of healing or at least improving the relationship with our fathers, we must risk going against the emotional logic that we have relied on to protect us from hurt. To bury or ignore our hurt or to remain angry or distant ourselves offers a protective shield. It seems to make sense that getting into the muck of these painful feelings or relinquishing our emotional defenses can only heighten the pain and perhaps worsen the contact with our fathers. The beginning steps of healing, however, lie in facing the hurt. What feels like quicksand is really the foundation from which we can bring about change.

There are two levels on which we need to seek healing—externally with the father and internally with ourselves. The external process involves reconciliation. We must be ready to fully acknowledge the failure to be connected to our father and experience the pain that characterized the relationship. At the same time we have to try to put these feelings behind as we seek a new connection. Reconciliation is about wanting to build bridges back to our father through healing the emotional wounds instead of nursing them. It is about restoring or strengthening our own love for him, seeking the blessing or validation we have missed, improving the quality of our contact, and identifying the ways in which we are inseparably bonded with him.

In his quest to find his legacy from his own father, author Philip Roth identified different items he thought he really wanted as a simple inheritance to define his bond with his father. Ultimately, he realized that his true inheritance came with his willingness to care for his father as he died, to feel a love strong enough to bypass traditional sensibilities and old hurts so that he could even clean up after his father's incontinence.

Roth wrote: "You clean up your father's shit because it has to be cleaned up, but in the aftermath . . . everything that's there to feel is felt as never before. . . . There was my patrimony: not the money, not the tefillin*, not the shaving mug, but the shit."

Roth's reconciliation came when he stopped looking for some gift from his father that would validate their connection and when he could freely give of himself to his father without expecting anything in return.

Roth's discovery of his patrimony came through his willingness to make a journey—inward and outward. He had to carve time out from a busy schedule to fly to Florida and be with his father, after he determined that his father needed him and he needed his father. He had to reach down deep and call upon all his patience, selflessness, tenderness, strength, and forgiveness to build the bridge that took him to the foot of his father's grave.

The reconciliation we are talking about, then, is as much with ourselves about our father as with our father. Unquestionably, if our attempts at building bridges are responded to in kind and if our father is willing to hear and accept our concerns about the relationship as valid, it makes the process of reconciliation satisfying and complete.

Most relationships will not heal this way. Whether our father is dead, living in Brazil, or unwilling to let a conversation get beyond the box scores in today's sports section, there is a great deal of internal healing and growth that can take place. Like Philip Roth, we can find our own peace or resolution that allows us to reach out regardless of the outcome. Resolution means we have achieved an internal reconciliation that frees us from the frustrating grip of anger, blame, hurt, shame, and self-deprecation for the relationship's failings and lost love. We can achieve this inner healing even if our efforts to change the relationship have little or no success. We cannot, however, expect to secure an external reconciliation with our fathers if we do not do the work internally to prepare us for this journey.

In the past few years there has been a great deal of emphasis on ritual as a means to promote healing in relationships with fathers. Men in particular have engaged in meaningful structured gatherings, sharing primitive rituals, poetry, and tears to deal with their grief at their dis-

---

*Tefillin: Leather boxes containing scriptural passages worn in prayer by Orthodox Jews.

torted masculinity and their unfulfilled paternal bonds. But more is needed than ritual to accomplish the healing that is needed with fathers. We have to be willing to actively and sincerely take the steps needed to make the journey to our father and, as with any difficult trip, to accept the rugged conditions we might face along the way.

While most of us deem ourselves willing travelers, it is easy to fool ourselves into defining the trip we want to take instead of preparing for the journey actually before us. The first step in this preparation involves facing the barriers we ourselves erect that make it unlikely we can reach the desired destination and that we may then use to avoid making the journey at all.

All too often, we miss the opportunity to test out the degree of healing that can be achieved because of our beliefs and attitudes about our fathers. In addition, we may be handcuffed by mistaken notions about how to go about healing the division with fathers, which then results in misguided efforts. Moreover, the healing process cannot begin without the simple readiness to truly let it occur. Many of us believe we are more ready than we are and are unaware of how we hold ourselves back.

Self-Defeating Attitudes

It is natural to feel ambivalent or fearful about whether our efforts to achieve change with our fathers can work. Unfortunately, we may let our beliefs act as a rationale to avoid our discomfort. We may even convince ourselves that change is simply not possible; that our father is an old dog who cannot be taught new tricks.

Obviously many fathers are resistant to change or even to facing the reality that their relationship with their children was not all it could or needed to be. It may also be true, though, that the father we see today is not the same as the father we knew as we grew up. We may be operating from the distorted view that he must have been an "old dog" then and he still is now. We may be seeing him in static, one-dimensional terms.

Psychiatrist William Appleton relates an anecdote in *Fathers and Daughters* about a woman whose father was cautious about her relations with boys as a teen and gave her the message not to trust them. She was surprised to find at age twenty nine that her father expected that she would be sleeping with her lover. Circumstances change, children change, and fathers themselves may change with the times.

I have heard many clients explain their surprise at changes they encountered in their fathers, especially in response to careful efforts at reconciliation. The changes are not necessarily earth-shattering. Usually they are basic, like being able to carry on meaningful conversation or the father initiating contact. Sometimes they include the father's recognition of and regret for the earlier years of distance.

Some fathers simply seem to "mellow" in their later years, particularly when the pressures of work and being a provider ease up. What is dramatic about these changes is in how the new behavior compares to the past and in how the changes reflect an opening for further growth.

It is commonly believed that fathers will not talk about their feelings and therefore will be incapable of changing. Consequently no dialogue could occur that would bring about healing or greater closeness. We have likely seen fathers avoid their feelings for so long that we cannot imagine they could ever open up. Part of our fear is that their inability to deal with feelings means they won't be able to hear the feelings we do voice.

It may also be true, however, that we have our own discomfort about being open with our fathers, but find it easier on ourselves to focus on how they can't express their feelings. It is also true that many children grow up conditioned to protect their fathers from the discomfort they are presumed to have about talking on an emotional level.

This protectiveness of fathers also may take the form of trying not to hurt them. Children often operate from the belief that "all that can come from bringing up the past is for him to be hurt." They then avoid expressing any of their own hurt so as to not hurt their father.

Ron, for example, wanted desperately to be able to feel a closeness with his aging father before it was too late, but he couldn't overcome the image he had of his dad breaking down in tears and succumbing to terrible guilt for his mistakes with Ron. What Ron couldn't imagine was that his father might welcome the opportunity to voice his guilt and regret. Ron's avoidance of hurting his father may have fostered both of them being stuck in their own pain. If we want to bring about change with our father, we need to relinquish our penchant to protect him and, in fact, let him be the parent. That is indeed what we need from him and why we would seek reconciliation.

Behind this concern with fathers' reactions is the belief that to examine what has happened in the relationship will inevitably be seen as blaming them. Children are reluctant to be critical because they feel they are being disloyal as well as hurtful toward their father.

Children may be reticent to find fault with their dads for different reasons. Many men especially regard criticism of their father as running counter to the goal of the adult male becoming responsible for his own life. Children may see their judgment of their father as unfair if they hold to the belief that the father tried to do his best. If they are attuned to his weaker side, they want to protect him from hurt. If they are focused on his power, they may fear that he will react in anger.

Kyle had entered therapy after his years of working with his unreliable father and covering for him had led to depression. After months of avoiding the discomfort he felt at discussing his father in therapy, Kyle finally got the message: "I need to remember we're just talking about understanding, not blame. I need to understand what that word 'understand' really means, so I can stop protecting and defending and freezing up whenever anything comes up about what my father might've done wrong."

What Kyle realized was that he could examine his relationship with his father and come to terms with how he was affected by it without having to focus exclusively on what his father did wrong. Healing relationships does require honesty; it doesn't require bludgeoning with blame.

Of course, many fathers are quite uncomfortable relating on the level of honesty and self-examination required to improve their relationship with their children. They may react with antagonism or out of hurt when the quality of the relationship or their behavior in it is called into question. Their initial discomfort or negative reaction doesn't necessarily mean they are unwilling. Nor does their ineptness at responding on a feeling level mean something can't be gained from trying. We may have to give an old dog more time to learn a new trick, but if he knows it's important, he may be more willing to keep trying.

We tend to interpret what may well be an inability or difficulty to respond in a new way as an intended rejection. To us it may seem patently obvious and elementary that a father would interact with his family if he loved them. Our fathers, however, may not have understood that they were needed this way, that more was expected of them than being a provider. Moreover, many fathers could not function in a more expansive way as we grew up.

June's father came home night after night and headed straight for the couch. On weekends he rarely consented to go places with the family. June took this unwillingness to do things with her as not wanting to be around her. It never dawned on her that her father was sometimes too exhausted or other times too hung over to join his family in activities.

In fact, there was some reason to suspect he was afraid to go out; that just to get through the work week and do the basics involved with having a family was in itself an enormous strain, which he tried to relieve with alcohol. June reacted by pulling away herself. She was determined to show her father that if he didn't want her, she didn't need him. Many fathers are predisposed to believing they aren't needed anyway, so such a reaction reinforces their view.

If we assume a father's passivity means rejection we may not only misread him, but we will react to the perceived rejection in ways that add a confounding element to the relationship. We may try to reciprocate with rejection, or, as commonly occurs, we may take on a passive stance ourselves and wait for him to make the first move. We can easily rationalize that after all, he's the parent and he's older, so it should be up to him. Fathers can initiate the healing process and some do, but if they were likely candidates to do this, the distance would not have persisted in so many relationships.

A great deal gets in the way of fathers being the initiators. Not only may a father's pride prevent him from stepping down from his parental pedestal, but his age can work against him, too. Just as our fathers were raised with a traditional conception of their role and therefore did not expect to be more involved at home, they were also not exposed to self-awareness and emotional openness as acceptable male behaviors.

Talking about emotional distance and working to improve a relationship are foreign concepts to most of these fathers. Therefore, they would not likely initiate the healing process, let alone have the awareness or sense of how to begin. Even though younger fathers today have been exposed to different expectations and a broader spectrum of behavior, many still find it difficult to operate in the realm of feelings and sensitivity.

Moreover, because of the power we experience or attribute to many fathers, for example, those who fit the autocratic, abusive, or ideal types, we regard them as being in control of what happens in the relationship. We may want to protect them from hurt, but we still may see them as in charge.

It is not easy to shift from the child's dependent, relatively powerless position with such fathers even when we have arrived at adulthood. We may not accept our own adult power. Perhaps more important, it is hard to conceive that our fathers have lost any of their power, especially over us. With the passage of time fathers, particularly those who have been autocratic or abusive, become more and more like the Wizard of Oz. Their voices boom and their directives resound from their spot behind the curtain. Pull back the curtain and they are not only of human dimensions, but perhaps quite insecure at the prospect of their illusory power being exposed.

Some children despair of ever having an impact on the failed relationship with their father. As a result, they feel their best alternative is to cut themselves off. Through maintaining their own distance from the father they hope to establish an identity that no longer relies on him for emotional needs or validation. Their independence is seen as the path to self-acceptance and as a protective shield against further hurt by the father.

In reality, severing ties usually is a way to justify pulling back from the father without dealing directly with our feelings. In most instances we are under an illusion if we believe we have to sever ties with our father in order to be an independent person. It is also illusory to think that such an action will of itself make us stronger as an individual.

In August Wilson's overpowering play *Fences*, about the shattered dreams of a black former ballplayer, the hero's son has an emotional exchange with his mother about his decision not to go to his father's funeral:

CORY: I can't drag Papa with me everywhere I go. I've got to say no to him. One time in my life I've got to say no.

ROSE: ... Whatever was between you and your daddy ... the time has come to put it aside. Just take it and set it over there on the shelf and forget about it. Disrespecting your daddy ain't gonna make you a man, Cory. You got to find a way to come to that on your own. Not going to your daddy's funeral ain't gonna make you a man.

Since so many children saw their fathers use distance as a way to cope with feelings, it is not surprising that they would behave the same way. Certainly children need to escape a father's sphere of influence for some period of time to catalyze their transition into adulthood. This is not the same, however, as using distance from the father as an emotional barricade.

A pattern that is probably far more common among children struggling with disappointment and frustration at the quality of connection with their fathers is to feel they have already made significant efforts to repair the relationship. These perceived efforts at reaching out are then used to rationalize no longer trying. Unfortunately, these initiatives are often predictably inadequate to the task. This is true not just because our fathers are intransigent, but due to the attitude behind the attempts or a naïveté about how those efforts could affect another person, particularly a father.

When we are hurt by a relationship our attempts to repair it may be colored by a one-sided view. We see only ourselves as the injured party or believe we are the only one making any effort to address the situation. Fathers, too, may be hurting, though they are so often adept at masking and denying that hurt. They also may be reaching out in their own way or at times when we are not ready to receive them. When we assume that we are the only one trying, we set ourselves up to become resentful quickly if our outstretched hand is seemingly ignored.

Children commonly are either not aware of their anger or else feel justified in holding on to it. Their initiatives may then be infused with passive or direct resentment, yet they expect their fathers to still make efforts to change. Charlene said to me, "I'm so angry at my father and frustrated with him. I can't understand why he won't change after all the feedback he's gotten!" The feedback consisted of a lot of hostile criticism about the father's own long-standing pattern of hostile criticism. Dishing out the same behavior to a father that created the hurt and resentment is not likely to offer a clear message or an incentive to change the behavior. It will elicit the same hurt response in the father or a defensive posture on his part.

The anger we have tried to bury is bound to come out in our interactions with our fathers and serves to push them away or put them on the defensive. They are not likely to be able to connect the anger with their own behavior unless it is clearly, directly, and constructively delivered. We can let out anger in this constructive way only if we are prepared to relinquish it, not hold on to it. An enormous difference exists in how anger is experienced when the child is prepared to let go of it rather than stay angry until she gets what she wants. Fathers won't view demanding anger as a desire to be close. What's more, we won't be getting what we really want either, so we will entrap ourselves in our unhappiness.

Historian Philip Greven, in his book about the religious underpinnings of punishment, *Spare the Child*, relates the story of Allen Wheelis, who was harshly disciplined as a boy by his bedridden father. One day, in utter frustration, Wheelis poured out a torrent of his pent-up anger, telling his father how mean he was and that he hated him and wished he was dead. After that outburst and the silence with which it was greeted, Wheelis says: "The rage passed and I became miserable." In their hurt and anger, children may believe that if they can only dish out some hurt to their fathers or convince them how wrong they were, they will themselves feel things have been equalized. With this kind of parity they think they can be at peace with the past and ready to reconnect.

Sometimes children feel justified in holding on to their anger or expressing it because they are, in effect, merely evening the score. Geoffrey Wolff said it simply and directly at the conclusion of *The Duke of Deception*: "I had felt betrayed by my father, and wanted to betray."

Besides representing a reflexive desire to give back the hurt we have received, this type of anger also reflects the belief that a show of strength is the best way to counteract the power we believe our father possesses. We use our anger as a means to guard against the father's seeming capacity to control the relationship and continue to inflict hurt. We act as though the best defense is a good offense. The faulty part of this strategy is that even if it gets an overbearing father to back off, it does not engender closeness or bring resolution to the pattern of conflict that has plagued the relationship.

Another way to try to even the score with fathers is by winning their acknowledgment that our behavior never justified their failure to relate to us. If we can erase their presumed negative view then the relationship itself will be healed. Franz Kafka, in his book-length letter to his father, was using this approach to balancing the ledger between his father and himself. He believed that if he could convince his father that he was blameless within the relationship, the two could achieve a lasting truce.

It is possible to even the score with some fathers—either they are willing to let the child vent without upping the ante afterward or they agree to zero out the scoreboard and declare neither at fault. Unfortunately, the former tactic is likely to inject new hurt into the game and therefore keep it going; the latter may result in old hurt being buried only to resurface in the future.

Successful reconciliation usually entails a renunciation of blame—an internal realization that blaming holds on to anger, causes distortion, and blocks healing. When we are ready to stop blaming, we don't have to even the score; we pack up our bats and head for home.

Throughout her adult years, Renee had geared herself to meet her autocratic father head-on to stifle his attempts to control her. Finally, after a visit from her father for which we had amply prepared, she took on a different perspective: "I can see now that he stays stuck in his angry outlook as a way to cope with the world. I used to regard that anger as power; now I know it comes from the weakness he's so good at concealing. I realize I don't have to answer his attacks at all."

Renee's father didn't become a softer, more loving parent, but when she let go of having to maintain either a good offense or a good defense, she had a sense of power and freedom she had never felt around her father before. She at least felt she could be around him, even if they weren't close. Psychoanalyst Linda Leonard arrived at essentially the same understanding in *The Wounded Woman*, her book about father-daughter relationships, when she realized, "In rejecting my father, I had been refusing my power." She was understanding that to sustain her anger at her father for the way he had hurt her was to push away his positive qualities and not just his negative ones. She could derive personal strength from embracing those positive traits.

Often we don't relinquish our self-defeating attitudes about our fathers because we simply aren't ready ourselves to take the risk. We resist taking steps that might be healing because we fear being rebuffed or having our efforts fail. We may also hold back because we are not prepared for what it means from our end to no longer have the distance between us and our fathers. We have found ways to adapt that allow us to tolerate our hurts and live with our anger and disappointment. We are determined not to be hurt anymore and are convinced that with our wagons carefully circled we won't be. If we truly open ourselves to the possibility of our fathers becoming accessible, we must then face expectations to do our part, to take risks and be vulnerable. We will have to behave in new ways that we are not used to.

Matt wanted to get to know his father better and to be known by his father, but the idea of calling him up and inviting him out to lunch was frightening. He was so rarely alone with his father he did not know what to expect. Matt thought about his fear and recognized:

> I'm not afraid of him as much as I am of myself. It was easy when I could put the blame on Dad and write him off as not interested. If he agreed to spend time with me, I'm scared I wouldn't know what to say. The burden would be on me to keep a conversation going. Maybe he's afraid of the same thing. That never dawned on me.

When we find ourselves holding back we need to examine our motivation carefully to be clear we are not simply being self-protective. All too often we justify halfhearted or coldhearted attempts at reconciliation and keep alive the focus on our hurt in the present because we are still trying to change the past. We cannot accept that we completed childhood without the fathering we wanted so deeply. We are not ready to move on.

It may feel like giving in to move toward forgiveness before we have allowed our rage free rein or received a sincere apology that recognizes the wrong done to us. So we look for our father to have the revelation that will awaken him.

Our concept of forgiveness, when we think this way, is too narrow. We need to accept the full range of our feelings about the disconnection in our relationship with our fathers, including our anger and hurt. But we need to use that acknowledgment to prepare ourselves to move forward, not remain mired in those feelings. Philip Greven, in *Spare the Child*, draws upon psychoanalyst Alice Miller's sage understanding of the nature of forgiveness even with an abusive person: "Genuine forgiveness does not deny anger but faces it head-on . . . only then will the way to forgiveness be open to me. Such forgiveness . . . is experienced as a form of grace and appears spontaneously when a repressed (because forbidden) hatred no longer poisons the soul."

This spontaneous forgiveness, however, comes only with considerable internal work to prepare us to move from the passive stance of a victim to a readiness to test the waters of change. We don't begin with forgiveness and then engage in the process; we go through the process, take an arduous journey, to arrive at the freedom and inner peace to be able to forgive. The path to reconciliation or resolution is through our own internal change and not through expecting our fathers to change first.

13

Preparing for the Journey

Recently I went for a walk with a friend and colleague. We were talking about how hard it is for someone who has been abused by a parent to overcome his or her anger and be open to any kind of closeness with that parent. My friend opened up at that point and told me how she had been abused by her own father. She admitted that for years she had denied the abusive behavior and then for more years had been so angry she wouldn't let him near her emotionally. She kept waiting for him to make the first move.

Much later she understood she was waiting not only out of anger, but out of hope and expectation. She desperately wanted the relationship to change. She was holding on to all her childhood expectations of her father and felt entitled to have them met. Finally, she realized that it wasn't going to happen that way. She could wait forever and he might never reach out his hand. She told me:

> I figured out that if it was going to happen, I had to do it. And I had to do it for myself, not for him. No matter what his response would be, it no longer mattered. I was going to reach out and make peace unilaterally, with no strings attached and no expectations. I'm the one who needed it and I would gain most of what I needed if I just did my part.

My friend didn't reach this epiphany through some mystical intervention. It took a great deal of hard work.

Part of this work for my friend involved overcoming the natural inclination to believe she was entitled to a good relationship with her father; that it was an inalienable right and therefore she shouldn't have to put herself through the demands of trying to make the relationship a better one. When we wait for our fathers to take the lead in improving the relationship it is no different than any other relationship where we hope the other guy will apologize or raise the flag of surrender first. Sometimes that strategy works, but it means we are putting the possibilities for fixing things in the other person's hands. That is a risky approach because it may not happen or may not happen in the way we want it to.

When we accept that we must take on the responsibility to bring about change if we really want it to occur, then we must also look at whether we still carry the kind of self-defeating attitudes that will block the way. To get beyond these we have some painful preparatory work on an emotional level. The preparation must be with ourselves so that we have worked on our own attitudes, arrived at our own clarity, and come to understand our own reactions and feelings enough to approach the act of reconciliation in a constructive frame of mind. To make peace, we have to want peace. To want peace we have to have dealt fully with the old feelings that saw our father as an adversary.

The film *Field of Dreams*, popular in the early 1990s, tapped into the pastoral romance of baseball and wholesome Midwestern values to capture the hearts of moviegoers. The film was really much more about the dream of reconciliation with a father than baseball per se, however. The hero, Ray Kinsella, an Iowa farmer, is told by a mystical baseball announcer, "If you build it, he will come." Ray listens to the voice and builds a baseball stadium on his farmland. One by one the Chicago Black Sox and Shoeless Joe Jackson materialize. Through this action Ray honors a dream of his deceased father's; in so doing, he creates his own opportunity to unite with the father he never really knew and to whom he had never taken the chance to extend an olive branch.

The building of the ballfield in the middle of an Iowa pasture and Ray's completion of the tasks assigned to him by the voice he hears offer a wonderful metaphor for how to make the journey of reconnecting with an estranged father. "If you build it, he will come" can be taken to mean that if we do our part to prepare and change ourselves, rather than look to our fathers to change, perhaps they "will come" after all. Indeed, in doing our internal preparation to ready ourselves for the work of reconciliation we may well become people who appear inviting to a father who has remained out in the cold. In this way, we increase the odds that he in turn will be receptive.

There are five steps, discussed in detail in the remainder of the chapter, that I regard as central to the self-work needed so that "he will come":

1. Reassess the relationship.
   - Take an inventory of your feelings about your father.
   - Re-examine significant family events and patterns, looking at your father's role and your behavior and reactions.
   - Learn about and take into account the context of your father's history and life apart from the family.
   - Reconsider attitudes and assumptions about your father.
2. Understand what has been lost in the relationship.
   - Examine the basic parenting needs your father failed to provide.
   - Recognize your feelings about these disappointments.
3. Experience your feelings of loss.
   - Recognize your feelings of anger associated with the disappointments and find constructive ways to express the anger.
   - Identify the complementary feelings that go along with your anger, particularly the sadness.
   - Allow yourself to grieve.
4. Look for the possibilities.
   - Distinguish your father's responsibility for the relationship failure from who must assume responsibility for reconciliation.
   - Identify positive traits in your father that you can value and connect with.
5. Determine your goals.
   - Clarify what you are looking for in the relationship.
   - Realistically assess what your father is capable of.
   - Assess what you are ready to put into the relationship.

As with any growth process, these steps do not follow unwaveringly from start to finish. They overlap and are interrelated. They reflect that this process of reconciliation, even at the outset, is layered and complicated. It is certainly not simply a matter of saying, "I'm sorry things have been this way for the past thirty years, but let's change them now." Even the first step of accurately reassessing the relationship can take a great deal of time and involve its own circuitous and difficult journey.

There were a number of years in my life when I merely went through the motions with my father. I had reasons to be angry at him for ways he had hurt me and my brothers, for his harshness, his lack of understanding, his unreasonable demands and expectations. Yet I could not turn my back on him. I was there for him in a dutiful way, maintaining contact and being helpful when needed. I was physically present, but emotionally estranged. I had convinced myself that I didn't expect more from the relationship.

This was my outlook about my father when I told my friend that I honestly didn't think I would be upset if my father died, as I related in "Author to Reader." When he told me that I was wrong, I did not believe him at the time. It was some months after this conversation that I related my story of the ladders and being sprayed by my father (recounted in the beginning of this book) to my office partners. Ending up in tears at that time taught me that I had been deceiving myself.

Regardless of what our dads are like and the nature of the relationship, we have lots of feelings about our fathers. We may hide these feelings from others and from ourselves, but they are deep and powerful. When we are aware of our feelings we may find ourselves caught in a quagmire of conflicting emotions: resentment, pride, disgust, sorrow, sympathy, yearning, rage, respect, disappointment, love. We are aware that on some level we are loved by our father, but we cannot feel it from him. We know we love our father, but, like him perhaps, avoid saying it directly; or if we say it, avoid truly letting ourselves feel it. Sometimes we can be so confused by this long-hidden mass of feelings that we cannot see the forest for the trees.

On a broader level, we may not only have hidden our feelings, but maintained a distorted sense of the nature of the relationship. We may have kept an ideal father on a pedestal and not recognized that he did not always deserve to be there. The abuse of fathers may have been transformed into mere strict discipline, the weakness of a father covered over, the absence too readily excused.

We may not recognize patterns of our own behavior in the relationship either: ways we jumped to protect our father or our quickness to blame him for everything that went wrong; how we were so keyed into winning his approval that we did not learn to achieve for ourselves or how we deflected his attempts to give encouragement; how we played the role of victim and left in his hands the power to judge and hurt us; or how we tried to make a victim of him when we fought back.

In August Wilson's play *Fences*, the wife of the protagonist tries to give her son perspective on his father and on the responsibility family members have in their relationship with him. She is hoping to help him move beyond his anger and rejection of his father, who has just died. She tells him: "I didn't know to keep up his strength I had to give up little pieces of mine. I did that. I took on his life as mine and mixed up the pieces so that you couldn't hardly tell which was which anymore. It was my choice. It was my life and I didn't have to live it like that."

To work toward healing our relationship we need clarity about our father's behavior and our response to him over the years, and we need to understand the dance we did together as we each struggled to maintain identity and self-worth. But perhaps most important, we must recognize and accept our part in the relationship. We must do this not from our perspective as a young child, indeed we were largely helpless to consciously shape the interaction with our father, but as the adult child. We must see the patterns of relating we developed out of our hurt or fear and our strategies for self-defense. We must take responsibility for those responses as adults and assess whether they are still appropriate or need changing.

In order to gain perspective on our own and our father's behavior as we grew up we need to re-examine family events and how both mundane and significant issues were handled. Siblings, relatives, family friends, family memorabilia, and parents can help us delve into the family history and reconstruct the dynamics of our relationship to our father. Group or individual therapy that encompasses exploration of family interactions can prove enormously helpful. In conducting this examination of family life it is important to shed the static version we have carried into adulthood and open ourselves to seeing through new lenses.

Two sets of lenses that will be useful are polar opposites. One allows you to view your father in the context of the whole family system in which he and you functioned. With the other you see him as an individual apart from the powerful influences of family dynamics. Within the family a father's influence is shaped by all the family members even as the rest of the family is affected by him. For example, some fathers feel excluded in their families by their wives' perceived domination, while others would seemingly never be involved if their wives didn't insist on it.

Below are some questions to ask yourself to help you reflect on the dynamics in the family that may have influenced the various roles your father played:

- Did the size of the family or special needs of individual family members place unusual demands on your father? A very large family or a developmentally disabled child, for example, could result in both added economic pressures and heightened stress at home.
- What did members of the family expect from your father? Was he sought after to help with homework, solve sibling disputes, or attend the kids' activities at school, for example?
- What were the roles your dad played in the family? Was he the sole breadwinner, the peacekeeper, the watchdog on spending?
- What was your parents' marriage like? Did your parents make decisions on an equal basis? Was your father active in determining their social life? Did they divide tasks on a traditional gender basis? How did your father show affection, anger, sadness with your mother?
- In what ways did you or other members of the family make it more or less difficult for your father to feel connected? In some families fathers are always invited ahead of time to participate in planned family activities, while in others the father may be invited only as an afterthought.

Charlene had for years carried out the unquestioning role of ally to a mother she felt had been mistreated by her father. She felt a justifiable anger at her father for leaving so many of the home responsibilities to her mother. When Charlene began to explore her anger in an effort to loosen its grip on her, she allowed herself to re-examine her father's relationship with her mother. She began to see that her father was not as unyielding as her mother painted him. Her mother was passive in ways that made her out to be a victim when she often had options available to her if only she would speak up. Becoming aware of this pattern freed Charlene from regarding her father as a villain and from having to hold on to her anger out of loyalty to her mother. She then became open to new possibilities in the relationship.

The pulls and demands of family life foster growth, but inevitably constrain who we are as well. It is important to look at your father apart from his conditioned familial behavior. Of course, fathers may exhibit dependence and helplessness when separated from their families, like those who cannot manage to cook and do laundry for a week when the family is away from them. A fuller picture of your father, however, requires viewing him apart from the normal routines and expectations of family life. What were his personal dreams and goals? Did these dreams become a reality, or did he sacrifice them for the well-being of the family? How did he behave in his private time, with friends away from the family, or in his work environment?

In sorting through his father's papers, Paul Auster, in *The Invention of Solitude*, was able to find an old letter of appreciation from one of his father's tenants. Some of the ledger was balanced for Auster by discovering that his father gave of himself to others, if not to his son. In rummaging through his own memories, Auster also recalled a time he fell in tar and came home a mess. That time his father could laugh and take him out for new clothes. A single memory like that can break ground with long-hardened feelings and invite a sense of closeness, as it did for Auster.

Another critical perspective for viewing our fathers is to be able to recognize when we are the projector and when we are the screen. We project so many attitudes and traits onto our fathers that reflect our interpretations and our need to see them a certain way. At best these are partially accurate; often they are gross distortions. We need to realize that many of our beliefs about our father's behaviors are only assumptions that have probably never been checked out.

I recall one man, for example, who always thought of his perfectionistic and critical father as being insufferably arrogant about his own knowledge. Together we traced some of the family history back to the paternal grandfather's behavior, and it became evident that the grandfather was even more critical than the father. I posed to this man the possibility that his father was far more insecure than he appeared and that his perfectionism was perhaps learned and came out of his own anxiety about doing things wrong around the grandfather. The idea that his father was insecure rather than arrogant left this fellow with the need to reassess many of his beliefs about his father's motivation and expectations in his treatment of his son.

Often we view fathers as more confident, for example, than they are. Caroline's parents were very active socially. She often heard her mother describe her dad as the "life of the party." Caroline envied what she believed to be her dad's ease with groups of people. She never took into account that his impoverished childhood made him fear being out of place with people of means, despite his success as an adult. His social skill was a front to keep others from guessing how uncomfortable he really was.

Fathers have sent their own messages that over the years have seeped into our consciousness and influenced our beliefs about ourselves. Some may be partial truths about us, but may also be distortions. One client who had worked hard on understanding his feelings about his father through writing about him said to me: "I need to remember that's me in the narrative that I'm talking about, not just Dad. It's a mirror on me of a lot of things in him."

Many fathers identify qualities in their children that reflect traits in themselves with which they are uncomfortable. One example is the father who sees his own sensitivity as a drawback for being strong enough to be successful in life. This father may have hidden his softer side, but been critical of his child for being too sensitive. The child then grows up believing there is something wrong with him or her for being this way.

The need to take a fresh look at the dynamics with our father extends to our beliefs about our own feelings and behavior and not simply about our father's end of the relationship. Most significant and common is the need to come to terms with how our father may have failed in meeting his parental obligation to us. We must consider what we depended on him for and how he responded to those needs. Moreover, each disappointment carried with it an emotional reaction on our part that is important to recognize. Exploring what we lost out on with our fathers is the second step of the self-work involved in preparing for reconciliation.

A young man named Drew had maintained throughout our conversations that his father had always been supportive and done all he could have asked for. Therefore, any problems he had and any unhappiness he carried were of his own making. Little by little it came out that Drew's father was very judgmental, though he was never direct about it. His disapproving attitude came with what he didn't say or with a particular look or question. As a result Drew learned he had to conceal particular aspects of his lifestyle if he didn't want to be judged.

There was a significant chunk of his life that he could not share with his father. He was not unhappy or ashamed of that part of his life. He was very unhappy that he couldn't be more open with his father and thus gain his full acceptance.

Until Drew allowed himself to face some things about his relationship with his father, he could not begin to recognize that anything was missing in that relationship. He had blamed himself for disappointing his father instead of realizing that he had been let down himself in some ways. He had not understood that a part of himself was lost in the process because he had to hide parts of himself that he valued but knew his father did not. He felt it was up to him to be a good son to his father and not his father's job to support him in being the person he was.

If we look to the basic needs we have from our fathers—security, guidance, affection, and validation—we will find the missing dimensions that cause us pain. When we weren't told we were good kids or taught how to fix things or helped with our fears, on some level we developed a longing, regardless of our conscious denial. To realize we lost something from our father, that there was something real to miss, can help us understand self-blame is not the answer. There is something to which we are reacting, so it's not just us.

When we experience a sense of loss about our fathers we are admitting that the relationship did and does matter. There is sadness to that acknowledgment of loss, but also satisfaction. It's better to know Dad matters than to have a father no more important than an appendix. If something was lost and it matters, it means there is something worth changing. Drew had believed his unhappiness was his own fault. When he saw that it came from a particular aspect of his relationship with his father, it gave him something on which to work.

To recognize that we have sustained a fundamental loss in the context of our paternal relationship is not a cold fact. It carries with it powerful emotional baggage. We have to recognize the loss with our hearts as well as our minds. It's not "just the way it was." We lost something important.

When I'm shaving and I nick myself, there is usually a little delay before the blood starts to flow. I kid myself and think maybe I got away with it this time. Maybe I won't bleed. It can be like this with our fathers. We would like to believe sometimes that we know we lost something but we don't have to feel sad. Unfortunately, we do feel sadness. When the father-child relationship is nicked or cut or gouged, there is bleeding. The blood comes in the form of grief.

Letting ourselves feel what we have lost with our fathers and giving expression to our sadness is the act of grieving. This third step is difficult for many, not only because they have suppressed their pain, but because it seems uncalled-for to grieve if our father is still alive. It also seems foreign to grieve for aspects of a relationship and not necessarily for a whole person.

Sometimes people will sit in my office and, after having worked up to it for weeks or months, let themselves cry and then sheepishly apologize for crying. I tell them that a father is worth crying for. We need to let out the grief in order to free ourselves to move forward, to get unstuck from the emotional distortions that come with keeping emotions suppressed. It is no different from the natural healing process that comes with grieving the death of a loved one. When people do not go through an appropriate mourning, they become knotted up with their feelings of guilt, remorse, and regret. It spreads throughout the rest of their being like a cancer. Here we are talking about partial deaths, but these, too, merit grieving.

Often the path to our grief winds first through our anger. Our hurt and disappointment may be more readily expressed in this form or may be known to us initially this way. In *The Wounded Woman*, Linda Leonard related a mythical tale, "The Courageous Girl," about the redemption of a father. In the tale the youngest daughter of a blind man goes on a dangerous journey to secure the medicine needed to cure her father. To do so, she must wrest the medicine from a three-headed, raging monster. Leonard interprets the tale this way: "Redemption of the father invariably seems to require facing monstrous rage and aggression, both one's own and that which the father himself was unable to integrate."

Regrettably, we can get stuck in our anger just as we can in our self-blame. As I have already noted, this unyielding anger can block us from recognizing the possibility of change. To work through our anger we have to find ways to express it constructively, but first we have to truly understand it.

Jules Henry, the noted social anthropologist, made the point in *Pathways to Madness* that anger is not a pure emotion, but an amalgam. We're angry-hurt or angry-frustrated or angry-sad. We need to learn that entwined with our anger at our fathers is our sadness. We need to give expression to both, but get mired in neither.

Charlene was a person who had been so bound by her anger at her father that it permeated all of her relationships. She had never felt free to let out her anger because her father's own tirades had always seemed so intimidating and ugly. What she found after being able to vent her anger in the safety of my office was that a new feeling emerged she had never experienced toward her father—sadness.

She had memories of how involved her father had been with her as a young child, and she realized that she longed for that kind of connection to him again. She knew she was missing something she had once had. She even recalled aspects of her father's life that she could sense would have been sad for him, and she could empathize. Recognizing her sadness then became a source of motivation to re-examine and work on the relationship.

One of the most helpful and productive exercises I utilize in my work with clients to help them express their anger in a constructive way and get in touch with the breadth of their feelings is to ask them to write a letter to their fathers. Before having anyone actually write the letter I spend considerable time identifying events and aspects of the relationship that may have been triggers for anger, hurt, and resentment. When people's awareness of these events has been heightened and they have been able to release much of the anger that has been stored up inside, they are then ready to work on the letter.

The scenario I suggest to establish a framework for writing to their dad is for them to imagine that their father is fully prepared to listen and to accept whatever they want to tell him. They are thus taking advantage of a singular opportunity to tell him whatever they need him to understand about themselves and the relationship. I urge them not to censor themselves and not to plan on sending the letter, though they may choose to follow up with some actual communication based on what they learn from the letter.

It can take weeks or months of exploring the relationship, seeking more information about your father, observing him if possible, and painstakingly searching within yourself to be ready to write a letter that says what you want it to say and speaks from a cleansed heart. This letter becomes an opportunity to organize thoughts and feelings. It expresses the full range of emotional reactions and raises the questions and doubts and wishes that have long swirled around the relationship.

I have included an actual letter from Todd to his father. Todd's letter demonstrates the kind of clarity and perspective gained with this letter-writing exercise when we have done our emotional homework and our readiness has ripened.

Dear Dad:

I remember riding in the car with you, I think you had picked me up from someplace, taking me back home, and we drove along silently. Maybe the radio was playing. Close to our street you said to me, "A penny for your thoughts, Todd." I was surprised, taken aback, wondering both what I was thinking about that I could share off-handedly with you, and where did that question come from? I wasn't used to your gentleness.

Somehow the preoccupied man was the father I pushed against. It used to make me very mad that you did not hear what I had to say, that I had to repeat myself. Mom added to this, letting us know you as a ruler, a father who would come home from bowling and really let us have it. I didn't like her anger, but I was more afraid of the threat that you represented.

I think I saw you as underneath Mom's certainty and opinionated vibrancy. I think I saw you become a servant for her. In my eyes this looked like losing your self. I didn't see the service in it; I saw a man throwing himself away. I didn't like that. But I also took it as a model; when I was married I thought it necessary to do everything for my wife. I didn't like that either.

We kids giggled at your funny stories, songs, and actions, but I was afraid of you, too. You scared me with your temper. I always wanted to be good, and sometimes it was obvious that you didn't understand my intentions. I was reminded recently of your term, "freeloader." I found a bird's nest up under the awning once, and wanted to stop the yard work in order not to disturb it. You got disgusted, maybe called me a "freeloader." I didn't like it. I felt hurt, not known.

What do I remember as good—going to the circus, sitting in the third row, center, just the two of us on my birthday. Going for drives in the car after work, in the summer, all of us. All of the presents you would buy for us, all of the cookies and ice cream, the coffee cakes on Sunday.

Some of this became the acts of service which I eventually dismissed. The circus stands out as a rare and profound time with you, alone.

I was always aware that alcohol was a power in our lives. It was to me another in the many routines I saw you do each day: get up, kneel down to pray, fill up the sink with water, shave, get dressed, put on a tie, sit at the table with a cup of coffee with milk, half a grapefruit and newspaper, and then leave for work. At 5:30 you would return home. Mom and you would have a manhattan or two, I don't remember, and then after dinner you'd go off to the store or to take a nap, then do dishes, do your office work or water the lawn. I don't remember how often or if every night there were bottles of beer to go with these evening activities, but I do remember beer.

It was part of the routine, but I never liked it. I was afraid of it. Maybe I did not want the compulsion I saw in you. But I also wasn't comfortable in the model of scatteredness I found in Mom. So where did that leave me?

I never questioned your loyalty or devotion to us. I learned a lot about offering love to other people, being generous in all ways. You didn't seem to care what others thought of you, your dress or manners, and I respect that now, but again it was hard to see this. I didn't want to look at you. I was afraid of you.

I think your structured personality set up a secure house for me to grow up in, but it also meant that I had to push against a lot of walls. Some of your resistance to my questions now seems like wisdom and some of it restricted me, did not allow me to become independent.

I don't know what it is that as a child scared me so much that I now lack faith in myself and my abilities. Our house had confusion, anxiety, and limits. I responded by trying to do away with all of this in my life. I wanted to be clear, calm, and capable. That is a solution, a rescue mission. It was a way to survive.

There was something missing. It is as if someone yelled too loud and I got shell-shocked. I went inside where it was quieter. When I was a little more secure, not much but a little, when I came out, most of you was gone. The powerful man in the world was gone, the social man was gone, the successful man was gone, and all I had before me was a dwindling man, falling back on the compulsion of habits, beer, and acts of service.

You continue to be a source of a confusing paradox for me: a spiritual man full of service who is hot-headed and full of bridled anger. A man who loves parties and fun and talks to people but who I am afraid to look at, that I am embarrassed by. I'm very confused by the example of your gentleness interspersed with something I didn't want to get near.

I understand your life as my legacy. I've been trying to pinpoint what it is that was withheld from me. I often presume that you had it and didn't give it, but maybe this isn't so. Maybe you never had it to give. Maybe I'm longing for something you didn't have to give.

I am looking for what was missing. I am looking for the skills that will allow me to move out into the world.

I can hear your last words to me: "Your mother and I believe in you, Todd." But why do I not believe in myself?

This is all for now. I send this with love.

Your son, Todd

Todd's letter reflects far more groundwork than could be apparent from reading it. He had to come to terms with the likelihood that his father was an alcoholic and that his dad had engendered considerable fear in Todd that hampered him in how he lived his own life. After acknowledging his fear and disappointment it became easier for Todd to see the good in his father.

This letter does not say, however, "Now that I see you more clearly, everything is wonderful." Todd recognized his confusion and mixed feelings. More important, he had opened a closet door on those feelings and as a result no longer had to hide from his father or hide his father from himself. He was less inclined to feel ashamed of himself for his reticence and his dependent side. He was more forgiving of his father even as he was more forthright about his father's weaknesses and honest about his power.

Todd's father was deceased, and so it was not possible to follow up the letter by actually talking to him. Had he been alive and not actively drinking I believe Todd could have addressed many of his concerns with him. He was ready. He was also ready to forgive himself and to take responsibility himself for what was indeed missing in his life—to give himself the validation his father could not offer until his dying words.

The emotional progression for Todd reflected in his letter would have taken him to the fourth step—to being ready to move forward and look for the possibilities in the relationship. At this point in our preparation for the journey we must separate whatever we see as our father's responsibility for the distance and dysfunction in the relationship from who will be responsible for initiating reconciliation. Paul Auster said of his estranged, deceased father in *The Invention of Solitude*: "We were fixed in an unmovable relationship, cut off from each other on opposite sides of a wall. Even more than that, I realized that none of this had anything to do with me. It had only to do with him."

We need to know that the barriers to a closer relationship may in some cases lie exclusively or at least largely with our fathers. This can free us from the self-blame and self-questioning that can make attempts at reconciliation seem pointless or impossible. There may be severe limits on what can happen in such an impaired relationship, but if one person in it becomes free from anger, resentment, and blame, it can clear the atmosphere enough to make a new beginning.

Far more often we have created a straw man out of our hurt and frustration, the father in whom we can only see bad. Much of the blame or anger we have been carrying may be displaced from ourselves onto him. Sam Osherson in *Finding Our Fathers* exhorts that "for a man to grow up he must find the good and the strong in his own father." The importance for Osherson of seeking a positive connection with a father is tied to the role of the father in shaping a son's identity. For a son or daughter, it is easier to move toward reconciliation if he or she can go beyond the negatives to see one's father's redeeming qualities and the possibility of allying with those things that are good in him. After all, it is difficult to move closer to someone whom we can't respect or have good feelings about.

It is unfortunately true that even when we are looking for something positive to latch on to, it is not always easy to find. The weight of a father's abusive behavior or his absence or his critical attitude may have buried the good. Sean spent weeks talking about his father before he got to a positive memory. For a brief period his father was the troop leader for his Cub Scout group, and he took them on some fun camping trips. This one recollection took an edge off Sean's bitter view of his dad. He knew his father had another side.

Another man, whose father had been terribly abusive, could not feel anything positive, but in recalling how his father had endured years of oppressive factory work, he could feel a modicum of respect. He could also link his own stubborn determination with his father's character.

When we find some way to value our fathers, we soften our own pain about them. They become more human, understandable, and accessible. We have reasons to want to connect to them. When a father alienated from his child experiences that child mellowing toward him, his own pain is likely to be eased. He becomes more approachable and perhaps more willing himself to approach.

We have reached the endpoint in our emotional preparation when we can see our fathers more fully and honestly and are willing to assume the responsibility for initiating healing because we want to change ourselves more than our fathers. It is at this stage that we must take the step to determine what we really want from the relationship and what is realistically possible to achieve.

As the mother in the play *Fences* told her son, "It was my choice. It was my life and I didn't have to live it like that." She was looking at the past. The future in our relationships is also our choice—not exclusively, but substantially. Relationships, just as with any other situation in life, are far less likely to change in the way we desire if we do not define and set our sights on what we hope to accomplish.

I often hear people voice a sincere desire to make peace with their fathers and then get lost in a morass of old hurts that seem to need to be redressed. Ron was like this. He had for years bottled up the hurt from his autocratic father because he feared hurting his father with the rush of recrimination he expected to pour out. He had imagined that his father had to understand all the ways he had wronged Ron in order to get their relationship on track. In time, once he had himself given expression to how wounded he felt, Ron realized that he didn't have to dump all these grievances on his father. He simply needed to know that he could be in charge of who he was in the relationship, that he didn't have to be controlled or intimidated anymore.

Getting our hurt out, either by ourselves or with a supportive third party, isn't always sufficient to give us clarity about what we need to do with the relationship with our father. We may have a residue of anger or pain that we cannot get past unless we bring it up directly with him.

We may have questions we need answered about our father personally or about his behavior toward us or others in the family.

June realized she was not ready to risk more with her father until he could tell her why he had moved in and out of her life all these years. She had specific questions she wanted to ask him about what had led to the divorce and what made him so angry at certain times. She said: "If he was willing to answer those questions for me I knew he was also ready for a changed relationship. If he could do that, I thought I could let go of the past. So I decided my next step was to ask him to help me let go of the past by answering my questions."

Here are some key clarifying questions you can ask yourself before approaching your father:

- What old wounds must you address with your father before you can move any further toward reconciliation? Do you need to talk with him about acts of abuse, absences or unavailability at important occasions, or disturbing criticisms?
- What do you need to get from your father—acknowledgment, apology, understanding of your feelings?
- Are you ready to spend time with your father? What kind of time: the two of you alone or only with others; recreational, conversational, or intimate time; occasional or frequent time together; For long or short periods?
- Are you ready to show him affection? To ask for affection from him? To receive affection if it is offered?
- Are you ready to be honest with him about your present feelings? What about feelings from the past?

All of these questions represent decisions you make about the nature of the relationship. If you regard them as choices and not just questions, then you realize you have considerable control over the shape of your relationship. You do not determine your father's own choices and responses, but you can do a lot to influence them. You do not have to await his actions passively. When you are passive you may believe you are innocently waiting for him to show his hand, but in fact your passivity can shape his reactions as much as any other kind of conduct.

Reconciliation can take many forms. You may want to have an idyllic, openly loving relationship with your father but find that either you or he or both of you are ready only for more modest goals. It is help-ful to have a realistic sense not only of your own readiness but of your father's, of what he can tolerate in the way of intimacy and perhaps confrontation. It is far more critical, however, to know what you are prepared to do than to guess at his readiness level. You may be quite incorrect about where he is or, more likely, how he might change with the right cues or constructive gestures on your part.

One of the most common roadblocks to a successful journey is to be drawn into the past. Not only do we have a difficult time letting go of our feelings about old wounds, but we may look to our fathers to play out a role in the present that is anachronistic. We may still want him to fulfill the basic functions we needed from him as we grew up. We may look to him to help us curb our own out-of-control behavior or bail us out of financial jams. We may want him to point the way when we are confused or lead the way when we are lost. There are, of course, spe-cial circumstances when it is appropriate as an adult to seek such parental support from a father. In general, though, the degree to which we routinely continue to count on our father for any of these basic childhood needs is a measure not only of his earlier failure, but also of our inability to overcome it.

Even the acceptance and affection we will always want and need from our fathers takes on a different context if we are not healed in regard to the past relationship. It is the acceptance and affection of our dads that we usually most desire when we seek as adults to reconcile. If the relationship is not healed, however, we tend to seek approval and love to validate our own identity rather than for their own sake. Many sons and daughters become stuck at this juncture. They cannot fully heal without receiving their father's validation or come to terms with the fact that they will not receive it.

Mostly what people truly need and want from their relationships with their fathers is uncomplicated and fits with adult needs. They want to feel some degree of closeness; spend time together free of long-standing ten-sions; carry on normal conversations and know they are listened to and appreciated; spend time together and not feel like strangers; get to know who their fathers are and have them know who they are; hear directly that they are loved; and be free to tell their fathers they love them.

When people aren't clear about what they want, when these basic desires do not come into focus, there are a couple of simple questions

I often ask that seem to help bring clarity: If you could have the ideal conversation with your father, what is it you would most need to have him understand about what you want from him? Or, if you or your father were expected to die, what would need to happen for you to feel at peace with him?

If we start with inflated, romanticized ideas about a fatherly relationship that rights all the wrongs for all the years or achieves perfect harmony, we set ourselves up for disappointment and the continued cycle of resentment. We must not require that our fathers remake themselves to engage in healing the relationship. In helping people work on their own ties with their fathers, I explore with them what their father's relationship with their grandfather was like. Usually it was considerably worse. I remind them that in one generation we can only expect to travel so far.

When you work on your own feelings and attitudes toward your father, you can reach a point of clarity and peace within yourself about what you need from him. As a result you will be more open and accessible yourself, which in turn will invite a greater degree of receptivity from your father. He may eventually be more able to come to you, but initially the hope is that he will be more willing to let you in when you come knocking yourself.

In the preface of *The Wounded Woman*, Linda Leonard relates how her father changed from a loving father to an alcoholic and how she came to reject him as a result. The act of writing her book started her back toward her father. At one point she decided to put on the ring he had given her for her twenty-first birthday, his one gift to her in the midst of years of disconnection. Wearing the ring helped her to feel closer. She knew then that she had to write her personal story of her relationship with her father, which moved her from her theoretical understandings to positive feelings she had long buried. She was ready to let him back into her life when she could see through his negative traits to what symbolized his specialness: "My way back to the magic of my father was to allow these images to live in myself." Her experience reminds us that the door opens from the inside as we begin our journey back to our fathers.

14

Starting the Journey

I awoke and I imagined the hard things
that pulled us apart
Will never again sir tear us from each other's
hearts . . .
My father's house shines hard and bright
It stands like a beacon calling me in the night
Calling and calling so cold and alone
Shining cross this dark highway
Where our sins lie unatoned.

"My Father's House," Bruce Springsteen

I indicated in *Author to Reader* that I had worked on my own relationship with my dad over a ten-year period. I want to share some of that experience with you in the hope that it may help guide and motivate you in your own journey. When I hear friends or clients despair about ever making progress with their fathers, I let them know my dad was in his eighties when our relationship began to change.

I lean backward in my seat and stare out across an expanse of clouds that separate the brilliant sky from the anonymous land below. I am flying to Miami, Florida, to take part in a panel discussion at a national conference. I am also due to meet my father in Miami, where we will share a hotel room while I attend the conference and then go on for two days to his condominium north of Miami. This trip is unusual and tension-laden for two reasons: I have not spent more than an hour or two alone with my father that I can remember in almost twenty-five years; and I have decided to invite my father to sit in the audience of our panel discussion. The last time my father heard me speak in public was my high school graduation speech.

My mind wanders back to those high school years when he and I were the only ones left at home. These were rich years for me personally as I made the most of wonderful friendships and a fine school environment. I had constructed a life that had been designed to please my father, yet cordon him off from real involvement with me.

He has never been an easy man to be with. His childhood had been harsh and ascetic both emotionally and materially. My mother's death at thirty-five, leaving him with three young sons, had stunned and bewildered him. His view of life was jaundiced, but he maintained a demanding standard for his sons, perhaps in the belief that we would thereby be spared the hardships he had encountered. He did not understand how painful his critical, exacting nature could be and that his sons were achieving in spite of it, not because of it.

I remember the ladder incident, described earlier, when I became outraged at his disregard for my being. When I sprayed him with the hose it marked a kind of emancipation at the time—one of the few times I stopped being a good boy and let him know, albeit indirectly, that I was hurt and angry and tired of being taken for granted. At that time, and for years after, I thought I could do without him; that my best strategy to avoid further hurt was to keep him at arm's length. In college I returned home only for short visits and stayed with one of my brothers. I kept my father perfunctorily informed. During the turbulent years at Harvard in the late sixties one of my brothers worried about me, the other was always prepared to rescue me, and my father was always kept in the dark.

Twenty years ago I had managed to convince him not to come to my college graduation because I dreaded being embarrassed by him. Now I was inviting him for the first time to hear me speak as a professional. I had no idea how he would handle it or how others might perceive him or how I would relate to him in such a setting. What was really new for me was that I wasn't going to try to control it. I wasn't going to per-

form for him or anyone else there. I wasn't going to cover for who he was or be on guard against what I knew he could be.

I come out of my reverie in time for the landing and feel my grip loosen on the armrests. I know I have made an important decision. I have decided to let him into my life and find out what will happen.

As it turned out the panel discussion was more than I bargained for. There was a small turnout, and therefore it was clear from the outset that my father would not be set off anonymously somewhere in a crowded room. We formed a circle of chairs, and everyone sat together with no separation at all between presenters and participants. My father sat next to me and proudly introduced himself to the group as having come to hear his son. For my part, having no buffer between myself and my father initially made me uneasy. My fears were intensified because in such an intimate setting there was a higher risk of somehow being embarrassed by my father.

Once we moved past the preliminaries, I relaxed and focused on the task ahead. I felt bolstered by the warm reception my fellow panelists gave my father and by their supportive recognition that something special was happening today between a father and son. The theme of the panel discussion was on the use of stories in therapy and how the stories of men and women tend to differ.

At one point I related a personal vignette about what it had been like to grow up without a mother. As I told my story I was not conscious of my father being next to me. As I finished, however, I became aware that the eyes of the group were focused on my dad. Then I heard the sniffles from my father and turned to see tears in his eyes.

I had seen my father cry before on occasion, either about my mother's death or my brother's. It had always seemed to be about his own pain, which was, of course, ample. I don't remember him ever before showing such recognition and empathy for my pain. In fact, I doubt that I ever expressed anything about my own pain to him. I didn't quite know what to do and can't recall clearly what I did, although I think I started to put a hand on his shoulder and then reached for his hand.

Someone in the group tenderly asked him if he could express his feelings—again probably something which had rarely, if ever, occurred for him. He explained that he had never heard me talk about my mother's death as it affected me and that he realized he had not understood what *it was like for me. He said that he didn't know much about children or what to expect from them; that he had responded as best he could, but he realized now that there had been much more to being a father than he had comprehended.*

Obviously the group was touched by this glimpse into the emotional scrapbook of a father and son. The discussion went on, but the course of history with my father was altered. I felt a hopefulness about what might possibly take place between us that I had never felt before.

After the conference we made the two-hour drive back to his home and began our forty-eight-hour marathon of being together. While in the car and with the open spirit of the conference still with us, I started asking questions about his reactions to the panel discussion. My father tried to answer honestly, but it soon became apparent that I was asking in my language about subjects that were familiar to me. Whatever had touched him emotionally with the group had shrunk from his consciousness. We couldn't get back on track.

Over the past five years or more I had made a point of getting my father to talk about our family and his personal history. This had always been neutral territory that interested me and about which he enjoyed talking. Once back at his condominium I pursued this tack once again, but was determined to take it to a more personal level than in the past.

I started with an innocent question: "What was your favorite period of your life?" His answer, while I should have expected it because it fit with everything I knew about him, nevertheless stunned me. "To be honest," he said, "I never really knew happiness. There was always something, some troubles."

So there it was—a plain, dumb fact staring me in the face. He had never known happiness, so, of course, he was not able to show happiness. The lightness, the softness, the sensitivity, and warmth we wanted during all those years were not a part of his repertoire.

He readily started talking after this remark about more of the history behind it. It amazed me that after forty-two years of knowing this man and numerous conversations where I probed his mental archives, I was for the first time getting a clear picture of what his childhood was like. Having the time and the patience, since nothing else demanded our time and we had no distractions, was an important factor in allowing his story to unfold.

I had always known that the Polish village in which he grew up was situated inside the front lines during World War I and saw the Russian and German armies seesaw back and forth. Since I was little I had heard the story from time to time about the Russian soldier who threatened to shoot my grandfather as a spy for opening the rear bedroom door while their house was occupied.

On this day I heard for the first time that my father's home burned down for the second time when he was eleven, and the family lived in the cellar of an abandoned dwelling while my grandfather built a new home. Just as the family prepared to move into their new home in time for Passover, probably in 1915, the Germans descended and the town fell under siege. Shortly afterward, the Russians retook the town and ordered the inhabitants to vacate it. My father became a refugee in his homeland until the end of the war.

Five years after that, he became an immigrant in America. I imagined myself, or better yet my own children, at eleven facing the terror and chaos of war and being uprooted repeatedly through the growing-up years. I understood better the insecurity that characterized my father's early years and that became the psychological underpinning for much of his adult behavior.

The next day my father hauled out his motley collection of family pictures and memorabilia. He had saved my entire correspondence with him from college and graduate school, as well as much of my brothers'. He wanted me to take all these home. He was passing along to me what little of the family history was documented.

Amid the familiar pictures of my childhood years were photos from his young adulthood in America. In little two-by-two inch black and white pictures here was a father I never knew. My father at the center of a cheerful camp group in upstate New York holding the medicine ball—my father who had never played catch with me in all my years. My father standing casually by a sports car smiling, with two pretty women in a scene somewhere in Arizona. My father perched tall on a mountain peak in the Rockies, barechested and looking dauntless. These were sides of him I had not known—a playfulness and boldness and free-spiritedness that I could not readily connect with him, but which warmed my heart.

By the next morning I could sense his mood shifting toward melancholy, in sync with the darkening sky and thickening air as a rainstorm approached. I felt his sadness at my leaving reverberating in my bones.

I could tell how much I meant to him despite his inability to articulate it. He surprised me, though, by telling me: "I really enjoyed this. We never have time like this together. Just the two of us. We should do it more often." He busied himself after that trying to locate other items he could send home with me.

I sat alone for a few moments and reflected on the importance of this visit, this healing time together. I looked up at the calendar on his wall and noticed that it was still on April, though it was well into May. Time is meaningless for him these days of living alone, I thought. He comes alive with our visits. There was a saying on the calendar: "Sometimes a path cut through hard stone leads to a soft life." Not his. I was glad for this visit and allowed myself to embrace the idea that it had meant a great deal to me and not just to him. It had been a fair exchange. I thought to myself: I give you a son, you give me a father.

A few months later my father came for his annual summer trek north. There was clearly a carryover of companionship from the spring visit. I was more at ease with him. He was different with me in some subtle ways. He was listening attentively to me when I talked and with an involvement that seemed new. He asked questions about what I was doing or about my friends or our family life that showed me he had been taking in what I had previously told him and that conveyed his own sense of involvement in my life.

One evening I arrived home to a joyful reception by him. My father was so happy to see me, he was walking down the driveway with a smile even as I drove up. He had been working on a set of window boxes for us and had the air of a person absorbed in a labor of love. He followed me into the kitchen and we got caught up on the day's events. My wife and children were out for the evening so I pictured the two of us having dinner together and more of that time alone he had prized.

As I started preparing the dinner, I looked around and realized he was gone. He had returned to his work on the window boxes. I told him to take a break and join me, but he waved me off and told me he needed to keep working, though he had plenty of free time to complete that project.

At first a familiar angry reaction started to seep in. I was being ignored again, as with the ladders, as with so much of childhood. Then a different perspective came to me. I thought about the innocent, lov-

ing countenance with which he had greeted me. This man was now so consumed by getting a project done he would pass up this golden opportunity to be together. He would certainly have wanted to have that time, too.

It dawned on me that it was a compulsion that kept him working away during time that would otherwise have been precious to him. He had to get his job done and done right, as he had always had to do. As a child around him I experienced this behavior as a demand for perfection. Now I could see this compulsion was his response to his own childhood—to the chaos and the insecurity and the sternness of that solemn-faced grandfather who blankly stared at me from my father's bookshelf where his lone picture was placed.

It wasn't about me at all. It was about establishing the little bit of order to his life that was familiar to him. That was such a fundamental force in him that it overpowered all the rest. He couldn't be with me until he got his work done. From him I, too, had learned that I couldn't be okay until I got my work done. It wasn't about love. It was about survival. Then and now.

A few days later as we drove to the airport I noticed that I didn't have the sense of relief I had always had before when a visit was over and we had gotten through it without any lasting conflict. This time he was leaving town, but not exiting my life. At the airport as we stood around somewhat anxiously waiting for his flight to depart he looked suddenly vulnerable to me. I pictured him returning to his empty condominium and its contrast to our life-filled home.

We heard the boarding call and it jolted us. My father thanked us for the visit and remarked about how fortunate we were to have such wonderful friends and how he had appreciated being included with them in our lives. He gave my wife a tender, loving hug and kiss such as I had never seen him give anyone before. He was a touch less tender with me, perhaps to ease his pain.

As he walked down the ramp into the hull of the plane he looked agonizingly alone and fragile, yet, I thought, incredibly courageous. He would go on with his life and continue to be a survivor amid whatever life dealt him. I felt a deep sadness for the loneliness that was enveloping him. I was also aware of the freshness of that emotion. I could feel sad for him. I could miss him. I, too, could feel alone as he left. Tears came of their own volition. At first a mere welling up, but as I sat down

and let it come, a full torrent. I ached, but also there was a definite con-
sciousness that I wanted to rejoice at having these feelings at last. It
was a long journey home.

The personal story I have just related does not reflect a completed journey. Perhaps the work to heal relationships with our fathers is like the twelve-step programs for people who have addictions. We are always recovering, never recovered. The relationship will surely require continuous effort if the problems have been severe and the emotional distance prolonged.

As I look back on my own experience with my father I see that there was no single true starting point for the journey toward healing. There were multiple transition points where I became more aware of my own feelings or clearer about him or more resolute about my intentions. Each of these transitions reflected movement in the direction of healing.

There is, however, usually a definable point when we shift the focus of our efforts at reconciliation from preparation to overtly attempting to alter the relationship itself. For me this moment came when I chose to invite my father to sit in on the workshop. Much followed from that decision. It required me to face my feelings more directly and to recognize that I wanted to work on changing the relationship. I had conceded that change might be possible and that I had to explore that possibility.

15

First Steps

To prepare for our journey we reexamine the past, take stock of our own feelings and behaviors, vent our anger, experience our pain, grieve what we have lost, and reassess what we want in the future. To do this inner work, we reflect, ask questions, talk, write, cry, and dream. Finally, we reach a point when we have done all the inner work we can without moving outside ourselves and interacting with our father. We need to discover what is actually possible with him. We need the taste of reality to verify what we have learned and tell us whether we are on the right track.

As with virtually any challenge in life about which we are anxious, taking the initial step is the hardest part. Ron had worked with me in therapy for almost a year, largely trying to sort out his father's impact on his life and hoping to find a way to overcome the limitations in their relationship. He was terribly worried about coming on too strong and hurting his father. Ron had so many different thoughts and feelings that he feared he would overwhelm his father, but he was himself overwhelmed.

For several weeks Ron kept planning to take the first steps and open up to his father about his desire to heal their relationship. We did practice runs where he talked through what he might say depending on how his father responded. He would leave with the best of intentions and come back the next time sheepishly explaining his inability to follow through. At one point he finally acknowledged, "I just can't get over the threshold. I don't know how to start."

Ron was a college professor and taught writers' workshops in the summer. I asked him what he advised participants in his workshops when they complained of writer's block. He didn't hesitate to answer, and he instantly got the connection. With a nodding smile he said, "I know. Just start. You can say anything at all to begin with, just get it going any way you can." There are no perfect openers.

When there has been no communication at all for some period of time, simply to initiate conversation can be a meaningful beginning. Otherwise, just to talk is inadequate. When you can get past the initial icebreaker you must find a way through what you say or the tone you use that conveys an openness, if not a clear desire, to change and develop the relationship.

One way to signal your interest in connecting with your father is to initiate contact in ways that don't normally occur. Often these ways are shockingly obvious and easy, except for our own discomfort with what is unfamiliar and therefore awkward. When I tell people to simply arrange a lunch or breakfast or event or try conversing with their father when he answers the phone instead of letting him turn the call over to their mother, they sometimes look at me dumbfounded, as if to say, "It's that easy! No, it can't be."

Besides meeting over food or beverage (don't make the mistake of going for a drink with a father who may use the opportunity to abuse alcohol), any chance to talk without interruption and alone will do: just going for a walk or driving somewhere or inviting him to do something you used to do when you were younger, such as fishing, golfing, or working on a project.

Matt surprised his father one day by calling him at work and arranging to visit him later that day. This was something Matt could have done a hundred times before, but he never thought it was the right thing to do. He assumed his father would either be upset or uncomfortable. Over the years it had always seemed unfair to Matt to see his father go off to the factory and return at night so depleted. It was as though his dad left for a forbidden land where family members were excluded, only to have him furloughed for the evening but under strict orders not to talk.

Now as he waited in the reception area for his dad to meet him, Matt was so nervous his palms began to sweat. The look on his father's face changed all that in an instant. It was obvious he was thrilled to have Matt take time out of his own busy schedule to come out to the factory. He proudly showed Matt around the physical plant and introduced him to his buddies. Afterward Matt realized the gesture itself of coming there said far more about his father's importance to him than any words spoken that day. At that point in their relationship it was a wonderful way for Matt to have gotten the message across.

For Matt the fact that he chose a dramatic and unusual way to alter the typical pattern of relating to his father made it unnecessary to spell out his purpose. The act spoke for itself. This will not usually be the case. Fathers may be surprised to be invited fishing after not having been for a long time, but that doesn't mean they will hear the request as wanting to change the nature of the relationship.

Any situation that brings you together with your father can still be used to maintain the status quo. It is essential in most instances that you make the point of saying to your father why you are initiating contact. It need not be a statement that dredges up the pain of the past, nor does it require a sentimental gushing forth. It can be as basic as: "Dad, I really enjoyed this time together. When I asked you to have lunch I was doing it because I want to see more of you and have us know each other better than we have. I hope you'd like that, too."

A prolonged physical distance and/or ongoing state of conflict with a father calls for a different forum to be used to connect with him and a more delicate approach. Many are tempted to write their father as an initial step because it frees them to voice their upset without having to face his response on the spot.

While letter-writing is an excellent exercise for consolidating feelings about a father and a fine way to maintain communication between two people who are close, it is not an ideal vehicle for healing a discordant relationship. With letters we lack the opportunity to get the immediate feedback that tells us we have been understood and permits us to correct misunderstandings. Sometimes, however, the mail is our best or only choice, particularly because it can provide the safety needed to be honest.

For Andrew, the only way he felt he could initiate reconciliation with his father was through an exchange of letters. This mode of communicating assured Andrew control over what he said and prevented his father from interrupting, dominating, or not listening to Andrew's full message. The letters slowed the process between them because neither could respond immediately as in a conversation. Also, the balance of power was shifted in a constructive way since Andrew felt more in control of the process.

The primary drawback to this approach was that Andrew felt so free to vent his anger and frustration he overlooked the need to spell out the underlying positive nature of why he was initiating his correspondence, that is, to try to alter the destructive dynamics in the relationship so he and his father could become closer. Since Andrew reviewed the letter with me I was able to point out this oversight.

While our preparatory work will have allowed us to gain perspective on our anger so we are oriented toward letting it go, reconciliation or resolution for ourselves may well require addressing our anger with our fathers. At issue is timing and how to present our anger in a constructive fashion. To lead with our anger or with blaming statements is the surest way to bring on defensiveness.

There will be ample opportunity to get anger out if an atmosphere of trust and consideration is established. To do this, we must first make clear to our father that our intentions are toward making peace; that we are willing to hear his point of view and we want to know and understand him better; that we are voicing our feelings in order to get beyond our hostility and to bring about an improved relationship.

When you are ready to spend time with your father, it is important to remember that the father you are ready to meet is not necessarily the father you have avoided. Fathers normally mature and change with the circumstances of their lives and the stages of their psychological development. For example, as was pointed out to me by a colleague, the father who was immersed in building a successful career and therefore was underinvolved with his young children might at a later point be a willing and wonderful mentor for his adult children.

Matt, who had always found his father inaccessible, was delighted to encounter a playful, relaxed side of his father in retirement that made the idea of doing things together inviting. Observing this side of his father helped Matt understand that a significant part of his father's inaccessibility was related to the stresses of daily work.

It may also help stimulate new patterns of relating to interact with your father in an environment outside of the usual family dynamics. You may both be a little uncomfortable initially, but also less prone to the old routine behavior that may have sustained the distance between you. Sylvia was shocked at how different her father acted when her mother went on a long trip. He didn't act in his usual scattered, histrionic fashion, and he demonstrated more initiative and confidence than she had ever seen. She turned to him for advice and felt supported by him in response—a totally new experience for her with him.

For many, being with your father on a one-to-one basis is an astonishingly rare event. Intimacy requires private, individual time. Much of the distance that characterizes father-child relationships can be sustained because of the lack of such time together. One-to-one time, whether over breakfast, on a walk, or in the car driving to a ballgame, allows you to speak directly to your father without the potential interference, jealousy, or judgment of others. It also puts you in the position of being your own spokesperson to your father about your feelings. There will be no distortions or inaccurate portrayals of your feelings by others, and your father will be able to hear and ask for himself what is important to you.

Direct contact with fathers, unadulterated by the input or perceptions of others, also will help you gain your own accurate picture of your father. As Robert Bly and others have pointed out, sons and daughters have too frequently learned who their fathers were through their mothers. A mother's perceptions, for example, may be a well-intentioned way to bridge the gap between father and child, but could also be an exercise in bitter venting. In either case, the children are deprived of the bonding that comes with directly gaining personal knowledge of their fathers. Siblings, too, may have their own agendas or points of view that complicate rather than clarify the relationship.

Relying on an intermediary* to conduct the work of relationship-building with our father, whether it is learning more about him or attempting reconciliation, undermines our goal. Utilizing someone else to carry our message can convey to the father that we are afraid to speak up ourselves. It also can promote the sense that the relationship requires insulation and hence continued distance. It is not only the father's thinking along these lines that may be reinforced, but our own as well. In addition, we lose the psychological validation to be gained by voicing our own concerns and facing our father directly in an adult manner.

Using an intermediary may not work because the communication may get garbled in the process. It also may never occur. Kafka's famous

---

*None of this is to suggest that a family therapist would not prove helpful. Indeed, a therapist would seek to open and support direct communication with a father as well as identify ways to overcome impediments to such communication.

Letter to His Father illustrates this danger. Kafka anticipated a negative reaction from his father to his heartfelt letter, which expressed much hurt but also a desperate desire to repair their damaged relationship. Perhaps as a result of this anticipated response, Kafka gave the letter to his mother to transmit to his father. She chose never to pass it along. Soon after Kafka died, apparently without reconciling with his father.

Some people complain that they can never get their fathers to be alone with them or that their mothers or even siblings won't respect their need for privacy. In these situations you need to be direct and tell your father that you want some one-to-one time with him or tell your mother or sibling that you have some personal matters to discuss with Dad and you believe it will go better for both of you if no one else is around. In most instances, especially if you are kind but firm, others will respect such a wish.

When I made my trip to Florida and spent time with my father the problem was obviously not having time alone, but rather how to feel comfortable with and make use of that rare time together. I have found in my work with clients, as well as through my personal experience, that one of the least threatening and most effective ways of taking steps early on toward reconciliation is to find out more about one's father, beginning with his experiences growing up.

There is a point in *Field of Dreams* when Ray Kinsella first sees his father on the ballfield with the Black Sox players. He is observing him as a man still in his youth. He realizes that by the time he knew his father he was already seeing a man worn down by life. It is not only after a day's work that we get our father's temperament instead of his teaching, as Bly put it; to a significant extent we get the temperament produced by the years of experience that preceded his becoming a father.

As children we mock our fathers for using a standard line such as, "When I was your age I walked six miles to school even if it was twenty degrees below zero." Children do need to know what their fathers' earlier lives were like, however, in order to understand their behaviors as a father and man.

To know about a father's personal struggles, his failures and successes, and the events that tested or traumatized him humanizes him in our eyes. To see our fathers in multidimensional terms permits us to apply a different, more understanding perspective to their behaviors. To place our fathers in the context of their own lives "detoxifies" them for us, as psychologist Sam Osherson put it in *Finding Our Fathers*. It means our image of them is not dominated by our pain. Osherson quotes a statement made by Robert Bly about his own detoxifying shift in attitude toward his father: "I began to think of him not as someone who had deprived me of love or attention or companionship, but as someone who himself had been deprived . . . to see him more as a man in a complicated situation."

In a men's group I conduct one of the members acknowledged with regret: "I never was able to love my father until after he died. It was only then I was able to see him in human terms."

Children who grew up in the shadow of their father's power commonly find it difficult to overcome their inflated views until the father's aging or death brings home the reality of his underlying frailty. Some never get beyond their childhood perspective.

Some children are reluctant to get to know their father in more human terms for the opposite reason. They do not want to see his weakness. They may fear that their efforts to uncover more about him will open an old wound. I recall the son who would not ask his father about the mysterious circumstances surrounding his grandfather's death because there was some hint of scandal about it. He assumed he would expose his father to unwanted shame.

Another woman feared that knowing about the sadness in her father's past life would reinforce her feeling responsible for him in the present. This was something that had impeded her for years. It did not dawn on her that having such knowledge might allow for a new closeness that could free her of that binding sense of responsibility.

When we steer clear of our father's pain we are likely to be stuck with old projections about his inability to deal with such hurt, and we surely maintain our distance from him. We may expect that hearing about our father's past struggles will make it hard for us to seek his support for our own legitimate needs and that we will then become further lost within the relationship. In fact, we may find out more about his resilience, not simply his vulnerability, which may free us to be closer to him.

There is, of course, the risk that what we learn will highlight a father's dependence or leave us feeling obligated to take care of him. I have yet to see a relationship, however, where the impact of such knowledge was more binding than what had already been inflicted by ignorance or the denial of the father's neediness.

Like Paul Auster's father in *The Invention of Solitude* or Germaine Greer's in *Daddy, We Hardly Knew You*, some fathers' lives have been so reclusive or their past has been so hidden that great perseverance and extensive research are required to uncover their histories. With most fathers, though, to obtain a more human picture of them is not at all difficult. It starts with asking questions, being an objective journalist or historian in search of a good story.

It used to surprise me how little many people know about their fathers' lives. I know now that fathers almost characteristically say little about themselves, including their personal histories. Others may have talked freely about themselves but given little sense of how they were affected emotionally when things happened to them. Most lack awareness of the feelings connected with the events they experienced. When asked in an interested, receptive tone most fathers will either eagerly begin to relate their stories or at least make an effort to answer a child's questions.

"Tell me about your childhood," is too broad a request for many fathers. They may not be used to talking about themselves in a personal way. Like a self-conscious adolescent speaking to an adult, they may respond with clipped, unrevealing answers.

It will help to ask neutral but specific questions to start with and then move to more personal or charged questions. For example, don't start with, "Why did your parents hate each other?" Rather, try, "Can you tell me what your parents were like as people? How did they try to raise you?" Below are some of the approaches you might follow:

1. Get as detailed a picture of the family tree as possible.
2. Identify the significant people in the family and learn what made them important.
3. Identify major family events—deaths, divorces, illnesses, feuds, achievements, successes, failures, how people entered the family and who left it.
4. Explore what your father's parents were like as parents: how they gave affection; how they disciplined him or his brothers and sisters; who their favorites were, who was out of favor, and how he knew about these attitudes.
5. Trace as much as possible what your grandparents' lives were like, because that will shed light on the temperaments they brought to their son.

6. Ask what your father's childhood was like: what responsibilities he had; who gave him support and attention; what the milestones of his life were and how his family responded to them.

What we find out when we are able to locate our fathers in the time and setting that shaped their lives can be astonishingly dramatic or elegantly simple. Yet this information can shed a light on our fathers that alters our whole experience of them. Paul Auster unlocked the terrible secret that his paternal grandmother had murdered his grandfather. His father's withdrawn nature took on a different meaning after this discovery.

Ron's visit with some elderly relatives gave him the opportunity to hear how rigid and demanding his grandfather had been with his father. It made his autocratic father seem more easygoing in comparison. He no longer saw his father's controlling nature as directed against him personally but recognized it as a learned family trait.

Charlene's impenetrable wall of anger toward her father began to crumble when she heard him relate a tender story about his disappointment one Christmas when there had not been enough money for the gift he had dreamed of getting. A father becomes more real when we learn about the path he followed before we came into his life. When we can talk with him about his personal history he becomes more accessible to us and it is easier to talk to him about what he is like now.

History-taking with our father exposes us to the general structure and fabric of his life. Initially it may feel safest and most comfortable to focus on the externals that shaped him and what he had to contend with while growing up. The next step is to go deeper, to get an appreciation of how he was affected by his life's experiences. We can move from asking factual questions to probing how he felt at the time and how he feels now about the various aspects of his personal history.

In *Iron John*, Robert Bly writes: "If we adopt psychological thinking toward our father, we can bring out of ourselves forgiveness, complication, humor, symbolic subtlety, and compassion. The heart begins to melt."

To adopt psychological thinking toward our fathers means that we admit our fathers have their own emotional lives. They may never have expressed it to us and they may still be unwilling to reveal it, but they all have their own pain and their own vulnerability. We have to face it to begin to see it. Linda Leonard found through her writing of *The Wounded Woman*:

> I had to really look at him, to try to understand his side of the story, his aspirations and despair. No longer could I dismiss him from my life as though I could totally escape the past and his influence. Nor could I simply blame him as the cause of all my troubles. . . . When I looked in the mirror I saw my father's face.

Desi Arnaz Jr. had the extraordinary experience of portraying his own father in the film *The Mambo Kings*. He described what happened to him as a result: "Playing my father was a cathartic experience. I not only was able to capture certain positive feelings I never knew were there between us, but I was also able to let go of certain negative feelings that have been buried deep within me all these years."

These feelings of closeness and identification ideally emerge when we secure a deep emotional understanding of our father. Unfortunately, not many of us get the opportunity to have such a psychological union with this man. Most commonly we only obtain occasional glimpses into our father's emotional life. Perhaps through the tears he shed at his mother's or father's gravesite or in a vulnerable moment before we left home for college he gave us clues to the softer side he normally kept hidden.

As our fathers age and are less concerned about maintaining an image, when they know their parenting job is mostly done and the pressures in their lives have eased, many become more relaxed about revealing themselves. They are open to answering inquiries about aspects of their lives they would never have talked about before. They can enjoy passing on something about who they are.

We can make it easier by encouraging them to do what is familiar as a way to ease into the unfamiliar. For example, if we ask our father to talk about his feelings, he may become instantly ill at ease. When we coax him to tell us stories about his life, and we listen or watch for the feelings, they'll be there. I am reminded of the news producer I saw recently on television who explained that as the assassination of President Kennedy was being reported, the commentators and staff dared not show their feelings. As he related this story almost thirty years later, tears rolled down his cheeks.

One man whose father was a thick-skinned, unyielding person, never expected his dad would reveal anything to him, but he decided to try.

He was surprised to find that the first time he asked his father about his early family life, his father talked about the emotionally stark existence in which he had been raised and how he felt he had never had a childhood. The conversation didn't suddenly alter their relationship, but both the poignancy of what his father said and the fact that he was willing to voice it to him led this man to stop viewing his father's gruffness as a form of rejection.

It is not always possible to get your father to discuss his emotional life. Some aspects of his life may remain too painful for him to talk about or he may not be able to unlearn a long-standing pattern of keeping his feelings contained. To understand his pain may require you to extend yourself into his life and stretch the limits of your empathic abilities, to answer the questions yourself to which he is unable to respond.

As an example, Geoffrey Wolff perceptively asked himself whether his grandfather ever said healing words to his father. Once he asked the question he knew the likely answer and it shed light on his father's destructive behavior. A client recalled how his father had handled the death of one of his other children and recognized that he had never been the same after that. This recollection helped him overcome the intimidating image of his father that predated this tragedy.

In Julia Alvarez's novel *How the Garcia Sisters Lost Their Accents*, the father rips up a speech one of his daughters has proudly written about educational reform. This seemingly outrageous, authoritarian act takes on a different meaning when the daughter retraces her father's terrifying experiences under the Trujillo dictatorship back in the Dominican Republic. She understands that he feared her outspokenness would endanger the family. It was no longer an action aimed at destroying her own integrity. When we can project ourselves into the lives of our fathers we humanize them and usually soften our views of even their harshest behaviors.

16

Addressing Old Wounds

Learning more about a father's earlier life and trying to gain perspective on how his experiences in the past shaped him as a parent is normally an effective and safe way to begin rebuilding a sense of connection with him. Seeing things through his eyes to some degree will likely take the edge off our hurt and anger.

There are many instances, however, where the discord between fathers and children cannot be healed by spending time together without addressing the history of the relationship itself. There may be deep wounds that were part of the past—physical abuse, a nasty divorce, alcoholic behavior, too many years of unexplained withdrawal—that cannot be pushed aside and yet are extremely difficult to talk about.

While professional help could aid the healing process in such problematic situations, most people are reticent about inviting their fathers to come in to see a therapist with them. Many people bypass the opportunity to promote healing through the guidance of a family therapist because they believe their fathers would never agree to such a radical step. Many dads would react this way, but a surprising number would not. When the idea is posed as an invitation to join you in work you are doing to help yourself or as a sincere effort to help you understand each other better, many fathers are willing to extend themselves despite the discomfort they may feel. When I encounter resistance to professional intervention, I encourage people to talk to their fathers on their own in natural settings.

Sometimes out of the desire to put our tension behind us we rush prematurely into confrontation, as though we can settle years of misunderstanding with one heart-to-heart talk if we get right to the point. I remember one man who was encouraged by a colleague at his company to just ask his father point-blank: "Why didn't you ever love me?"

On the surface, it might seem like asking such a question would be wonderfully cathartic and would get right to the crux of the matter. Few fathers, however, would accept the accusation they did not love their children. Obviously such a blunt approach would in itself be hurtful from the father's end, no matter how poorly he had in fact carried out his parenting role. Such a question would predictably lead to a defensive posture at best.

In fact, the father who was asked the question did react angrily. The son continued to feel misunderstood and it was years before either was ready for another try.

In another instance, a therapy group encouraged a victim of considerable paternal abuse to head over to his father's house and let him have it. Father and son had not seen each other in several years. The son came by unannounced and poured out his anger of thirty years in one long diatribe. This emotional ambush was no more effective than the kamikaze approach mentioned earlier. No matter how wrong a person believes he is, he will likely respond defensively if he has been put on the defensive and he will reject the person who has rejected him. This example also highlights, unfortunately, that mental health professionals do not uniformly give sound advice on how to attempt reconciliation.

The late television news commentator Eric Sevareid once said: "In candor is the greatest form of tyranny." While it is essential that you approach your father with honesty about your feelings, honesty without tact and without attention to your father's feelings will continue the cycle of hurt. It may be true that your father has been a bastard all these years or that you have regarded him as a coward and a failure. But telling him so punishes your father without providing feedback he can respond to. You may expect that it will feel good to get your anger off your chest, but when the cathartic release leads to more hostility and keeps doors of communication shut, the catharsis will close in on itself.

You can be honest and open without bludgeoning your father. For example: "Dad, for a lot of years I've kept the attitude that you were mean to me. I don't want to feel that way anymore. I want to try to put aside my bad feelings about you, but I need to talk about them first."

The man who ambushed his father was filled with rage at the abuse inflicted on him. That was the truth. It was also true, though, that he felt overwhelming sadness at how he had been treated and how he had missed the nurturing of a father. Ultimately it would have been far more personally healing for him to go beyond venting anger to expressing his sadness and other feelings. As long as he held on to the anger, he maintained a guard against anyone who might hurt him. His father, who was still an alcoholic, probably would not have been capable of responding much better to the sadness. A more complete expression of this man's feelings, however, would have left him more at peace with himself and certain that his effort was not misguided. He might have tried something like the following: "For a long time I've been terribly angry at you for lots of things that happened when I was growing up. I need you to know about my anger, but I realize that I also need you to know I think we both missed out on a great deal. I have so much sadness, too. Maybe you do, too. I hope it's not too late to make some changes."

The best way to begin is not to point an accusatory finger at your father, but rather to acknowledge how you have been feeling about the relationship. Rather than defining or interpreting his behavior or intentions, state your experience in honest, nonjudgmental terms. For example, try: "I have felt for a long time that I wasn't really understood by you. I wanted you to know me better and take more time to ask me about myself and really listen to my answers. I didn't get that feeling very often growing up."

Don't say: "You never tried to understand me. You didn't want to know me. You didn't ask me anything about myself and if I tried to tell you, you never listened anyway."

Often clients will say to me something like: "Oh yeah! Just tell him for the last thirty-seven years he's caused me terrible pain and now I've spent two years in therapy trying to undo the damage." Again, you can state your feelings directly without having to skewer your father. It won't help to understate or overstate the reality. If you say what you mean, you will be more likely to avoid confusion and guessing games at a time when you can ill afford misunderstanding.

Being direct about your concerns is important because you can't expect your father to be on the same wavelength as you. You have been thinking about what you need from him for a long time and are certainly much clearer on the subject than he could be. Because you remind him about a painful moment in your history does not mean he will know you were hurt then unless you tell him.

Bringing up past hurts also does not translate into his understanding that you are prepared to forgive him. You have to say: "I want to let go of that hurt and I can forgive you for it, but I need to hear that you at least understand how I might have felt at the time." Don't leave the important things to chance. Say them, but with the appropriate degree of force. Don't use a sledgehammer's overkill or an eyedropper's timidity.

I usually spend time with clients rehearsing how they will approach their fathers when they feel ready to begin addressing old hurts. I do this because when we think through what we want to say and how to say it beforehand, we are more likely to avoid falling into the old patterns of communication that have been destructive or ineffective.

Practice is helpful not only with finding constructive ways to bring our hurts to a father, but also with how to invite closer connection and express positive feelings. For example, instead of saying: "It's time that you stopped being a stranger with me," see how it feels to say, "I'd love to have the chance to get to know you better."

Positive statements in relation to a father may feel foreign and therefore do not come easily to many children. The practice helps them recognize that this level of communication may be possible.

Some people find the idea of such preparation insulting. One man said to me after an emotional role-play: "It seems so absurd. That's the one person with whom I'd want to feel I wouldn't have to do that." He recognized in saying this that he was engaging in wishful thinking about how he hoped things would be and not admitting how they were.

Practice helps provide perspective on what we're doing. I remind people to think about why they're making this effort in the first place. It's usually to be closer and to promote healing. That takes healing words and a tone that invites closeness. And it takes work to reach the point where we can overcome the past enough to approach our father with a message of reconciliation.

Addressing the real issues of concern involves a serious emotional risk. Stating what we mean or what we want can make us vulnerable. If I say that I want to know that my father loves me or believes in me or wants to spend time with me, I of course run the risk that he will tell me he doesn't. As I have already noted, most of us deep down believe

that our father loves us; the question is whether he will risk acknowledging it and whether we will ask.

For one man the process didn't even begin with words. It started by
his deliberately giving his father a hug every time he ended a visit. This
was a dad who had never been overtly affectionate to his children, yet
the practice became contagious. This dad started hugging all his children and eventually told them he loved them. What began as greater
physical openness gradually led to a richer, more intimate relationship
for this father and his children. It was as though the father had been
holding back his feelings for his family and breaking the barrier of
physically demonstrating his affection released the dammed-up feelings.

Dana had cut off all but formal communication with her dad as her
initial step in dealing with his past abusive behavior. She worked on
how to create her own security around him, but wasn't ready to test her
new skills. She was determined, though, that she would end the relationship altogether if she did not feel safe with him. Part of her reluctance to spend time alone with her dad was her fear that he had not
changed and that she would indeed be forced to stop seeing him.

She also worried that she would not know what to say to him about
the years of abuse if she had the chance. She hoped to be able to forgive him and tell him she still loved him, but didn't know if the right
words would come out. When she found out he was diagnosed with
prostate cancer, even though it appeared he would be fine, she was
finally able to break through her reluctance. When in doubt about
revealing these risky, true feelings, it is important to remember that
delay in doing so can mean we will be too late. If we would regret
something going unsaid for eternity with our father, then the risk of saying it is surely worthwhile.

To move forward with our fathers may well require relinquishing old
patterns of behavior, such as being timid, needy, or overly protective,
which we normally used in our approach to our fathers. We behaved
this way in order to hold on to his approval or to avoid his criticism.
For many, it is easier to overcome their own hostility with their fathers
than to stop the behaviors long used to seek his approval. It can be scary
to stop trying to please a father, to not be daddy's little girl or golden
boy. Indeed, it will probably be necessary to sacrifice some positive
feedback from a father in order to gain a more honest, personally satisfying relationship.

To change the familiar pattern of the relationship will require asserting oneself in ways that in themselves can feel risky and out of character. When his father was dying of a brain tumor, Philip Roth had to take charge of a parent who had always been domineering. The shift was palpable and dramatic in this case: "Do as I say, I tell him—and he does it. The end of one era, the dawn of another."

It would be easier in the case of a serious illness to be strong with a father because the shift in power is so obvious. Usually the power balance in the relationship can be altered in less dramatic fashion. This may mean setting limits with a father's intrusiveness or control, setting boundaries on those areas of your life in which a father can be involved, requesting that your dad initiate more of the contact, stating your needs clearly and directly to him. It may mean backing off and letting your father know that he is expected to carry his weight in the relationship. At times you run the risk of hurting your father through honest feedback in the short term in order to change the long-term relationship.

In many instances, though, what we fear will be hurtful is not as hurtful as we anticipate. It may well be something the father already knows and feels bad about. Dana encountered this reaction when she finally approached her father about her need to feel safe with him. He did not apologize for his past behavior, but he understood the importance of respecting her needs in the present and why she was voicing her concerns. Disclosing your feelings can be like lancing an infected wound— there is pain, but with the promise of healing.

Skillful risk-takers consider ahead of time what steps they can take to improve the chances that their initiatives will be successful or to reduce the probability of failure. Two such steps with our fathers are: (1) finding out what they recognize and feel about the very hurts or concerns we want to resolve with them and (2) being clear and limited ourselves regarding the range of issues we choose to bring out.

The best way to get another person to hear us and not to be defensive is to show him that we are as willing to listen to his point of view as we are to voice ours. While we may be all keyed up to unload our frustration or anger or hurt, if we can begin with a readiness to find out our father's perspective, we may inform our own view and perhaps defuse some of our strongest reactions.

This might occur, for example, if our father validates some of our concerns before we have to voice them ourselves or if he gives us information about his life that helps us understand the way he behaved at the time he hurt us. We must recognize that we have known about our own feelings for years, but we may know little about his feelings or our knowledge may be inaccurate. We need to start with a readiness to learn, ask questions, and listen; then we can require the courtesy of reciprocity.

For example, we can say:

> I have had lots of hard feelings about our relationship over the years that I want to be able to talk over with you. But I realize that as much as I feel justified in my feelings, you have a point of view about which you feel justified, too. Before I start telling you my feelings I'd really like to hear how you've viewed our relationship over the years.

What we know about our father is what we experienced from him, not his intent or what he perceived or felt about his own actions. Healing can come more readily if we can get to these levels with him, but only he can supply this information.

When people write a letter to their father, an exercise described in "Preparing for the Journey," they pour everything out in one burst of honesty and emotion. Sometimes these letters are written in a single sitting, though often they are composed painstakingly over several days or even weeks. To get it all out at once is usually cathartic and to have it on paper to review either alone or with a therapist provides perspective on the whole relationship. But for us to gush forth all the feelings and concerns that have built up over years and which we have brooded about and hashed over for weeks, months, or years would utterly overwhelm our fathers. They will not understand where much of our feelings are coming from. They may not share the same memories. They are not prepared the way we are to discuss this emotionally charged subject.

If our interaction is to be more than a brief thunderstorm of catharsis and we hope for an improved, ongoing relationship, we need to keep talking about these accumulated personal concerns. We will also find that if we start with the core hurts and the basic desire to overcome the conflict and distance of the past, we can then afford to let many of the lesser concerns go unsaid. We don't need to expose every wound to heal the relationship. Rather, if we have emotionally prepared ourselves we will have determined what hurts we really need to reconcile with our father to let go of the past.

Even with the most earnest preparation for reconciliation, many find it difficult to stay with the realistic goals that they have accepted in the abstract. When they anticipate actually talking with their fathers some get cold feet and back away from dealing with their true concerns. They define their goals for their paternal relationship in minimalist terms: "I'd just like to be able to call him up once in a while and have a pleasant conversation." They are back to playing it safe.

Others continue to expect too much: "I want to have him treat me now like he should have when I was a child." They are still unable to relinquish the good daddy of their fantasies. When pushed for what they really want, the minimalists invariably recognize they want more and the idealists would be quite comfortable settling for less.

Often individuals have a distorted image of what they need to do to address their fathers. Many picture an emotional summit conference taking place with their dads. This inflated view leads naturally to either backing away in discomfort or bringing a comprehensive agenda to match the scenario of the summit. Certainly some situations do call for a dramatic confrontation with a father; most do not. The work of reconciliation requires far more attention to creating a tie with one's father than focusing on why the distance existed in the first place. Thus, it is not an explosive summit meeting, but patient, modest interaction over time that is the heart of reconciliation.

One woman said to me with a touch of relief in her voice: "I always thought I'd have to have some kind of big talk with him. I realize now I need to have a lot of small talks with him. I need to start acting with him the way I've been wanting to and not wait for him to start acting different first."

Indeed, the way we approach our father with our feelings and desire to improve the relationship is an opportunity to enact change and not to just talk about it. We need to view our efforts to communicate about what needs to be healed as an opportunity to demonstrate what the changed relationship could look like in the here and now, not in the distant future when we and our father have both undergone a magical metamorphosis.

A final caveat about how we approach change in the relationship is that we may be inclined to counter the extremes of the past by going in the opposite direction. With a father who has been autocratic, we may want a period of complete freedom; with an abusive father we may want to lash out instead of being a victim. As another woman perceptively put it: "The pendulum had to swing in the opposite direction before it could come back to the middle. But I realize it's a different middle than it was before and I don't even know yet what it will look like."

Figuring out what we want that middle to look like is an essential part of our journey. Ultimately, to truly test out the possibility for achieving meaningful change we must go beyond good intentions or natural inclinations. We must thoughtfully determine the destination we want to arrive at, but we must also go beyond what we know intellectually and explore our own emotional depths. With unbending honesty we must examine our own motivation and our own part in the evolution of the relationship.

As Linda Leonard discovered in her writing of *The Wounded Woman*, it was not enough to complete her chapter on "Redeeming the Father." That only caused her to feel more pain. She had to go deep within herself to discover the strength of spirit to overcome the distance she, too, had allowed to prevail with her father. It is this kind of strength that is required to go the distance with our fathers, as the mystical voice in *Field of Dreams* would tell us.

17

Completing the Circle

I saw again what I had seen when I was a child, in love
with my father as with no one else.

The Duke of Deception, Geoffrey Wolff

When *Time* magazine selected Ted Turner as its "Man of the Year" in 1992, its editors knew they were choosing someone who had walked the edge of self-destruction. They also knew that the model for such self-immolation was Turner's father. Ed Turner was an overpowering father who abused, pressured, and humiliated his son in the name of ambition. When his father committed suicide, Ted Turner said "that left me alone, because I had counted on him to make the judgment of whether or not I was a success." Turner sought success for years by following his father's pattern of being driven and becoming a drunk.

Finally, with the help of a psychotherapist as well as medication, Turner began to turn his life away from the brink of disaster. As *Time* put it, "Taking the biggest risk of his life, Turner confronted the dark legacy of his father and prevailed." The result was a man who began to enjoy his family, who became openly affectionate, who his children found could have fun for the first time, and who could establish his own priorities for his life. Certainly there were multiple factors in this life reversal for Ted Turner, but coming to terms with his father was assuredly at the center of it.

The dramatic transformation of Ted Turner represents a hopeful picture of the kind of change that is possible when we confront the legacy of a troubled relationship with our fathers. This example, with its heroic figure, can also create a distorted impression about what it takes to come to terms with a dysfunctional father relationship.

The journey we are talking about is not the stuff of fairy tales. There is not any guaranteed direct correspondence between the effort we put in and the outcome. By traveling a treacherous pathway to a faraway land or slaying the designated monster we do not get the king's blessing and inherit the kingdom. The rewards that do come generally take time and are usually of a modest nature.

Diane had struggled over several years and through many therapy hours trying to come to terms with how uncomfortable and intimidated she had been around her father. The change within her was gradual but steady. Eventually she reached the point where she could be herself around him without walking on eggshells. She could stand up to him in a conflict without gearing herself up for virtual warfare. Despite these internal changes, in her mind nothing had changed in how her father related to her. He was still demanding, insensitive, impatient. She continued to feel that the relationship offered her nothing positive and that her energy must be directed at avoiding the negatives. She saw no reason to be hopeful that he would change.

One lazy Sunday afternoon on a visit to her parents' home Diane found herself alone with her father. For the moment he seemed reasonably relaxed. Without any forethought she proposed an uncharacteristically personal question to him: "What was the most worrisome thing that ever happened to you, Dad?" She got back a surprising and wholly uncharacteristic response. Her father went into a lengthy description of the hardships in his childhood that she had never heard before. She had never in her entire life heard him be so frank and open.

There is no way to know what brought on the magic of that moment—the lazy breeze and relaxed atmosphere of a summer day, the fact that Diane had become more relaxed and real around her father and could approach him differently, or her dad's mellowing out as he approached retirement. Probably all were factors, along with Diane's readiness to start a meaningful conversation and work at continuing it once her father proved responsive.

This level of interaction was not sustained in their future encounters, but Diane's ideas about what was possible in her relationship were altered, as were her feelings about her father. He seemed softer and more accessible. His harshness not only had a context, but had a counter side that at least existed, even if it made only infrequent appearances.

Some months later, Diane's father suffered a heart attack. Diane had wondered for a long time how she would be affected by her father's death. With the actual threat of losing him she could feel clearly for once that it would be a loss. She offered her own perceptive explanation: "I guess the caring came back that was there before the pain became too great." It wasn't that her father was so dramatically different; it was the real potential that he could be different that allowed her old feelings to emerge.

The pattern for Matt was quite different. If he was intimidated by his father it was by how sphinxlike his dad was, not by any sense of threat. Matt had inched closer to his father in modest increments. He began by trying to engage him in conversation on the phone before his father would abruptly turn the call over to Matt's mother. Next, Matt invited his father to play golf. Visiting his father at work was a bold step. Finally, he summoned the courage to ask his father to lunch.

The first time they struggled to fill forty-five minutes with small talk. A number of months and several lunches later, there was a warm flow to the conversation. That lunch followed a family reunion that had put Matt's father in touch with some old relatives and fond memories. It was Matt who started to feel at a loss for words; he wanted to hear his father go on and on, but wasn't sure how to keep him going and whether it was all right to do that. A few months later it was Matt's father calling to confirm their next lunch. He would skip his weekly poker game afterward so they could have more time together.

No one path takes us on the journey to our father. The path depends on change in us and preferably in our father as well, but change takes different forms. It may be a slow, bit-by-bit evolution. It may be sudden and sizable, occurring after a long period of resistance. Change may come the way the bamboo plant grows, with a prolonged stage of underground growth to form a root structure, followed by rapid visible growth once the root system is in place. The pace and nature of how we may change won't necessarily match or be in sync with what is possible for our father.

One must remember that the agenda for change is ours and may not be our father's. When two people are motivated by and clear about sharing the same agenda, change occurs more quickly. When the desire and focus are more unilateral the change is going to occur more like osmosis. Moreover, we can't expect to change a relationship that has likely been off track for years in one or two efforts. Rather, we must plan on repeatedly approaching our father, as Matt did, and after each attempt assess what did and didn't work, taking note of the progress made.

With fathers who are inept at relating socially with their children their learning will be incremental. We ought not to measure change with a father by our standard for other relationships, such as peer friendships. Perhaps a father initiating an invitation to spend time together or his listening better or his putting down the newspaper when we're trying to have a conversation will signal that he's making an effort and that we're beginning to get through to him. One of the most satisfying developments for me in my interaction with my father occurred when he began to be more attentive to the events in my life and to follow up on those events from week to week. I experienced that interest as an expression of his caring and not just improved communication.

There was a significant improvement in the quality of my conversations with my father, but his greater demonstrated interest did not come through every time we talked and did not wholly characterize individual exchanges. We must be prepared as we work at reconciliation for the obvious yet difficult to accept fact that the improvement in our connection with our father will be imperfect.

The good news in this dose of reality is that imperfect often turns out to be much more satisfying than expected. Small changes, in contrast to what the relationship has been, can make an intolerable relationship tolerable or a tolerable relationship pleasurable. This slight shift may seem minor when taken as a change in individual behavior, but it is major in the context of one's life. It is also true that incremental changes may accumulate and lead to significant changes when seen over time.

Matt was taking stock of some of the ways he thought things were changing: His father called one day to tell him he had almost bowled a 300 game; his brothers were commenting that he was spending more time with their father, which meant his father must have been talking about it; he found himself thinking about his father at odd moments. These changes did not seem dramatic in themselves, but when Matt contemplated how each compared with past behavior, he realized that fundamental shifts were taking place.

As you attempt to hold in check your expectations for change in the relationship, it is helpful to remember the pattern with which people typically learn. We don't learn new behaviors with constancy and unremitting movement forward. We make gains, then fall back a bit into old habits or mistakes, then move beyond the point we earlier had reached. This is the normal learning curve. Allow you and your father to revert to past patterns and to get off track. What is important is not that you regressed, but being able to bounce back, to be resilient in your learning and behavior with each other.

When we ask our fathers to work at improving our relationship with them, let alone to work at being closer or more intimate, we are dealing with concerns and behaviors that are still relatively foreign to the average man of their generation. Tending to relationships and dealing with emotions have tragically been designated in our culture as women's work. Change is still occurring slowly on this front. If you imagine your father trying to learn a foreign language with you, you'll have the proper frame of mind for tolerating his discomfort and being patient with any ineptness he displays.

The ideas about the journey to our father offered so far in this and the preceding five chapters have been of a general nature. They apply to most fathers where the relationship has been characterized by distance or lack of connection. No one has a universal father, however. We all have to figure out how to come to terms with the unique character of our own fathers. In Part I, fathers were typecast according to common patterns of behavior that also were primary sources of the failure in their relationship with their children. If we look again at fathers in terms of these patterns—power, weakness, and absence—we can get greater clarity regarding specific steps that will help us overcome the failure to connect.

18

The Path to Reconciliation With Overpowering Fathers

The greatest challenge in overcoming the troubled relationship due to distortions of power is to stop attributing so much power to that father. When we are children our fathers can be that overpowering. They can be abusive without hope of containing their twisted anger; they can control without limits; they can dominate by their image of perfection. A child's options are limited and every one carries a high emotional price tag. The task as an adult is to recognize that the power imbalance that existed can only continue if you let it.

Fear is the great enemy of change with powerful fathers. Out of fear we may allow ourselves to continue to function as a victim to his abuse, as a lackey to his autocratic behavior, as an inferior to his perceived success. Out of fear we avoid confronting our fathers with their impact on us.

In most instances, when we stop letting our fear dominate our own behavior, we discover that our father is not nearly as powerful or perfect as we thought him, nor are we as powerless. Once we can remove this aura (which, of course, is like saying, "once the hero has slain the dragon"), the remaining work is more about learning to use our own strength than about our fathers changing.

If we recognize our own strength and see ourselves clearly, we don't need to change our father. It is consistent with what the martial arts teach—if we know how to use our own force, we won't waste energy trying to overcome an opponent's force; we'll use our strength in our own behalf.

Autocratic Fathers

The power struggles we have likely engaged in for years with autocratic fathers show how our child's perspective on a parent's power can create distortion and block change. The controlling nature of the autocratic father is really a mask for his own insecurity. We have to free ourselves from our natural inclination to find a way to resist him.

If we see the controlling behavior as his problem, we will realize that we neither have to be submissive nor engineer a coup and topple his authority. The options are not the black-and-white, obey-or-disobey with which the authoritarian personality lives. Often children of an autocratic father are concerned about stripping him bare of his integrity, as though he must be in charge or he becomes nothing. They then ignore their own integrity lost by being submissive.

There are healthy, constructive options for the seeming paradoxes posed by the autocratic father. Rather than obey or disobey, take the focus off his views and make your own choices: "Dad, I see what you mean and that probably would work for you, but that's not the way I need to do it."

Choose the level of closeness that is right for you at the time rather than letting yourself feel smothered or keeping him at arm's length to avoid the times he doesn't respect boundaries. Know that you can set your own boundaries: "That sounds like an inviting offer, Dad, but I want to be home early tonight, so I'll accept for dinner and pass on the movies."

Many autocratic fathers will not respond in a supportive way, either because their own needs are too great or because they lack the self-awareness and insight to change old behaviors. It takes a willingness to risk making them unhappy to find our own comfort level of relating to their need for control. The lure of giving in to avoid an argument or to retain their approval is hard to resist, but the short-term comfort and stability exact a long-term price.

Many find it difficult to stand their own ground because they feel they will only be able to hold their position if they are willing to engage in mortal combat. In reality, to maintain our own integrity and positions merely requires standing firm. Nothing aggressive is needed. We do better keeping our feet firmly planted than by digging in our heels.

Renee turned the corner emotionally when she discovered this fact on a visit to her father:

I found out I didn't have to say one word when he criticized me. I always used to start defending my way, as though until I convinced him, it wasn't all right for me to do what I wanted. Now I just let him rant and I might say something, but I might not—I know I don't need to. I don't need a good offense or a good defense. There's tremendous power and freedom in that realization.

A further discovery came for Ron when he deviated from his usual routine of remaining passive in the face of potential conflict with and disapproval from his father. In one particular encounter over how to repair the kitchen faucet, Ron showed his father he understood his father's thinking behind one of his dictums, then proceeded to explain that he had another point of view. Afterward he reflected on how this new approach affected him:

> What I realized was that in the past I was letting my father be a know-it-all. That meant I knew nothing. When I let myself voice my own opinion, whether he liked it or not, I felt like a whole person. That reinforced for me that I was a different person than him and was entitled to have my own way of doing things.

The critical step in learning how to get beyond your father's control is to stop sacrificing your own identity to please him and meet his expectations. Sometimes we have to become painfully aware of just how much we are losing ourselves by trying to hold on to his approval.

One exercise I suggest to heighten this awareness is to spend several days carrying your father's critical or controlling voice around with you. Every time you take an action or make a decision write down (or at least think about) the judgment or reaction you would get if your father were there looking over your shoulder. After the exercise remind yourself that it is now your decision whether you continue to carry that voice around with you. If you start being your own parent and knowing you can make your own choices, you won't have to blame your father or keep a distance from him.

To honor your own identity is the path to the emotional freedom that will in turn allow you to take down your own protective barricades. For a son, this means no longer trying to be a miniature of your father. For a daughter, it means not trying to be the good daughter. For both, it means being your own person.

The irony in this shift is that often fathers will respond supportively when their children present a firm, confident sense of themselves, even when such behavior contradicts their own way of doing things. Those fathers who can't feel good and be supportive initially will usually come around in time if their children hold their ground. Often autocratic fathers have been too caught up in their own internal struggles to see their children clearly. They most likely do not recognize that their off-spring feel controlled, and they lack awareness of how their children perceive their power.

For some time Andrew limited his communication with his father to their written correspondence. Finally, he took the bold step of inviting his father to a therapy session. In that meeting, Andrew was able to express to his father how overwhelmed and powerless he had always felt around him. His father's response was not to recoil in anger, but to tell Andrew that he had never known he felt this way and had in fact always seen Andrew as so confident and mature he never imagined he wouldn't speak up for himself. He told Andrew he was glad that he could tell him this now. Andrew's new problem became learning how to use his own power with a father who was willing to contain his.

Obviously not all autocratic fathers will abdicate their throne. If you recognize and come to validate your own identity, however, no one can take that from you. The inner security that comes with this growth can allow you to be with your father, regardless of his controlling nature, without being intimidated, dominated, or diminished.

Ideal Fathers

With ideal fathers we again lose out when we allow ourselves to be in an inferior or passive role. Our failure to approach an ideal father keeps him on a pedestal and thus maintains distance. If a sincere attempt is made to overcome the barrier, most ideal fathers will welcome their children.

In a way, this is a validation of what the child perceived about the father all along. If he is exemplary, he will certainly want his children to be close to him. On the other hand, if he rebuffs his children, that suggests petty motivation and narcissism, which reveals a major flaw that questions his Olympian standing. The most confounding challenge for the child of the ideal father is to break the mind-set that the father is so good, his failure to connect is justifiable because the child is unworthy in comparison.

Only two fundamental attitude shifts are needed to allow for reconciliation with the ideal father: relinquishing the view of the father as perfect and rejecting the view of oneself as inferior. For daughters, this is a challenge that has been made more difficult by the patriarchy in our culture. Male success has too long been valued at the expense of women. Daughters have had to overcome not only familial but social strictures about their own self-worth. For sons, the struggle is intensified by the inherent pressure to be like one's father. To be different from an ideal father is readily defined as falling short. To be less than him is to be a failure and thus to weaken the bond with him.

Whatever social or psychological pressures exist, the path for overcoming the disconnection with an ideal father begins with self validation. When you are clear that you have the right to define your own abilities, to set your own standards, to be the only judge of yourself, you take away the power of the father that keeps you at a distance.

There is nothing to fear in the ideal father if his strengths are simply his particular character traits and you have your own special qualities. If you are centered in how you view yourself and your own goals and choices, that is, if the source of those views comes from within you, neither your father's example nor his judgments can diminish you. Your father becomes a helpful role model, but not the standard for your existence. It may take a substantial effort at personal growth, but it is up to you to validate yourself so that you become free to approach your father in a healthy way.

In order to see ourselves more accurately and positively, we have to arrive at a more realistic, balanced picture of our fathers. Gene had an extremely difficult time letting go of the idyllic view he had always had of his father. His dad died when Gene was just entering adulthood. His death deprived Gene of the opportunity to have an adult's perspective on his father.

Gene's older sister, however, was instrumental in conveying to Gene that there were other sides to their father. She saw him as distant and unaffectionate and felt her own intimate relationships and self-confidence had been undermined as a result. Accepting a partial validity to his sister's outlook opened a crack in the veneer of his father's perfection for Gene. This in turn made it possible for him to begin to be less demanding and more accepting of himself.

With that self-acceptance Gene gained the capacity to see his father favorably but in human terms. He no longer felt diminished by his image of his father. The positive reinforcement that goes back and forth between self esteem and a balanced view of the father promotes the possibility of a changed relationship and assures an inner resolution regardless of your father's accessibility.

Abusive Fathers

With fathers who were abusive, it is more difficult to break out of the emotional cycles of the past. The defenses a child develops to survive with an abusive father can remain as an almost impenetrable shield as an adult, making reconciliation difficult to achieve. When the adult child faces the reality of the abusive past, no matter how the father has changed, the residue of feelings will continue to complicate and hinder closeness.

Mike's father had always had a temper, but he had stopped reacting violently by the time Mike was eight or nine. Over the years Mike's father gradually mellowed and also learned to reach out and be supportive. By the time his father died suddenly at sixty, Mike could honestly say he loved his father and felt a deep attachment to him. Mike's grieving of his father's death was intense and heightened his sense of wanting to honor his father's place in his life.

In spite of this healing progression Mike was stunned to hear his response to a friend shortly after his father's death. The friend asked Mike what stood out most for him about his father. Mike reflexively replied: "He hurt me."

It was befuddling for Mike, who knew he loved and idealized his father, to realize that he also knew in his heart he still could not fully forgive his father. What Mike needed to see was that he had had two fathers—a loving one and an abusive one. Therefore, he had feelings about both. His feelings had to be divergent to be real, and that was going to be confusing. He needed to allow both sets of feelings to coexist.

Mike was fortunate to have had the opportunity to see a positive side to his father that he could readily love. Martin was only six or seven when his father deserted the family. As a result, Martin not only was deprived of having any positive vision of his father, he also never had the chance to experience himself in relation to his father's rages as anything but a tiny, powerless victim. The emotional wounds from abuse in a young child are ingrained in the soul and psyche of that child. Without experiencing himself or herself in any role but the victim with the father, the child will carry this unchallenged self-image into adulthood.

To alter the victim pattern of relating to an abusive father these children end up struggling more with their feelings about themselves than about their fathers. They must overcome the shame they carry for being a victim and seemingly giving their fathers reasons to victimize them. That sense of shame prevents them from believing they have the right to be treated differently.

Abused children often are held back from pursuing reconciliation by the reservoir of anger they have carried and by their fear. The anger is difficult to relinquish because letting go of it can mean losing the hope that the past can be changed. For some, letting go of one's anger is equated with forgiving behavior. To forgive without retribution feels like a violation of one's integrity.

In addition, fear exists that one may again be abused. For daughters the raw physical vulnerability to hurt may well continue long after any actual abuse occurs. This overpowering fear can make it difficult to emerge from the victim role. Sons may experience this same fear, though the physical threat of the father usually lessens as the child gains adult male stature. Sons, however, are perhaps more prone to a kind of self-victimization and compounded shame if they did not see themselves stand up strongly against an abusive father. In keeping with their model of masculinity, boys believe they should encounter assaults bravely. Thus, they fear exhibiting fear and feel shame when they do.

Abused children tend to have little faith that they can ever find comfort in their relationship with the victimizer. They may believe that their only hope for coming to terms with the abuse is to confront the father with the cruelty and destructiveness of his actions. Such confrontation may be necessary as a means of emerging from the role of victim and overcoming the fear and shame carried for so long. These confrontations, when delivered with reciprocal rage and the intent to hurt, seldom achieve the desired end. To behave this way is to behave like the father, which feels shameful.

It is constructive to confront the father by delineating how you were hurt and making clear that you will never allow such treatment again. Establishing your integrity in this manner will help you affirm yourself without tearing at your father's need for his own image as a decent person.

To the degree that a father can retain and act from his own sense of integrity while apologizing for the past, healing can be achieved. If you are able to at least see the father in the context of whatever victimization led him to his own abhorrent behavior, some kind of reconciliation may well be possible. One woman remarked to me, "When I heard my father talk about how unprepared for parenthood he had been as a young man, it helped defuse a lot of my anger at him."

If you have made efforts to constructively confront or reconcile with a father who remains unyielding, you may be left with the option of maintaining distance to keep your own integrity intact. Under such circumstances you have to acknowledge your right to reject a father whose unwillingness to accept responsibility for his behavior threatens your emotional well-being. In this event, there is a unilateral sense of resolution that comes with protecting yourself and rejecting ever being victimized again. This resolution, however, is inevitably tinged with the loss of the relationship and your father's immutable status as villain.

19

The Path to Reconciliation With Weak Fathers

Children of weak fathers have not focused on protecting themselves from their own insecurity. Fear of the father is not, then, usually a critical interference with reconciliation, as it is with overpowering fathers. In the case of overburdened and troubled fathers, coming to terms with the issue of responsibility is central. With silent fathers, as with ideal fathers but for different reasons, validation of the self is at the heart of the emotional transition.

With all three of these weak father types the ability to achieve reconciliation or resolution requires being able to distinguish ourselves from our father. Whereas, with overpowering fathers we have to learn our own strength, with weak fathers we must understand that the father's weakness is not inherently our own. The largest role that fear does play with the weak father is the fear of ending up like the father. The distance that exists with these fathers often occurs because the child feels safer with it, as though a limited association will offer some immunity to the virus of the father's weakness.

Choosing to make the journey toward reconciliation with a weak father often requires overcoming a powerful inertia. For some, the unwillingness to move toward the father derives from the deep sense of shame about him. Moreover, many children of weak fathers have had to function on their own since they were little. Having been independent from an early age reinforces the belief that the father is not needed. This belief, coupled with an edge of bitterness about the father's role in necessitating such early independence, can create a wall of isolation from the father that is hard to climb over.

Overburdened Fathers

The years of feeling responsible for overburdened fathers can leave children with an approach-avoidance conflict. They may be unable to let go of this support role lest their father fall apart, yet be so weary of being responsible that the effort required to alter the relationship becomes one more burden. If the father's struggles are linked to physical ailments or special circumstances, such as living alone or work or family demands, the father's vulnerability can be impossible to ignore.

Daughters living with fathers who are widowed or divorced may feel trapped in a caretaking role if the father does not resume a normal social life. They become substitutes for a wife on a practical as well as a social level.

Offspring of fathers who operate family businesses, especially sons, often feel obligated to work with such a father in order to keep his dream alive. They may become apprentices to their fathers at an early age and deny themselves the opportunity for other work experiences that would give them career options.

These children face the dilemma of how to establish boundaries between their own needs and their caring and sense of responsibility for their fathers. It is common for these children to be out of touch with their own needs because they are so focused on their fathers and so concerned about what will happen if they withdraw their support.

Before they can begin to establish a healthier balance with their fathers these offspring have to find out, often through psychotherapy or codependency groups, that they are entitled to a life of their own. Once they account for their own needs, they begin to set limits on how much they will sacrifice for their father. By setting boundaries, they usually discover that their father can survive far better than expected without relying on the child as a crutch. Allowing themselves to have a life apart from their father and seeing that he can manage make it more palatable to be with him and reduce the need to maintain emotional distance as the only protection.

Leslie looked at me almost dumbfounded the day I suggested to her that she didn't have to spend Thanksgiving Day with her father and that she didn't have to explain why. The mere idea that she had the option to say no and that her father couldn't overrule her was empowering for her. In learning the full bounds of her freedom Leslie became aware that she had a full range of in-between options for governing her time with her father. She could spend as much or as little time with him as she wanted to and give as much or as little explanation as she desired. In the end she could say to him:

> Dad, I enjoy my time with you much more when I've been able to take the time I need for myself also. I've never been very good at that. I know you want me to take care of myself and be happy. That means sometimes I'm going to say no to you when I think you may be disappointed. Otherwise I won't do what I need to for myself. I hope you can understand this. It will make it much easier on me if you do.

Leslie discovered that she was more comfortable and more open with her father once she could count on her own limit-setting. She found that much of the time he could be supportive of her and that he did fine on his own. When he fell into old patterns of manipulation to draw her into her familiar caretaking role, she was much more aware of what was going on and less likely to assume that responsibility.

The ability to establish boundaries that protected herself without having to remain emotionally distant gave Leslie another gift in addition to a richer, intimate connection with her father. It helped her see herself more clearly in relation to his weakness. She understood she was a separate person. The strength she found in setting limits with her father helped her appreciate that her ability to handle challenges in life was not identical to his.

Troubled Fathers

With fathers who are troubled it can be more difficult than with overburdened fathers to put limits on the responsibility taken for them. Troubled fathers may tend to purposely or involuntarily intrude into the lives of their children, not just to appear to want help, because of their difficulty functioning. These are fathers who are not there when you need them, but who when you really need them are there with their own problems.

It is inherently difficult to achieve closeness with troubled fathers until they deal with their own problems. For this reason, it is all the more critical to limit how much you do for such a father. Your continued responsibility for his behavior can enable him to avoid facing his problems. It is extremely hard to allow your father to fall on his face, especially since it was humiliating and painful to see him do so when you were young.

Knowing what you will and will not do for him can help in several ways: You will be less likely to exhaust yourself and as a result become totally unavailable; you will not have to avoid being with him as much; and he will be left to his own devices more, which might lead him into further problems, but could also encourage him to seek professional help.

Children of troubled fathers, perhaps out of the fear of a genetic link and/or because of the seriousness of the dysfunction, will worry more intensely about being connected with their fathers. As with overburdened fathers, distinguishing your identity from his becomes essential for your own well-being as well as allowing you to sustain a relationship with him. You, of course, do share traits in common, even some aspects of his worst qualities.

With your awareness of who he is and who you are capable of being, however, you can act to insure that your life does not travel the same path as his. As you understand your distinctness as well as your sameness, you will be freer to be around him and feel more justified in limiting your responsibility for him.

Marjorie never had the opportunity to sort out her own identity or understand the nature of her schizophrenic father's problems while he was still alive. She lived with his ghost in her marital family for years, fearful for her children, her husband, and herself. She came to peace with herself regarding her father through first learning in therapy how to affirm herself. As she faced her fears and developed confidence in herself and her ability to manage her life, she no longer had to fend off the nightmarish belief that she would eventually become like her father. She was able to recall previously blocked frightening experiences with him, but also some positive ones, and thus she could recognize having had a father and not just a troubled father.

Marjorie said that she wished she had more insight into what had triggered his psychosis and how he experienced it, but the unfinished business she carried was not about that. She told me, "The one thing I

would want to tell him if he were alive today is how much embarrassment and fear he caused me in my life. But maybe I need to know that
for myself. I don't think I would be able to put that on him. He was
scared and embarrassed himself probably."

Marjorie would probably have never been able to reconstruct a close
connection to her father had he lived longer because he was so disturbed. Seeing her relationship to him more fully and honestly, however,
did allow her to feel some renewed sense of attachment.

Sadly, there may be aspects of our fathers that no amount of time
allows us to resolve directly. The peace and resolution we achieve are
at times due to our recognition that our fathers couldn't help who they
were, but that we most surely can help who we are.

Silent Fathers

After years of minimal connection, it is very difficult to find common
ground with silent fathers. Considerable discomfort occurs when you
are in an intimate situation with someone you don't know but to whom
you are supposed to be close. The awkwardness we feel often blocks
our attempts to overcome the problem.

After Robin's first concerted effort to begin a dialogue with her
father, she reflected: "It felt weird. I realized that this man I was so
close to in some ways, in other ways I didn't know very well at all. I
felt like I was supposed to love this man, but I didn't really know
whether I did or not."

Without Robin's knowing her father, his silence had made him weak
in her eyes. Robin needed to get her father talking.

In most cases, a fuller picture emerges from the father's conversation
that helps explain some of his apparent weaknesses while revealing
strengths. The father becomes more human and usually more inviting to
be with.

A deeper connection takes time to develop. Both you and your father
gradually will find more to talk about. It helps if you can reduce the
pressure on yourself and the expectations of him. Focus on trying to get
to know him better before trying to talk about your disappointments of
the past. Make use of the history-taking questions suggested in "First
Steps." Think about what you want him to know about you and start
telling him some of that personal information.

Children of weak fathers commonly do not receive validation from them, which is the most damaging emotional price these offspring pay. With overburdened or troubled fathers, the children tend to believe their fathers do not have the capacity to offer their blessing. Unfortunately, the children are still left with the fear of ending up like their fathers, which also undermines their self-esteem.

With silent fathers, the silence is often interpreted not as an incapacity to give validation, but as conscious rejection. Rarely is this an accurate reading. Taking this concern directly to the father can remove a huge barrier not only to the relationships but to an improved self-concept for the child. This can be done with presumption and hostility: "I never heard you tell me that you cared about me or believed in me!" Or it can be accomplished with a clear desire for healing as well as affirmation: "Dad, you've always been so reserved about expressing yourself, at least with regard to your feelings about me. I used to interpret that as my not being important to you. It would really help me feel better about us and maybe about myself to hear your views of me."

Often we may believe that the father does love and place confidence in us, but doesn't express it; that, too, can be confirmed directly. With fathers who remain emotionally blocked, it is important to pay attention to their actions and receptivity to connection regardless of whether the words we want to hear are uttered. You can perhaps learn more about why your father has such difficulty verbalizing his feelings. This will help you distinguish capacity from attitude. A sense of connection and validation is possible without specific words being said.

In the end, recognizing that we can validate ourselves, and indeed need to as adults, eliminate a major pressure on the relationship with our father. Freed of the expectation that he will somehow finally fill our need to be approved we can take in whatever forms of validation he can offer.

20

The Path to Reconciliation With Absent Fathers

As with silent fathers, children lack intimate knowledge of absent fathers and are inclined to interpret their absence as rejection. They commonly assume a burden of guilt for somehow causing the absence. Getting to know the absent father is both the inherent challenge and the way to pave a path toward reconciliation or resolution. Obviously, to learn more about the father we have to extend ourselves toward him.

Simply gaining knowledge about him, however, in many cases will itself make the father seem more accessible and dispel some of the misinterpretation of his motives. Even if we discover there is an element of rejection in the father's behavior, understanding him better will expose whatever emotional distortion could lead a father to reject his own child.

Pride is a powerful inhibiting force behind avoiding efforts at reconciliation with workaholic and divorced fathers. We find it difficult to accept a father's excuses when he chooses work or another woman over being with us or leaves the home. Children may see their efforts to reach out as chasing after the father. Any response by the father to our reaching out will be suspect because it had to be solicited. With this attitude the child rationalizes keeping a distance and deprives himself or herself of the opportunity to determine whether the father has absented himself consciously or whether his absence reflects an incapacity to be different, as is so often the case with silent fathers.

With a deceased father, children can readily rationalize why they do not need to work toward a resolution of unfinished business with the father and the significance of his loss. This avoidance again protects against hurt. With absent fathers, as with the other types, one can rarely find a way to overcome hurt without risking it.

Workaholic Fathers

One constructive step with a workaholic father is to convey to him that he is needed in your life. Many fathers allow themselves to be absorbed in their work at least partly because they greatly underestimate the importance of their direct contact with their children, not out of any intended rejection. Being told that they are and were needed can serve as a wake-up call and an invitation if these fathers are at a point in their careers when they are willing to ease up. With fathers who feel they must, for reasons of economic or career security, continue their imbalanced investment in work, the potential for reconciliation is limited.

Whether a father can change his work ethic or not, it will help to find out more about his history with work: What made work so important to him? What pressures did he experience regarding work and economic security? How did he feel about his job? How did he end up with a particular career? The answers to these questions are often not what you might expect or know about. Many fathers don't talk about these issues, especially on an emotional level. For example, it may be common knowledge that your father's family struggled through the Depression, but you may not know of your father's disappointment if he had to give up his own dreams to help support the family.

Some of the most driven fathers are men who were forced prematurely to play a large role in providing security for their parents and siblings. Drew's father had been in this situation as a young adult, but then went on to a highly successful legal career. Drew believed his father's determination and success grew out of the pleasure his work gave him. Only after his father retired did Drew find out his father had taken little satisfaction in his work all those years.

Sally had always pictured her father as hard-driving but self-confident. When she asked him about his years as a young man he told her about how tense and stressed he felt by having three young children and a job that required long hours on the road to build up a clientele and earn an adequate income. Having this fragment of information about her father's early years as a parent helped explain why his involvement with the family seemed so limited. His willingness to open up about the past suggested that he was ready for more intimate contact. Without any change in the relationship, Sally had learned something important enough to make her feel more at peace with her father's history of unavailability.

Divorced Fathers

A father's absence due to work can more readily be viewed in benign terms than absence due to divorce. Work is still recognized as an obligation, while divorce, even in the most destructive of marriages, will be seen as largely a choice. Children of divorce may well distance themselves from a father because they feel rejected and still carry the anger, hurt, and self-denigration that may attend a father's departure from the home. As long as the divorce is regarded as a rejection, reconciliation remains beyond the horizon.

Regardless of the child's own behavior, the father is typically seen as being responsible for the connection that follows the divorce. The task of reconciliation is made more difficult when the father seems to deliberately elect to create or maintain distance. Any overt distancing behavior adds salt to the wound of his having left home in the first place.

Moreover, divorce puts children in a victim role, which engenders feelings of helplessness about their ability to affect their parents' behavior. Thus, children tend to expect the father to demonstrate that he wants to maintain the connection, and any moves toward reconciliation will be regarded as his to make first. It is easy to understand, then, how an insurmountable emotional inertia develops about the relationship.

Reconciliation efforts are further complicated by mistrust of motives. The children may wonder whether their fathers are spending time with them out of obligation rather than devotion. Money issues not uncommonly cloud the interactions, with children fearing the father will withhold support and fathers feeling their kids want their money more than the relationship.

The wariness, mistrust, and mixed-up feelings surrounding the relationship with a divorced father make for an uphill battle to repair the torn connection. Healing interpersonal relationships requires the comfort or safety to be honest and genuine, to express what is really felt.

The often toxic atmosphere of divorce lends itself to reconciliation the way polluted air and acid rain aid the growth of vegetation.

The best way to deal with these layers of discomfort is to discard the passive role of victim and assert your influence on the relationship. Address your concerns directly. Tell your father about the questions you have had about his motivation to be with you since the divorce. Express the worries you felt or still feel about losing financial support from your dad and how this may have caused you to be cautious in your behavior with him as well as resentful. Pin your father down on his commitment to being with you and let him know you want that time together with him.

John could never bring himself to face his father with his feelings. A lot of this response had to do with the reality that his dad had so readily withdrawn from the relationship. John acted out of the belief that pushing things with his father would risk the little connection he had. He also needed to maintain the sense that he could manage without his father, since he had to do so often over the years. This made it impossible for him to let down his guard with his father. The outcome left John in a stagnant relationship and with an inability to live without the wall of self-protection he had constructed.

June, as noted in "Preparing for the Journey," was willing to risk being direct with her father. She asked the very questions that had plagued her over the years and offered her father a path for re-entering her life, but he was unable to take it. The benefit to June, though, was that she was able to let go of the past. She knew she had conveyed to her father her own readiness to make peace and she saw she could not expect the response she needed. By no longer looking to change the past and being freed of unrealistic expectations for the present, she felt at peace, perhaps like an adopted child who has found a disappointing birth parent and through this encounter with reality can lay to rest the haunting images of the dispossessed.

The outcome for Andrew was more hopeful and probably more representative of what is likely to happen. Andrew's concerns with his father were much broader than those surrounding the divorce, but the divorce had made it more difficult to overcome them. The distance that had prevailed kept them from knowing each other and being able to adjust their behavior and responses constructively. Andrew had reached out first by mail and later through personal encounters. His willingness to be honest about his feelings while listening to his father's views opened a new chapter in their relationship. As they filled in the gaps of knowledge about each other they slowly started to build a connection they had never had. They gave themselves a true second chance.

Dead Fathers

As with virtually all children whose fathers have died, Mike was left with a myriad of questions he would have liked to have been able to ask his father. He told me, "I feel like I'm punching at a ghost." In Mike's case, much of the pain came about because he had finally arrived at the good relationship he had wanted with his father only to have him die, depriving them of the chance to enjoy their connection.

Some of Mike's questions genuinely needed a response, but most reflected his hunger for connection. Mike learned during his therapy-facilitated grieving that he could ask those questions of his father; that death did not sever the connection, only the conventional, tangible form of it. He could pose the questions and know the answers if he focused inward and listened to his own accumulated knowledge of his father. He wondered, for example, what his father would think of how Mike had developed the family business or of his decision to send his daughter to private school. When Mike reflected on how his dad would have responded he felt more, rather than less, connected to him.

When death disrupts an unsettled or troubled relationship, we are likely to despair about altering the unresolved state of that relationship. Since we cannot talk to the father directly it seems nothing can be done to achieve healing. We can understand the Victorian lure of a medium for such people.

There are three approaches, the value of which is commonly underestimated, to achieving meaningful resolution with a dead father:

1. *Talking to others about your father, especially those who knew him well.* Being able to have such communication not only keeps memories alive, but provides information and perspective about your father that can heighten your sense of connection and your desire for it. Seeking out old friends or relatives of your father even years after the death can provide surprising insights. In addition, the connection to those who were connected to your father can feel like a partial bridge to him.

James found an old friend of his deceased father's whom he had not seen in thirty years. When he approached her, without a single word yet exchanged, she started to glow with her recognition of what she could detect of James's father in his son. She confirmed many details of family history and character for James. None were more important than when she later called him back to tell him with loving pride that, "You have become what your father would have been if he had been able to." This unsolicited feedback was almost as validating for James as it would have been coming directly from his father.

2. *Talking to yourself about your father.* You can use your own words to describe your relationship with your father. Writing letters, stories, poems, or songs will help you learn about your feelings and gain perspective. The act of giving any kind of creative expression to this vital person and your relationship with him will illuminate his place in your life. Looking at photographs, recalling memories, or participating in activities you used to share with him can have a similar result.

3. *Finding ways to honor and be honored by your father.* We honor our fathers when we celebrate their memory and integrate them in our lives. Daniel eventually came to a resolution about his father when he realized he had aspects of his father's generous, caring nature within himself, but he had to find his own way to put those characteristics into practice in his life. He started volunteering in a program for disturbed children and set up a scholarship fund. These were both actions that he knew would have pleased his father, but they also represented Daniel's own interests.

Honoring a father is a way to overcome a complex set of feelings—guilt, rejection, abandonment—that cloud the relationship that lives on. There are fathers who are difficult to honor because of their lifestyle or our lack of knowledge about them. Geri struggled for years with the disturbing knowledge that her father died as a result of his drug abuse. Becoming chemically dependent herself made Geri more like her father in a way, but made everything more difficult to resolve. Geri ultimately understood her father was too wounded emotionally to have done a better job as a father, but in other circumstances and with support, he would have wanted to be different, something Geri could honor.

It is important not only to honor our fathers, but to feel honored by them. To be honored by a dead father may seem like a strange concept. Receiving the blessing of a father, or knowing how he valued, loved, and appreciated us, is to be honored by him. This is what we most need from a father, living or dead. One of the values of talking to those who knew your father is that they may be able to relate the regard he had for you, but was able to tell only them. Exploring and reviewing your father's life as a parent may well reveal living testimony of what his children meant to him.

For those unable to capture their father's validation on their own, psychotherapy, psychodrama, role plays, or staged enactments can offer extraordinarily powerful ways to create the blessing never received. James had long had a concrete image of the formal blessing he had wanted from his father, so we attempted to re-create it. I stood behind James with supportive hands on his shoulders and verbalized the honest statements I could imagine his father would have wanted to say. I told him: "James, even though I never was able to say it, I always felt you were special. I am proud of your intellect, of your wonderful professional accomplishments, and most of all, of your kind, gentle, generous spirit."

James wept with tears of comfort. He could truly imagine his father saying these words, and he felt validated. It was the bar mitzvah, the welcoming into adulthood, he never had from his father. He felt at peace.

21

Reaping the Rewards

> Then, with acceptance of the wound came the tears of
> transformation and a natural healing that can lead to love
> and compassion.
>
> *The Wounded Woman*, Linda Leonard

It is hard for many of us to accept how much healing can take place
when we take steps to repair the frayed connection with even the most
difficult of fathers. We can be so rooted in our negative outlook that we
not only resist the idea of a changed relationship, but lose sight of those
parts of a father that we can respect, honor, or value, the parts to which
we would want to get closer.

When Bill became aware of how emotionally inaccessible his father
had been throughout his childhood, he immersed himself in identifying
the ways in which his father's disappointing character had created problems in his own life. He could focus only on the negative ways in which
he was like his father and tried to change them.

Ironically, one day an old neighbor commented on how Bill had the
same optimistic frame of mind as his father—always a friendly smile
no matter how he felt when he greeted a person. At first Bill could feel
himself start to push away the compliment, then he took it in. It felt
good to allow himself a positive identification with his father. He realized this was a quality he had always liked in his father.

Much of Bill's disappointment in his father centered around the lack of meaningful support he gave Bill beyond his mere presence at athletic events. When Bill reached the point of wanting to move beyond his hurt to finding out if he could alter the relationship, he understood that he most needed to know whether he could break through his father's detachment and obtain some of the support he had needed earlier in his life and still wanted. It felt risky to let himself be vulnerable and directly ask his father to respond to his needs. Bill knew that following the code of silent acceptance he had with his father would lead nowhere. To change this pattern he had to be willing to take charge of the opportunity and to acknowledge his part in allowing the relationship to drift.

Bill planned a visit to his father with the express intention of creating a different mode of interaction. When his father started to put the television on in preparation for their usual uncommunicative time together, Bill was faced with his first challenge to staying in charge of the opportunity. With some trepidation, he told his father that he needed to talk over some things with him and that the distraction of the television would interfere.

Bill was willing to share some of his own struggles with his father, an important aspect of his effort to connect with him. These personal problems did not involve his father; rather, they gave his dad a chance to be a father just by listening. Instead of talking about connecting, Bill was actually doing it. He told his father exactly what he needed from him as he started to unload his own concerns, namely, for him to listen and not feel he had to solve the problem.

Afterward, Bill told his father how much it had meant to be able to have such a conversation with him and that he intended to do this more often. He did not blame his father for the lack of dialogue that had characterized their relationship, but rather owned the fact that he as much as his father had allowed too many opportunities to be missed in the past. The conversation was the longest they had probably ever had about something personal and meaningful. When Bill got up to leave, his undemonstrative father gave him a warm hug and told him he loved him.

When Bill drove home after his milestone connection with his father he was overwhelmed with tears. The rush of emotion certainly felt good in a way, but it wasn't that simple. Later, as Bill tried to understand his feelings, he explained:

My tears were for a lot of reasons. For one thing it seemed so strange at forty to be getting the father I'd always wanted. It was a bittersweet feeling to be receiving now what I had needed as a kid. Part of my tears were about the loss, about not having had that father when I was little. The tears were also ones of joy about at least having him now, especially after I worked deliberately to make it happen. I'm still trying to make sense of what it's going to mean for him and me.

What this reconciliation meant for Bill, and means for many others, was obvious in some ways and subtle in others. It was clear that it felt good to have his father be supportive and be capable of responding the way Bill had long wanted him to do. It was apparent his dad could be more of the father Bill had wanted. Bill also discovered, however, that the closeness with his father was not the same as that with a mother. The nurturing that comes from a father may not be as open and expressive as is often the case with a mother's but it can carry its own unique tenderness and caring. As Bill recognized and accepted this difference, he could experience his father's nurturing way as equally satisfying.

Bill was less sure he could count on his father's continued accessibility and support. He didn't know how close their connection could become or how much of the hurt from the past could be healed by a changing present and future. Bill understood it would take time to get answers to these questions and that in the meantime he would have to continue to be active in setting the tone for their interactions. Having these questions on his mind, though, reflected the progress that had already occurred.

The Rewards of Reconciliation

As we work on repairing the connection with our fathers we experience unanticipated new freedom in relating to them. We gain in the form of freedom *from* and freedom *to*. In the course of the journey to our fathers we gain perspective about them and ourselves that frees us from feeling controlled, judged, or measured by them. We no longer fear that they will misuse their power with us or that we will attribute power to them that they do not have over us.

We become freed from the fear that blocks our engagement with them. We become freed from bearing inordinate responsibility for their weaknesses and from having to hide from them in shame or hide our shame from them and from ourselves. And we become freed of the misinterpretations and distortions related to their absence that lead us to also pull away.

As one man told me with a kind of startled gratitude upon returning from a visit with his father: "I actually spent time with him on this visit. Just the two of us. And when I was around him I believe for the first time I can recall, I felt relaxed. I wasn't worried about his reactions. I could be myself. And I think he was more mellow, too, because he could tell I wasn't uncomfortable with him."

Indeed, the positive shifts from the child's end will start a pattern of positive interactive loops as father and child feed off the improved atmosphere between them.

The changed environment that comes with overcoming the emotional constraints opens up a new world of options with a father. We become free to be with a father who is no longer experienced with intimidation or shame or rejection. It is not only easier to be with such a father, but it becomes more possible to receive from and learn from him. When Bill's father hugged him, Bill experienced that show of affection in a wholly different way than he might have in the past. He did not question his father's motivation and he did not tighten up out of his own ambivalence. It was all right to take something from his father instead of having to deliver whatever it took to secure his silent approval.

The freedom to receive from a father includes being able to learn from him. The distance and the tension associated with the relationship have been barriers to learning what a father can teach us, from the practical to the social. As the relationship heals, we become receptive and are able to listen.

Sylvia had always wanted to learn her parents' native language and more about Hungarian culture and her roots. In the course of coming to terms with her father's weakness she planned her first trip to Hungary and asked her dad to help her learn the language.

Our openness to learn readily shifts to sharing more of our own knowledge and interests. Moreover, many fathers allow themselves to be taught by their children once they find their children want to learn from them.

The emergence of a closer relationship and the newfound freedom within it has a further cumulative effect; it fulfills the long-desired need to be validated by the father. The validation may come in the direct form, as with Bill, where a father can put words and action to the pride and love he has felt but to which he has not previously given expression. The needed validation may not come as directly or may take different forms.

For Andrew, whose father had always been demonstrative with his affection, the validation he needed was for his personhood. He needed to be recognized by his father, not just loved. He told me: "An object can be loved. I needed him to know me, to be able to listen to what I had to say from start to finish and show me he understood and considered it as important as what he had to say back."

When Andrew finally learned that he could get his father to listen to him and to know him, it felt wonderful. A healed connection with our fathers in itself provides a fundamental affirmation. We feel valued and recognized by our father and in turn better able to appreciate him. There is a sense of wholeness and stability that is restored by his involved presence.

Another unity that takes form through the journey to our fathers is between our masculine and feminine selves. As Linda Leonard worked on her writing and her redemption of her father, she discovered: "I had a masculine figure in myself who liked me as a woman. No longer did I have to be the innocent sweet daughter or the super-competent wonder-woman."

By redeeming her father in her own eyes, she was able to embrace the masculine strength for which he stood. In accepting the positive parts of her father's image, she was freer to accept herself as a woman simultaneously. She no longer had to prove herself through overstating her femininity to her unaccepting dad.

Men can be liberated in inverse fashion when they heal their father relationships. The self-acceptance they gain and their changed attitude toward the father mean they no longer have to redeem themselves or their fathers through distorted attempts to prove their manhood. Thus, they are freer to embrace the feminine side that is part of all men. They can extend their nurturing, sensitive, creative side into the world without apology and know it as equal in strength to their masculine side. For sons and daughters, the synergy of masculine and feminine allows them to enter their other relationships with greater clarity and confidence, and those relationships are richer for it.

Resolution and Its Rewards

Sadly, the sense of unity and harmony to be gained through our journey does not necessarily occur through reconciliation with our father. While we may find a way to "redeem" our father and release the toxic feelings that have justified our own alienation, we may not always be able to reconcile with him. Despite our best efforts, not all fathers can change or they may not be ready to change when we are ready for them to do so. Some fathers cannot relinquish their own pain or anger, some cannot overcome their own emotional blindness, some will not let themselves risk. When fathers remain emotionally inaccessible or if they are physically out of reach or deceased, we have to settle for something other than reconciliation.

The process we have talked about is still worthwhile and transforming. Going through it carefully and fully brings us to a point of inner resolution regardless of what happens with our fathers. We will know we have made the full effort, and we will learn a great deal about ourselves and some about our fathers. We will understand where our own responsibility begins and ends. We will know we are part of a lineage that can be honored as well as disavowed. There is growth and there is healing even in the journey that takes us to a personal resolution but not to a reconnection with our fathers. Indeed, the most significant changes may not be in our father at all, but rather in ourselves and how we are with others.

We need to understand that the work before us is never solely with our father. The emotional burdens that come with the lack of connection to our fathers can pervade and distort our relationships with ourselves and with others. How we deal with our feelings, how we relate to other members of our family, how we handle our love relationships and friendships with men and with women, and even our patterns of work behavior are all shaped by the failed connection. Therefore, all these aspects of our life will be influenced by any resolution we achieve.

The journey to our fathers can have a particularly profound effect in many instances on how we view our mothers. As Guy Corneau noted in a presentation on his book *Absent Fathers, Lost Sons*, a son can't re-own what his mother gave him until he resolves his masculinity, and that path is through his father. Corneau's point is that if a son is unsure of himself as a man he will be inclined to distance himself from his mother as a way of bolstering his masculine image.

Both sons and daughters may distance themselves from or blame their mothers because of a distorted view of their fathers. A silent, overburdened, or workaholic father may seem like a martyr around a wife who is angry and seemingly demanding with him. An ideal father may maintain his illusory perfection at a mother's expense. Mothers may be blamed for not defending or supporting the child of an autocratic, abusive, or troubled father or for driving away a divorced one. These projections of blame occur often as a way to discharge feelings about a father who is too inaccessible or intimidating to approach directly.

When a father is seen more accurately and in human terms, the mother also can be viewed without distortion. Robin had always regarded her gentle, reserved father as a saint. When he slumped in his easy chair every night after work, she felt sorry for him. And when her mother barked orders like a drill sergeant to keep things flowing at home she envisioned her father slumping even deeper into his chair to escape her bitchiness. She believed his passivity was a result of her mother's dominance rather than the other way around.

When she could see her father beneath the glow of his halo and herself experienced the frustration of trying to rouse him into interaction, it put a different spin on her mother's dominance at home. Robin was more respectful of and less put off by the strength her mother exhibited.

The shift in perspective isn't always positive for a mother. Larry had always been so blinded with rage at his emotionally abusive father, he disregarded the qualities in his mother that he didn't like. When he heard his dad describe how unhappy he had been in the marriage, it cast a different light on his father's moods at home. His father's frustration with his mother did not justify his father's behavior and, of course, it called into question why he remained in such an unsatisfying marriage, but it also pushed Larry to look more closely at his mother.

In the process, Larry realized that some of his own behavior that he disliked was associated with his mother and not his father. The result, however, was not to start him on a campaign to vilify his mother and rewrite the family history. Rather, he became more direct and honest with his mother, too. While his feelings weren't all positive, his relationship became more based in reality.

Views of siblings can change also when our picture of a father becomes more accurate and balanced. In acknowledging the abuse or problems or controlling nature of a father we can recognize that siblings in the family will have been affected differently and perhaps more severely by the same behavior. Some people discover that an older sibling took the brunt of a father's anger to protect the younger brothers and sisters. Sometimes the behavior of a sibling, perhaps jealousy or resentment, becomes more understandable in the context of the father's treatment of that sibling.

Larry had been so focused on protecting himself from his father's wrath, he had not appreciated how his younger sister and brother had been affected. His sister had been a brilliant student and a shining success in her teaching career, but his brother had been plagued by emotional problems. Larry had neither appreciated the scope of his sister's achievements nor been particularly sympathetic to his brother. While Larry found that any reconciliation with his father was limited, his resolution about that relationship brought him to reexamine his sibling relationships. Through sharing his personal journey with his sister, a closer relationship rapidly evolved. He also became more involved with and supportive to his brother.

When the father relationship remains an open wound, relationships with any family member can become imbalanced. Siblings can be leaned on or lean on others for the basic needs that a father should provide. They can be used as a buffer to a father's problematic behavior.

Mothers may feel forced to substitute for the father and compensate for his shortcomings. They may feel more comfortable at doing so with a daughter. Mothers may be particularly concerned about counterbalancing the father's lack of involvement with a son and as a result the mother-son relationship can become laden with tension.

When sons are connected with their father, they are less fearful of being consumed by their mother. Because they feel stronger, more self-accepting, and more confident about managing their lives, they are not so threatened by closeness with their mother. They no longer need to project blame onto either the "bad" father or the "smothering" mother. The way they react to their mother is not as affected by what their father thinks or does. They are also, as Corneau suggests, freer to love their mother.

For daughters as well as sons, coming to terms with their father builds the confidence to become involved in other relationships in a more secure and open fashion. The carryover extends beyond one's own family to intimate relationships generally. In the movie *Memories of*

Me, Billy Crystal's girlfriend tells him point-blank, "You make really good love, but then you can't hold my hand." She suggests to him that maybe that comes from his inability to face the love and hurt he carries toward his father. Once he has made peace and reconnected with his father, he is able to tell his girlfriend he loves her. For a change, this is not purely Hollywood hokum.

Men and women carry the barriers to intimacy with a father into their intimate relationships. For daughters the most formative learning experience about relating to men comes from their fathers. When Sally understood that being shortchanged with men was directly related to the experience she had with her father, she determined not to let this sort of relationship occur again. Her resolution led her to end a destructive relationship with a man rather than hold on to it.

Learning from our journey to our fathers goes beyond protecting ourselves. We make healthier choices of partners, selecting people who meet our needs rather than people who carry on the legacy of failed connection. As Sylvia grew stronger in setting limits with her father and valuing herself within that relationship, she started dating men who treated her in a manner consistent with what she now expected from her father and required for herself. Her next serious partner at this point was someone who stood out for his sensitivity and gentleness, not the uncaring ambition and drive she had been drawn to in the past to make up for her father's weak behavior.

While for daughters the father relationship is the paradigm for intimacy with a male, it is commonly the only standard for intimacy for sons. How they relate to other men as well as who they allow themselves to be with women is shaped enormously by the father. So much of the constraint about getting close to other men goes back to the lack of closeness with a father. A son is given permission to get close to other men when he either feels his father's acceptance of their own connection or recognizes that his dad's avoidance of closeness was a flaw in the father. He can then experience closeness himself.

I have seen many men able to go beyond the superficial camaraderie that tends to characterize male friendship after they have seriously tried to come to terms with their father. When Mike came through his period of grieving over his father's death and faced his pain over his father's abuse, he focused on deepening his ties to the two males in his life with whom he felt the strongest bond. He wanted more intimate friendships because after realizing what his father meant to him he felt the need for close male connection in his life. The work of arriving at this realization had opened him to new levels of emotional sharing, levels that he had never felt safe in approaching before. He did not want to close himself off again.

Matt had a startling epiphany one day: "Eighty percent of what I know about my father came through my mother." He started to do something about that by making deliberate efforts to spend time with his father. In building his connection to his father, Matt found other male figures in his family whom he discovered were important to his father and thus to his knowing his father. It became important to Matt to meet these uncles and cousins for himself. In the course of building bridges to these family members, Matt reflected on his prior pattern of seeking older male mentors outside of the family like coaches, teachers, and ministers to fill the hole he experienced inside:

> During those years when my father never had much to say to me and gave me no feedback, I see now that I was thirsting for somebody male to relate to and teach me about life. I was so sensitive to any criticism from these different mentors, because anything negative matched up with what I believed my father thought—that I just didn't cut it. I see how it all fits together now. I'm amazed at how encompassing this father stuff is. It impacted on my whole life.

Matt also joined a men's group as a result of the insight he gained about his pattern of connection with men. This group represented a chance to be with male peers instead of finding mentors to look up to.

While daughters are heavily shaped in their choice of male partners by their fathers' example, sons are probably more influenced about how to relate to the women they do choose than about the choice itself. Adult heterosexual men today are often in a quandary about how to act with women. Their fathers typically maintained traditional, male-dominant marriages, yet these men likely have relationships with women who are schooled in the equality and growth-oriented messages of the women's movement. For many, this poses a psychological bind. To secure the type of partnership acceptable to a woman today, they must behave in ways that are antithetical to their fathers' example.

Establishing emotional closeness with the father can erase this bind. It shifts the focus of relations from hierarchy and status to understanding and knowledge of each other. It is difficult to carry on a relationship under these latter terms without seeing the injustice of patriarchal inequality. Men who have healed their relationships with their fathers or have resolved that such closeness was the right way for things to be are more inclined toward parity with women. They are also more open to and comfortable with intimacy in general. If it is acceptable to have intimacy with a father, it is acceptable period.

From the attempts at improving their relationships with fathers, sons and daughters both learn a great deal about how to make intimate relationships work. The skills needed to overcome resistance, fears, and distorted expectations and to achieve understanding with a father readily apply to relationships between couples. Perhaps it is conquering the fright about overcoming emotional barriers that most enables us to be more skillful with intimate connections in general.

The journey to our father encourages a reexamination of our role as parent as well as partner. The journey commonly raises awareness of lost time and opportunities. With this awareness we are motivated to spare our children covering that same territory with us. As Matt told me, "I sure don't want my own kids to be saying about me someday what I've been telling you about my father."

Again, for sons the insights about their role as a parent are more direct because of the psychological identification with a father. Adult sons are better fathers as the result of the learning and emotional growth they acquire in making their journey. For daughters, working on reconciliation more typically heightens their appreciation of what type of parent they want their husbands to be rather than the type of parent they want to be.

Inevitably, as we examine our parenting behavior we recognize some of the negative patterns that existed with our fathers. After all, we teach what we know. The later in the process we learn about our own paternal relationship, the less time we may then have to alter destructive patterns with our children. This can cause considerable consternation for older, adult children.

It is easy, however, to lose sight of the important ways in which we have progressed from the relationship our fathers had with us. One man in a group, struggling to come to terms with his worry that he might be too late with regard to his son, was comforted by the thought: "At least I understand my son, where my father never understood me."

Men are making progress as fathers. Today most men are present at the birth of their children, while thirty years ago this involvement was almost unheard of. Being engaged in the birth process has certainly helped many young fathers to be more fully involved as a parent when their children are young. Fathers are not only changing diapers and giving baths far more than in the past, they are gradually learning to stay involved as their children grow, attending school conferences, taking children to the doctor, and being more interactive and emotionally open.

Much of the growth in father involvement in the past thirty years can be attributed to the women's movement, but it is also an outgrowth of men facing their relationships with their fathers. In their efforts to connect with their fathers many sons as well as daughters are hearing for the first time that their fathers regretted their choice of priorities and their immersion in work.

One further reward that can come with making the journey to our father is a clearer sense of priorities. When adult offspring say they do not want to repeat history and they intend to be involved with their children, they must also mean that they are willing to alter their work patterns. Some are getting the message, but the change is slow and there is little societal support for it.

A little more than a year after his father died and about nine months since I had last seen him, Mike called about doing some more work with me. The catalyst was the fact that he had just recovered from a lengthy illness that he was convinced related to his father.

I suspected that Mike's serious illness allowed him to identify and somehow stay connected with his father at the time of the first anniversary of his death. Mike found this idea an interesting thought, but believed he was simply working too hard. He had resumed an unrelenting, overtaxing workload a couple of months after his father died, at least in part to preoccupy himself so he wouldn't be thinking so much about his father. The accumulated stress had compromised his health.

Mike reflected: "I didn't just lose a father, I lost touch with myself. My father always worked like a horse and now I've been treating myself like a horse. No more." Mike was determined to start paying attention to himself, to stop living in a perpetual state of numbness.

Mike followed through with his self-learning. He began reducing his travel time for work, cutting down on his work hours, and planning to do work at home so he could be with his young daughter more. Mike realized, however, as he tried to achieve a better balance in his life that his overworking was not simply mirroring his father's long-standing behavior. He was working so hard because he was still trying to prove himself as a worthy son.

It became apparent to Mike that despite the earlier grief work he'd done in relation to his father's death, he was not really at peace within himself about his father. This awareness moved him to reexamine his father's abusiveness when he was a child. He realized how his father's anger had frightened him and how in general his father had intimidated him. Mike had felt as weak to himself as his father had felt powerful to him. He had felt defective for upsetting his father so strongly, and he had concluded that he would have to work harder than everyone else to make up for his shortcomings.

Mike could again appreciate the ways in which his father had changed and become his chief supporter by going back to his oldest, deepest hurts and grieving over what he had lost as a child in having an abusive father. This time around, though, he could see that he was not dependent on his father's support, which he now missed so badly, because he was weak. He understood that he felt weak because he hadn't dealt with how afraid his father made him feel and why he had been so afraid.

Mike and I met a few more times, continuing to discuss his changing relationship with his father over the years and the changed relationship he wanted with himself. Mike then took a break for several months. When I next saw him there was a tangible transformation. He was clearly more relaxed, and he carried himself with more confidence, not with the slightly hunched look of a burdened man. His smile was easy and spontaneous, and he stayed in direct eye contact with me rather than frequently having to look away to break the intimacy of our interaction.

Mike was pleased with the concrete steps he had taken with his life. He was continuing to take better care of himself, exercising regularly and eating in a healthy fashion. He worked at night at home even less and had further cut back on his work travel. He was setting boundaries with his road customers by telling them after a dinner together that he needed time to regroup, instead of staying out late to appease them at the expense of his own well-being. He explained: "I trust in myself more. Believe in myself. So I don't have to work to please others. I can do what I want or need to do, not what they want, and they'll accept it most of the time. If they don't, that's okay, too. I'll be all right."

This newfound ability to stay true to himself and his own needs was linked for Mike to the work he did on his father. He told me:

> I'm in touch with all my feelings about my father now—the anger, love, fear, disappointment, dependence. I've finally found the line inside myself, though, that tells me how much of me is him. I found where he stops, and I exist outside his influence.
>
> I used to look at my customers as these huge figures and be intimidated by them, like they were my father. Like I wasn't good enough to deserve their business. I don't feel that way anymore. I can get angry now at my daughter and not be afraid I'll turn into a monster. Anger no longer equates with being out of control for me.
>
> I feel really free these days. I'm not going to be dwarfed by who my father was, nor am I afraid of carrying that dark side of his power. I can love him for what he was and love myself for who I am.

In *The Wounded Woman*, Linda Leonard described her own and other women's transitions as they worked on healing their father-daughter relationships. One woman in therapy with Leonard had a series of dreams that reflected the progression of her struggle to break away from an autocratic type of father. One of the later dreams involved the death of the father and being called to cross a river with an unfinished bridge. Leonard made the following interpretation:

> The death of the father symbolized the end of his rigid reign, and now she was called to cross over to the other side of the river to a new side of herself. The bridge to that new side was already partly built, but she had to get into the water to cross all the way. For her this meant to get into the flow of life and her feelings.

Leonard noted that as this woman got into the flow of her life, the image of her father in her dreams became a more accepting one. The lesson illustrated by this woman and Mike is clear. The journey to our fathers ultimately becomes a journey to ourselves. The work toward resolution within ourselves in relation to our fathers leads to self-acceptance. This self-acceptance in turn transforms our relationship to our fathers.

It is not the father who must die to free us to grow, it is the dominance of a destructive and paralyzing image of the father that must meet its death. When we fully commit to making our journey, which encompasses coming to terms with ourselves and our role in the relationship, we do not have to reconcile with our fathers for profound internal changes to occur.

In most instances we will discover we have become freed from our anger. Not that we will no longer have any anger with our fathers, but we become free of the misdirected, excessive, inappropriate anger that often characterizes an unresolved paternal relationship.

The shift may be like that of Diane who first had to vent the anger apart from her father; or that of Kyle, who had to understand and accept his anger before he could begin to let go of it; or like that of Andrew, who had to take the anger directly to his father and have it acknowledged and accepted. Renee figured out that she simply didn't need her anger any longer to defend herself. There are different paths, but the outcome consists of letting go of the compost heap of anger that distorts our behavior with our fathers, with others, and toward ourselves.

Anger is healthy if it is connected to the core feelings that are its source: our disappointment, hurt, sadness, sense of loss. If our fathers cannot change toward us, these core feelings will remain. What we overcome is our need to deny, silence, fruitlessly lash out with, or helplessly suppress anger out of the frustration and self-victimization that come with not facing the disconnection with our father. Accepting the totality of our feelings toward our fathers means we are not chained to our anger in a toxic way. Indeed, as Mike learned in relation to his daughter, we can be freer to experience our anger in general as a healthy emotion that will not destroy ourselves or others. The freedom we gain opens us to new ways to experience ourselves and others.

When we have greater clarity about our feelings toward our fathers, we not only see our dads more clearly but have more accurate self-perceptions. As Mike demonstrated, we can lose touch with ourselves when we feel the loss of a father. Along our journey we gradually regain the capacity to value and to be ourselves. We learn that our perceived deficiencies were related to how we were treated by our fathers and to our fathers' own weaknesses or distorted behavior.

For Andrew, the experience of bringing his feelings to his father taught him that he indeed was capable of standing up for himself with anyone. Renee felt freer to be herself with others when she no longer believed she had to be so on guard with her father. James told me, "I no longer carry around the mentality of a rejected son." Arriving at our own resolution about our father relationship puts an end to concerns about not having been anointed or validated. We are set on a path where only we have the right to judge ourselves and where that judgment can come from an unbiased but supportive inner jury.

Freed from the distorted self-views and views of our fathers that came with the lack of connection, we can establish more realistic yet positive expectations for ourselves, our fathers, and others. With some fathers this means no longer believing we are responsible for their behavior or their feelings—a role that is unrelenting and overwhelming to fulfill. It also means, as one woman said to me with joyful relief, "I no longer have a hole to fill in me, so I'm not driven to fill it everywhere I go."

Along the journey we have learned that while our fathers may have a great deal to do with the creation of the emptiness we have felt, for the most part they cannot fill it for us, nor do we require them to do so. Our resolution brings us to the point where we understand what we have needed from our fathers, but also the limitations of what they can give. Our growing ability to value ourselves validates our needs, but also allows us to believe in our own capacity to fill those needs more than in our fathers'. That also allows us to not look to others unrealistically to fulfill what our fathers and we could not.

Kyle had long had difficulty keeping reasonable limits on his work life. He did not feel he had the power, nor did he feel he deserved to work less hard. Finally he came to a recognition "When I stopped seeing my father as always in control and always right, I had to change how I viewed myself. It meant I should be in control and I could decide if I was right or not. So it meant I was free to define my own life."

For Kyle this realization resulted in giving himself permission for the first time to have fun, to take time off from work, to believe that being happy was a more appropriate goal than pleasing his father. Also, when he stopped looking for his father to provide him with all the answers, he could evaluate and better appreciate the guidance he did receive.

Freed of our distorted anger, empowered by being able to value ourselves, unencumbered by unrealistic expectations, we can arrive at peace within ourselves. When we discover either the capacity of our fathers to be our fathers or our own capacity to nurture ourselves, we no longer have to keep searching frantically for substitute figures to give us approval or fill in the gaps. We no longer feel we must prove ourselves through overcoming our fathers' distance or silence or misdirected power.

Phil, a participant in a men's group, had long felt he had never quite gotten enough of his father. He had never connected this feeling with his troubling inability to believe in himself, however. One day I asked another group member, Roger, to role-play Phil's father. Roger did a wonderful job of standing in for Phil's father, who was in fact deceased. He listened to Phil's confusion and pain as Phil wished his true father would have done. He disavowed Phil's inflated view of his father and his presumed masculine strength. He spoke of his own weaknesses and his hopes that Phil would overcome them in his own life. With hands on Phil's shoulders he voiced his belief in Phil and his love for him.

Tears rarely came for Phil, especially in public, but they trickled down his cheeks now. I asked Phil to express the message of his silent tears, expecting him to talk of his sadness about his lost relationship. But he was in a different place: "I feel at peace. Like the circle has been completed." These were tears of quiet joy.

Bibliography

Ackerman, Robert J. 1989. *Perfect Daughters: Adult Daughters of Alcoholics.* Deerfield Beach, FL: Health Communications, Inc.

Alvarez, Julia. 1991. *How the Garcia Girls Lost Their Accents.* Chapel Hill: Algonquin Books of Chapel Hill.

Appleton, William S. 1984. *Fathers and Daughters: A Father's Powerful Influence on a Woman's Life.* New York: Berkley Books.

Atwood, Margaret. 1989. *Cat's Eye.* New York: Doubleday.

Auster, Paul. 1982. *The Invention of Solitude.* New York: Penguin Books.

Baker, Russell. 1982. *Growing Up.* New York: New American Library.

Becker, Lou. "An Older Father's Letter to His Young Son" in Thompson, Keith, ed. 1991. *To Be a Man: In Search of the Deep Masculine.* Los Angeles: Jeremy P. Tarcher, Inc.

Bly, Robert. 1990. *Iron John: A Book About Men.* Reading, MA: Addison-Wesley Publishing Company, Inc.

Corneau, Guy. 1991. *Absent Fathers, Lost Sons: The Search for Masculine Identity.* Translated by Larry Shouldice. Boston: Shambhala.

Eicher, Terry, and Geller, Jesse D. 1990. *Fathers and Daughters: Portraits in Fiction.* New York: New American Library.

Erikson, Erik. 1963. *Childhood and Society.* New York: W. W. Norton & Company.

Feldman, Larry B., "Fathers and Fathering" in Meth, Richard L., and Pasick, Robert S., with Gordon, Barry, et al. 1990. *Men in Therapy: The Challenge of Change.* New York: Guilford.

Gallagher, Tess, "My Father's Love Letters" in Stephen Berg, ed. 1983. *In Praise of What Persists.* New York: Harper & Row, Publishers.

Greer, Germaine. 1990. *Daddy, We Hardly Knew You.* New York: Alfred A. Knopf.

Greven, Philip. 1990. *Spare the Child: The Religious Roots of Punishment and the Psychological Impact of Physical Abuse.* New York: Alfred A. Knopf.

Henry, Jules. 1973. *Pathways to Madness.* New York: Vintage Books.

Kafka, Franz. 1966. *Letter to His Father.* Translated by Ernst Kaiser and Eithne Wilkins. New York: Schocken Books.

Kammen, Michael. 1991. *Mystic Chords of Memory: The Transformation of Tradition in American Culture*. New York: Alfred A. Knopf.

Leonard, Linda Schierse. 1982. *The Wounded Woman: Healing the Father-Daughter Relationship*. Boston: Shambhala.

Osherson, Samuel. 1986. *Finding Our Fathers: The Unfinished Business of Manhood*. New York: The Free Press.

Roth, Philip. 1991. *Patrimony: A True Story*. New York: Simon and Schuster.

Wallerstein, Judith S., and Blakeslee, Sandra. 1990. *Second Chances: Men, Women, and Children a Decade After Divorce*. New York: Ticknor & Fields.

Wilson, August. 1986. *Fences*. New York: New American Library.

Wolff, Geoffrey. 1979. *The Duke of Deception: Memories of My Father*. New York: Elisabeth Sifton Books.

Yablonsky, Lewis. 1982. *Fathers and Sons*. New York: Simon and Schuster.

Index